The Battle for Employment Guarantee

The Battle for Employment Guarantee

edited by

Reetika Khera

OXFORD
UNIVERSITY PRESS

OXFORD
UNIVERSITY PRESS

Oxford University Press is a department of the University of Oxford. It furthers the University's objective of excellence in research, scholarship, and education by publishing worldwide. Oxford is a registered trademark of Oxford University Press in the UK and in certain other countries

Published in India
by Oxford University Press
YMCA Library Building, Jai Singh Road, New Delhi 110 001, India

First Edition published in 2011

ISBN-13: 978-0-19-807062-7
ISBN-10: 0-19-807062-4

Typeset in Garamond
by SwaRadha Typesetting, Delhi 110 091
Printed in India at Rakmo Press Pvt. Ltd., New Delhi 110 020

Contents

Tables, Figures, and Boxes

TABLES

FIGURES

BOXES

Acknowledgements

This book is the collective effort of a now widely-dispersed team which included activists, economists, lawyers, NREGA labourers, and researchers, among others. Apart from the contributors, I thank Aparna John who did much of the work on compiling the extensive bibliography included at the end of the book. I hope that the hundreds of volunteers—from national institutions and local organizations—know just how much this book has benefited from their insights and hard work. For sharing their experiences with us, we thank all NREGA labourers and government officials. Institutions that hosted and literally 'housed' the research team include the Govind Ballabh Pant Social Science Institute (Allahabad) and Institute of Human Development (Ranchi). In Delhi, the Centre for Development Economics at the Delhi School of Economics extended research support. The National Commission for Enterprises in the Unorganized Sector supported the NREGA Survey in 2008. The rest of the work was funded by personal donations from well-wishers and supporters of NREGA.

Though the book is the result of the collaborative work of all these people and organizations, I am sure that all those who were part of this endeavour would like the role of Jean Drèze to be acknowledged, above all, for bringing us together.

Of all our young and committed volunteers, this book is dedicated to two who have lost their lives: Piku, killed by the CRPF in a fake encounter in Orissa, and Niyamat Ansari, killed by the Maoists in Jharkhand.

Introduction

In the early days of the National Rural Employment Guarantee Act (NREGA), when we participated in awareness generation drives in rural India, we were often greeted with bewilderment. That there could be a law guaranteeing employment to anyone who applies for it was beyond people's imagination and dreams. 'If the government fails to provide work, you are entitled to an unemployment allowance.' We thought that perhaps mentioning this provision would get them excited. But at times it made matters worse—being paid for sitting at home came across as a cruel joke.

Five years later, 'narega' (as NREGA is known in north India) has become a household word. It is probably better known—and understood—than any other Indian law. Every year, about 50 million women and men are employed under NREGA, according to official data. Nothing is given to them on a platter, but they are learning to demand their due—employment, minimum wages, payment within 15 days, and so on. The dream has not quite come true, but it has at least entered the realm of possibility.

Beyond the promise of employment, NREGA has other noteworthy features: there is a mandatory minimum share (one-third) of employment for women; work is to be provided within 5 km of residence; at least half of NREGA funds are to be spent by elected local councils; village assemblies select and prioritize NREGA projects; there are strict norms for transparency and accountability (for example, all NREGA documents are in the public domain); and workers are entitled to basic worksite facilities (including child care). Further, people are to be employed for the creation of productive assets such as approach roads, water-harvesting structures, contour trenches, and various works on private land (for instance, levelling or construction of wells).

This volume documents the early years of the NREGA—its achievements so far as well as the hurdles in realizing its potential for rural transformation. During this period, few representative surveys were undertaken. This created a gap whereby it was not easy to get a reliable and comprehensive picture of the situation on the ground. This gap may be remedied soon, to some extent, with the 66th Round of the National Sample Survey (pertaining to 2009–10), which includes a schedule on NREGA employment. Several other small- and large-scale surveys are under way, studying specific aspects of NREGA or trying to arrive at an overview of the programme at the all-India level. This volume, for its part, covers the early experience of implementing NREGA across much of the country. As a stock-taking of the first five years, it also highlights the challenges that lie ahead.

BATTLE FOR EMPLOYMENT GUARANTEE

A quick word on the title of the volume. To have such a law enacted was in itself a battle in the current political and economic climate. While that battle was won (partially at least, since the Act is a diluted version of what was initially proposed), it opened up the bigger battle: for the implementation—in letter and spirit—of the Act, and the realization of workers' entitlements. This is a battle at every step, in a number of ways. For instance, creating awareness of rights under the Act is the very first requirement of successful implementation of the law. However, as mentioned earlier, even this is a challenge—not just because the people concerned are often unable to read or write, but also because they tend to have little faith in the state.

Another major challenge is to develop a sense of accountability, which is sorely lacking, among functionaries responsible for the implementation of NREGA. The reaction of a Chief Executive Officer (equivalent of the Block Development Officer) in Kusmi block of Sidhi district (Madhya Pradesh) is a telling illustration. Unamused by the arrival of a team of English-speaking urban creatures, he came up with a range of imaginative reasons to dissuade us from proceeding. These included a lack of interest in NREGA work among labourers in that area; difficulty in getting food in the villages ('even I have to sleep hungry at times', he told us); the tall trees in the heavily forested area had shallow roots which, with the slightest breeze, could crush people; drunken village folk; snakes and scorpions; and so on. The message was clear—he did not want to be bothered with any questions in his little fiefdom.

This is just an anecdote, but the accountability problem looms large over all aspects of NREGA. In the course of these five years, we have found that those in charge of implementing the Act—the Block Development Officer, the Panchayat *Sevak*, the *Sarpanch*, and so on—do not necessarily empathize with labourers or share the vision of the Act. Often they are part of the corrupt nexus that sees the programme primarily as an opportunity to milk the system. Watchdogs, such as the police or the media, often belong to the same class and caste background as this corrupt nexus. Breaking this nexus has been an important part of the employment guarantee battle.

Lachhmanram Bhuiyan's story is a succinct illustration of this battle. A resident of Tumbagada village (Rabda gram panchayat, Palamu district), he applied for the construction of a well under NREGA on his small plot of land, and this project was sanctioned on 9 February 2007. One of the local contractors (officially banned under NREGA), Taslim Miyan, played an important role in getting the well sanctioned. When labourers began to demand wages, Lachhmanram asked Taslim to help him get funds released from the block. When Taslim did not help him, Lachhmanram sold one of his bullocks to pay the labourers. This continued—Lachhmanram sold another bullock the second time wage payments were due, and then four goats. After this, another resident of Tumbagada helped Lachhmanram file an application under the Right to Information Act to find out about his money. They learnt that Taslim had forged Lachhmanram's signature, and fraudulently withdrawn Rs 47,500 in his name. Lachhmanram did not give up. He filed a complaint with the district authorities, who sent it to the local police station for enquiry. A few days later Lachhmanram was picked up by the local police, kept in custody overnight, and beaten up for allegedly helping the Maoists and trying to become a *neta* (leader). Again, this is just one story, but it would be easy to cite many other harrowing experiences of this kind.

ORGANIZATION OF THE BOOK

This volume is organized into four parts. Part I presents a retrospective on the passage of the Act and a comparative summary of official NREGA statistics at the state level. As mentioned earlier, due to the lack of independent nationally representative surveys, one had to rely (with due caution) on government data in the initial years. The drawbacks of the available data are also discussed.

Part II is, in a sense, the heart of the book. The NREGA Survey 2008 (described in Chapter 3) undertaken in six Hindi-speaking north Indian states forms the backbone of this section. Apart from an overview chapter ('The Battle for Employment Guarantee'), thematic chapters discuss various aspects of NREGA such as the opportunities it has created for women and the remaining barriers to their participation, the pervasive threat of corruption and attempts to avert it (for example, through bank payments of NREGA wages), work incentives, and the role of NREGA as an opportunity for organizing rural workers. Part II also documents early signs, however faint, of the changes that NREGA brings, or can bring, in people's lives.

Part III presents more focussed case studies from a few states—Orissa, Himachal Pradesh, Chhattisgarh, and Tamil Nadu. The main message here is that state experience is shaped by a variety of factors: the political environment, administrative capabilities, and 'demand' for employment. Orissa and Tamil Nadu illustrate two extremes of the spectrum of state experiences. In Orissa, NREGA was still in the grip of corrupt contractors (protected by local netas), and delivering rather little for common people, when we visited the state in October 2007. Tamil Nadu, on the other hand, has steadily built robust institutional structures for NREGA and put in place extensive checks and balances.

The picture emerging from the studies presented in Parts II and III is, on the whole, relatively positive. It reflects the climate of energy and hope that characterized the early years of NREGA. Even at that time, there were regular stories of corruption and failure in the media, but these reports helped to take corrective action, and the general trend was one of steady improvement. Part IV qualifies this relatively optimistic appraisal with a discussion of recent setbacks and 'trouble spots'. Contrary to popular perception created by media reports, corruption is not the only or even the most serious issue that besets the NREGA today. In Part IV we try to shed light on other issues that are equally important. These include the lack of proper grievance redressal mechanisms or of accountability in the system, issues related to the payment of wages (especially delays in wage payments and non-payment of minimum wages), and, more recently (since the United Progressive Alliance [UPA] government assumed office for a second term), an unhealthy sort of politicization of NREGA.

The volume tries to give a flavour of the diverse NREGA experiences and issues across states. Inevitably, some important gaps remain. It focuses largely, though not solely, on the Hindi-speaking states. Outside that region, it covers field studies undertaken in Orissa and Tamil Nadu, and shorter field visits to Gujarat, West Bengal, and Andhra Pradesh. One of the main gaps in terms of regional coverage is the absence of a detailed study from Andhra Pradesh, widely seen as one of the pioneer states as far as NREGA is concerned. Apart from the gaps in regional coverage, at least one important topic remains largely unexplored. Though NREGA is primarily perceived as a social security programme, it can also play an important role in the creation of productive assets in rural areas. The issue of the productivity of assets created under NREGA is severely under-researched, and is only beginning to be an object of serious investigation (see, for example, Tiwari et al. 2011, Mahapatra 2011, Kareemulla et al. 2009).

The bibliography at the end of the book is not just a list of works cited, but also a potential resource of its own, in so far as an attempt has been made to include most of the available studies of NREGA.

THE FUTURE OF NREGA: THE BATTLES AHEAD

From being the 'wet dog at a glamourous party' in 2004, attacked fiercely in the business press, NREGA became, by the time of the 2008 global economic crisis, a welcome 'counter-cyclical' measure that could protect the Indian economy from the worst of the recession. At the 2011 World Economic Forum in Davos, the Indian government and business leaders began extolling NREGA as one of India's 'downturn-beating skills' (*Hindustan Times*, 27 January 2011). While this suggests that one battle, that is, against the hostility of the business sector, may have been won, actually all is not well.

In the first term of the UPA government from 2004 to 2009, the emphasis of the government was on laying the foundations of the programme. When the Congress Party came back to power in 2009, its electoral victory was widely attributed (rightly or wrongly) to the enactment of pro-people laws especially the NREGA. It was expected that in its second term, the UPA government would build on the foundations laid earlier and address what had thus far been termed 'second generation' issues. These included improving technical inputs for the programme (essential for creating useful and durable assets in rural areas), ensuring the provision of basic worksite facilities (for example, child care for women with young children), streamlining wage-related issues (especially delays in payments and the tension between minimum wages and piece-rate work), and putting in place grievance redressal mechanisms.

Instead, there seems to be a tendency towards an unhealthy politicization of the NREGA. 'Unhealthy' because there is an attempt by the Congress Party to earn political capital through superficial measures (such as prefixing 'Mahatma Gandhi' to the name of the programme). The expansion of the list of permissible works to include the construction of 'Bharat Nirman Rajiv Gandhi Seva Kendras' under NREGA is another such move, which has a more substantive effect on the NREGA. These construction projects violate several provisions of the NREGA—the ban on contractors, the mandatory 60–40 labour–material ratio, the provision for prioritization of works by the gram sabha, among others. Yet the Central Government attempted—with limited success—to impose this new and counter-productive priority on NREGA across the country.

Another ill-conceived 're-engineering' of the NREGA is currently underway. This is being done at the behest of the Unique Identification Authority of India (UIDAI), which is to issue a unique identification number to every resident, with biometric authentication. An attempt is being made to impose the use of UID in NREGA processes such as the distribution of job cards and the payment of wages, and even to introduce biometric verification of worksite attendance. The advantages of this proposed redesigning for NREGA workers are likely to be negligible. However, the potential damage is considerable, and could have lasting effects (see Khera 2011). For example, even if the UIDAI's ambitious targets are realized, it will only cover half of India's population in the next four years. In the meanwhile, millions of NREGA workers may be left without a valid job card. Besides, this re-engineering will reopen the door to private contractors, albeit with another name—'service providers'.

Meanwhile, the implementation of NREGA on the ground seems to be in danger of a major setback. Runaway inflation (especially of food prices), combined with the freezing of NREGA wages from January 2009 to January 2011, meant that the real wages of NREGA workers declined in this period. Instead of agreeing to the demand to index NREGA wages to the price level, the Central Government resisted this demand vehemently and succumbed only in early 2011. The scale of employment has also stopped rising in 2010–11, for the first time since NREGA came into force five years ago (even though there is still a large unmet demand for NREGA work). Delays in wage payments, caused by impediments in the flow of funds created largely by the Central Government, are beginning to cause fatigue among rural labourers and push them towards lower paid, more exploitative forms of employment in the private sector. These adverse developments indicate that even as hostility towards NREGA appears to have subsided, the Act's early achievements are in danger of being reversed.

Cementing NREGA's position on the political map would have been possible had its potential for mobilizing labour been realized. The hope, in the initial years, that NREGA would facilitate the formation of unions of some of the most disempowered sections of rural India is still in the realm of the possible. Aside from making NREGA more secure, labour unions can play an important role in fostering collective action on a host of social issues including health and education. Nowhere has this seed taken root, so far, in a significant manner. But as awareness of entitlements grows (and there has been much improvement in that respect over the past five years), it is still possible that NREGA workers will come together. Until such time as the NREGA establishes itself firmly on the political agenda, or labourers themselves build powerful organizations, the future of this historic law will remain uncertain. Whether it will live up to its promise or turn out to be another missed opportunity remains to be seen.

A recent encounter, in Surguja district (Chhattisgarh), with seven men belonging to the Pahari Korwa community, was like a glimpse of this promise. Pahari Korwas (a so-called 'primitive tribal group') are forest-dwellers, known for living on the margins on society. The men we met lived in the hills of one of the remotest villages of Lakhanpur Block. Yet, they were all familiar with NREGA, proudly showed their job cards and bank passbooks, and had all worked on NREGA worksites. We asked them how they had spent their wages. Often, people report that their wages are all spent on subsistence needs. Contrary to what we expected, one had invested his earnings in a bicycle. Another had put in some more money to buy a bullock. The third man said he had used his wages to repay a debt incurred when his brother was sick. As we went round the group another said he had set them aside to buy textbooks for his child's education; yet others met social obligations (for example, wedding expenses). Encouraged by their responses we asked them what work had been undertaken in that area. It turned out that the main activity was the levelling of their fields. They were pleased about this too and even felt that it could double their crop yields. It is experiences such as these that make the battle for employment guarantee seem worth fighting.

PART I

EARLY DAYS

1

Employment Guarantee and the Right to Work*

Jean Drèze

In a conversation with Mulk Raj Anand, way back in May 1950, Dr Ambedkar described capitalism as the 'dictatorship of the private employer'. I often remembered this expression in the summer of 2005, during the *Rozgar Adhikar Yatra* (journey for the right to work), as we travelled through some of India's poorest districts—Badwani, Banswara, Gaya, Nandurbar, Palamau, Puruliya, Sonebhadra, Surguja, among others. Everywhere we went, the rural economy looked like a graveyard and unemployment was the people's main concern. Seasonal migration (to distant brick kilns, tea gardens, or urban sweatshops) was their lifeline at that time of the year. At times, the local railway stations looked like a flashback to the days of the Partition—crammed as they were with desperate people on the move, with haggard looks, heavy loads on their heads, and scruffy children in tow. The predicament of casual labourers did not seem fundamentally different from that of slaves, except that they were driven by economic necessity instead of physical coercion.

EMPLOYMENT AS A CONSTITUTIONAL RIGHT

In the same conversation, Mulk Raj Anand asked Ambedkar why the right to work had not been made a fundamental right in the Indian

*Adapted from Jean Drèze (2010), 'Employment Guarantee and the Right to Work', in Niraja Gopal Jayal and Pratap Bhanu Mehta (eds), *Oxford Companion to Indian Politics*. New Delhi: Oxford University Press.

Constitution. Dr Ambedkar laconically replied, 'I was only one of the members of the drafting Committee'. The right to work ended up in the Directive Principles of the Constitution, along with other economic and social rights such as the right to education and the right to health.

The Directive Principles of State Policy were expected to be fought for politically. Article 37 of the Constitution explicitly states that they 'shall not be enforced by any court'. However, this does not preclude enacting laws based on these Directive Principles. In fact, the same Article goes on to say that these Principles are 'fundamental in the governance of the country', and that it is the duty of the state to 'apply these principles in making laws'.

Recent Supreme Court orders on mid-day meals in primary schools illustrate the possibility of building legal safeguards for economic and social rights. Today, every Indian child attending primary school is entitled to a cooked mid-day meal. This is a legal right, enforceable in court. Without these orders, it is unlikely that mid-day meals would have been extended to more than 100 million children within a few years. The Right to Education Act (weak as it may be) is another example of the possibility of framing laws that give concrete expression to the Directive Principles of State Policy.

Similarly, the National Rural Employment Guarantee Act 2005 (NREGA) can be seen as a step towards legal enforcement of the right to work. It is a limited step, especially since the employment guarantee is limited to '100 days per household per year'. Nevertheless the Act has much value as a tool of empowerment for rural labourers.

In particular, the Act can help to break the 'dictatorship of the private employer'. Today, rural labourers have no bargaining power. The fear of unemployment divides them and puts them at the mercy of private contractors and other exploiters. If rural labourers can get employment on public works at the minimum wage, as a matter of right, they will be able to demand minimum wages from private employers as well. Guaranteed employment on public works will also empower them to resist exploitative work conditions in the private sector. Further, the Employment Guarantee Act is a unique opportunity for them to organize and fight for related rights such as the right to social security.

The Employment Guarantee Act can also help to empower women by giving them independent income-earning opportunities. This point emerges in several studies of Maharasthra's Employment Guarantee Scheme (EGS), a precursor of NREGA. For instance, in her interviews with women working under EGS in the 1980s, Devaki Jain found that 'having once tasted the value of bringing home a money wage from their own labour, they had developed a sense of confidence and also release from the authority of the family and had started to gain the confidence to take up other types of work in the area' (Jain 2005). Similarly, in a recent assessment of Maharashtra's EGS, Aruna Bagchee (2005) argues that the payment of equal wages to men and women is one reason 'why the EGS was so popular among women labourers'. In areas where rural women are traditionally homebound, such as Uttar Pradesh and Bihar, the Employment Guarantee Act has an even more significant role to play as a means of empowering rural women and curbing gender discrimination.

The enactment of NREGA is a victory of sorts for Indian democracy. It shows that the underprivileged majority is not completely marginalized in this elitist political system. With adequate political organization, their demands sometimes prevail over privileged interests.

However, the real challenge is not the enactment of NREGA but its implementation on the ground. In India, as elsewhere, the history of social legislation shows that it often takes a long time for people to be able to claim their rights, even after laws have been passed. Some laws, such as the Minimum Wages Act 1948, have remained on paper for decades without making much impact, except in states like Kerala where labourers are vocal and organized. Similarly, NREGA is unlikely to succeed without sustained political commitment and public pressure.

A BRIEF HISTORY OF NREGA

The draft NREGA entered national policy debates in India a few years ago like a wet dog at a glamorous party. The enactment of a national Employment Guarantee Act was a long-standing demand of the labour movement, but it had never made much headway. In mid-2004, a series of unlikely events catapulted it to the top of the political agenda, at a time when privileged interests (notably those of the corporate sector and the so-called 'middle class') had an unprecedented hold on economic policy. Within a year, employment on demand became a legal entitlement.

It may be worth recalling some of the major steps that led to this breakthrough.[1] Though there is no obvious 'starting point', an important prelude was the campaign for an Employment Guarantee in Rajasthan, as an extension of the employment-based drought relief programmes launched in 2001 and 2003. This was also an opportunity to create interest in a national Employment Guarantee Act among leaders of various political parties, notably Sonia Gandhi, who was the Leader of the Opposition in the Lok Sabha at that time.

In early 2004, the promise of a national Employment Guarantee was included in the electoral manifesto of the Congress Party. This promise seemed to be neither here nor there, as most people (including Congress leaders themselves) were quite sure that the Congress Party would lose the next elections. As it turned out, however, the Congress came to power in May 2004 as the leading partner in the United Progressive Alliance (UPA) government. This alliance had the support of the Left parties, who were strong advocates of the Employment Guarantee. The Act became one of the main planks of the National Common Minimum Programme (NCMP), the official roadmap of the UPA government. In fact, it was the first item in the NCMP's list of policy commitments.

[1] For more detailed accounts of the genesis of NREGA, see McAuslan (forthcoming), Chopra (2010), and Lakin and Ravishankar (2006).

In pursuance of this commitment, the National Advisory Council (NAC) drafted a National Rural Employment Guarantee Act in August 2004. The NAC draft, which was actually based on an earlier draft prepared by concerned citizens, set the framework for all subsequent discussions of the Act.[2] However, this draft went through numerous changes and revisions before it metamorphosed into the National Rural Employment Guarantee Act 2005. On 21 December 2004, the government tabled a severely diluted version of the NAC draft in Parliament. This draft (the National Rural Employment Guarantee Bill 2004) was so weak that it defeated the purpose of a legally enforceable employment guarantee. For instance, the Bill left it to the Central Government to decide where and when the work guarantee would come into force. In other words, the government was offering an employment guarantee, but without any guarantee that the guarantee would come into effect! After being tabled in Parliament, the National Rural Employment Guarantee Bill 2004 was referred to the Parliamentary Standing Committee on Rural Development.

The National Rural Employment Guarantee Bill 2004 clearly fell short of the promise made in the NCMP. The response was a broad-based campaign to 'repair' the Bill and reinstate the crucial safeguards: irreversible guarantee, universal coverage, time-bound extension to the whole of rural India, assured minimum wages, and full transparency, among others. The NAC, the Left parties, and a wide range of organizations committed to the right to work played an active role in this campaign. This led to a series of amendments in the Bill, in July and August 2005, largely based on the recommendations of the Standing Committee, which endorsed most of the campaign's demands. The most contentious issues were settled in August 2005, in a frantic round of bargaining between the constituent parties and supporters of the

[2] Both the NAC draft and the 'citizens' draft' are available at www.righttofoodindia.org, along with extensive documentation of the debate that led to the enactment of NREGA. Note that the NCMP policy commitment applied not only to rural areas but also to 'urban poor and lower middle-class household[s]'. The extension of the Act to urban areas, however, is yet to be seriously considered.

UPA government, with the Left parties extracting some major last-minute concessions. Finally, the National Rural Employment Guarantee Act was passed in the Lok Sabha on 23 August 2005.

Interestingly, the Act was passed unanimously. Video archives give an interesting glimpse of this moving event. The Minister of Rural Development, Raghuvansh Prasad Singh, made a spirited speech in Hindi, ending with '*rozgar guarantee zindabad*' (long live employment guarantee) and a roaring applause. The Speaker of the House then proceeded to conduct the 'voice vote' on NREGA. When the time came for the opponents to say 'nay', there was pin-drop silence.

This political unanimity, however, was somewhat deceptive. While it would have been very difficult for any Member of Parliament to oppose the Act in public, there was a great deal of 'behind the scenes' opposition to the Act in the corridors of power, notably from the Finance Ministry. Further, this opposition was organically linked to a powerful 'anti-NREGA' lobby, very vocal in the corporate-sponsored media and related forums. The fact that this small lobby nearly succeeded in derailing the Act (and did succeed in diluting it in some important respects), in spite of its tremendous popular appeal, is a telling symptom of the elitist nature of Indian democracy. In the end, the opposition was dispersed, and the interests of the working class prevailed. But it was a narrow victory, and the possibility of a backlash against the Act (or, more likely, its quiet sabotage) should not be dismissed.

ASPECTS OF THE NREGA DEBATE

The NREGA gives a legal guarantee of employment in rural areas to anyone who is willing to do casual manual labour at the statutory minimum wage. Any adult who applies for work under the Act is entitled to being employed on local public works within 15 days. Failing that, an unemployment allowance (one-fourth of the minimum wage for the first 30 days, and one-half thereafter) has to be paid. Guaranteed employment is subject to an initial limit of

100 days per household per year, which may be raised or removed over time.[3]

The need for an Employment Guarantee Act has been questioned. Why is it not enough to initiate massive employment schemes? The main answer is that an Act places an enforceable obligation on the state, and gives bargaining power to the labourers. It creates accountability. By contrast, a scheme leaves labourers at the mercy of government officials.

There is another major difference between a scheme and an Act. Schemes come and go, but laws are more durable. A scheme can be trimmed or even cancelled by a bureaucrat, whereas changing a law requires an amendment in Parliament. Under the Act, labourers have durable legal entitlements. Over time, they are likely to become aware of their rights and learn how to defend them. A lasting Act also helps to create a consensus in the society at large, on the legitimacy of workers' demand for employment.

Opposition to the Act often arises from a failure to appreciate its far-reaching economic, social, and political significance. To start with, the Act can go a long way towards protecting rural households from poverty and hunger. One hundred days of employment at the statutory minimum wage is not the end of poverty by any means, but for people who live on the brink of starvation, it makes a big difference.[4] Second, NREGA can help to slow down distress migration to urban areas: if work is available in the village, many rural families will stop heading for the cities during the slack season. Third, as mentioned earlier, guaranteed employment contributes to the empowerment of women. A large proportion (about half) of NREGA

[3] For a reader-friendly introduction to the Act, see Dey et al. (2006). For the full text of the Act, and related documents, see www.nrega.nic.in.

[4] In a note on the financial implications of NREGA, the NAC pointed out that a net income transfer equivalent to 100 days' earnings at the statutory minimum wage would enable a large majority of poor rural households to cross the 'poverty line'. This should not be taken literally, since there are also second-round effects to consider, both negative (for example, foregone earnings in other activities) and positive (for example, multiplier effects). But it does give a useful indication of the potential impact of NREGA on rural poverty.

workers are women, and guaranteed employment gives them some economic independence. Fourth, the Act is an opportunity to create useful assets in rural areas. In particular, there is a massive potential for labour-intensive public works in the field of environmental protection: watershed development, land regeneration, prevention of soil erosion, restoration of tanks, protection of forests, and related activities. Fifth, the Act can help to activate and revitalize the institutions of local governance, including gram panchayats (village councils) and gram sabhas (village assemblies).[5] It will give them a new purpose, backed with substantial financial resources.

Last but not least, the Act is a means of strengthening the bargaining power of unorganized workers. This, in turn, could help them to struggle for other important entitlements, such as minimum wages and social security. The process of mobilizing for effective implementation of the Act also has much value in itself, as an opportunity for unorganized workers to organize.

Having said this, the financial implications of the Employment Guarantee Act caused much concern (in some quarters) at the time of its enactment. In a note on this issue prepared by the NAC in 2004, the cost of the Act was anticipated to rise from 0.5 per cent of India's GDP in 2005–6 to one per cent of GDP in 2008–9 (NAC 2004). This was based on the assumption that the Act would be gradually extended to the whole of India within four years, starting with the 150 poorest districts in 2005–6.[6] In the same note, the NAC argued that this was quite affordable, considering that there was much scope for increasing India's tax–GDP ratio—one of the lowest in the world at that time. This view has turned out to be largely correct: rapid economic growth and (until recently) a rising tax–GDP ratio have made it relatively easy to finance the Employment Guarantee Act as well as a range of other 'flagship programmes' of the UPA Government. In 2009–10, Central Government expenditure on NREGA

[5] At least 50 per cent of NREGA funds are supposed to be spent by the gram panchayats.

[6] In fact, the Act came into force in February 2006 in 200 districts, and was extended (in two steps) to the whole country by 1 April 2008.

was around Rs 40,000 crore, or 0.65 per cent of the GDP. This is less than the NAC estimate, but NREGA expenditure is likely to rise further in the near future—possibly quite close to the anticipated 1 per cent of the GDP. Meanwhile, the initial fears about the affordability of NREGA have largely subsided.

There is an interesting parallel here with mid-day meals in primary schools. When the Supreme Court directed state governments to start providing cooked meals to school children, in late 2001, the states pleaded bankruptcy—and their plea had a ring of truth at that time. The honourable judges, however, were in no mood to surrender and told them firmly to 'cut the flab somewhere else' [sic].[7] Within a few years, annual public expenditure on mid-day meals rose to more than Rs 5,000 crore. With a little help from adequate funding, the mid-day meal scheme became one of the best social programmes of the Indian government. Today, it has very few opponents.

Similarly, in the case of NREGA, money followed the law and not the other way round. Whether NREGA will achieve the same degree of success and acceptability as mid-day meals remains to be seen. But the financial hurdles at least have been largely overcome, and the programme does have a chance.

To the fiscal conservative, concerned with curbing public expenditure come what may, all this is perhaps a nightmare. But for those who believe that there is a case for much higher public expenditure on well-devised social programmes in India, there is an interesting lesson here about the possibility of using the law to gain a financial foothold for these programmes. The Right to Education Act is playing a similar role in the field of elementary education.

EMPLOYMENT GUARANTEE AND ITS DISCONTENTS

In *Manufacturing Consent* and other writings, Noam Chomsky presents an illuminating analysis of propaganda techniques in democratic societies. One of these techniques is 'flak'—a barrage of attacks on ideas that challenge the interests of established power.

[7] Supreme Court hearing, 28 November 2001.

The NREGA, no doubt a 'dangerous' idea, was the target of two waves of flak before it was passed. The first wave occurred around December 2004, when the National Rural Employment Guarantee Bill was tabled in Parliament. The second occurred during the monsoon session of Parliament, in July–August 2005, just before the Bill came back to Parliament with a series of amendments based on the recommendations of the Standing Committee on Rural Development.

As Chomsky observes, flak often involves personal attacks, and that certainly happened in this case. To illustrate, Surjit Bhalla—one of the most vocal opponents of the Act—attacked the so-called 'leaders' of the pro-EGA campaign as 'liars' and also accused them of being 'arrogant', 'ignorant', and 'brazen', among other colourful epithets (Bhalla 2005, 2004b). In a more sober vein, the advocates of the EGA were often called '*jholawala* economists' (Dasgupta 2005), as if there was something indecent about an economist carrying a *jhola* instead of a corporate briefcase.[8] One commentator extended this term to the entire NAC, dismissed as 'a bunch of jholawalas with their hearts in the right place but their worn out sandals walking the wrong way' (Singh 2005). She argued that instead of these jholawalas, the NAC needed 'people like Sam Pitroda', apparently forgetting that Sam Pitroda (a pioneer of the telecommunications revolution in India) was already in the NAC at that time.

Even fratricide figured in this merciless crusade. Jairam Ramesh, otherwise known as the 'poster boy of economic reforms', was called a 'turncoat' in the business media for supporting the EGA and related ideas (DNA, 7 August 2005). 'What is he smoking these days?', asked a dismayed member of the pro-reform brotherhood quoted in the article.[9]

[8] A 'jhola' is a cheap shoulder-bag, and a 'jholawala' is someone who carries a jhola.

[9] Jairam Ramesh, economist turned politician (currently Minister of State for Environment and Forests), is a leading member of the Congress Party, and played a key role in the drafting of the Congress Manifesto in early 2004, as well as of the NCMP of the UPA government.

Aside from personal attacks, deceptive statistics played a major role in this propaganda operation. Surjit Bhalla deployed some of his most spectacular hat-tricks to rubbish the Employment Guarantee Act. He even managed to show, based on a creative reading of the National Sample Survey (NSS) data, that 'poor agricultural workers had an unemployment rate of only 1 per cent' (Bhalla 2004b). Ergo, the EGA is not required. As the late Sudhir Mulji, who was otherwise on much the same side of the fence as Bhalla, soberly observed in the *Business Standard*: 'That the magnitude of unemployment is substantially higher than the one per cent inferred by analysts of NSS data is obvious to even casual observers if not to skilled statisticians' (Mulji 2005). It is worth adding that 'serious analysts of NSS data' were equally startled by this reading of the evidence. In a related genre, statistical hyperbole was widely used to produce scary estimates of the likely cost of an Employment Guarantee Act—more than Rs 2,00,000 crore per year, according to one critic (Debroy 2004a).

It is also interesting to consider the alternatives that were proposed by the opponents of the Act. One of India's leading economic columnists suggested dropping cash from helicopters instead of asking people to work for wages (Aiyar 2004). Another argued that 'the first best option would be to do nothing' (Acharya 2004b). A third commentator tersely wrote that it would be 'better to have unemployment insurance alone, without the employment guarantee' (Debroy 2004a), without explaining how a universal unemployment insurance scheme could possibly work in rural India. A fourth proposal was to take refuge in Section 80G of the Income Tax Act, which allows donations to charity to be deducted from tax: 're-examine 80G, tighten it, and direct it for rural employment creation' (Srinivasa-Raghavan 2004).

The least unreasonable alternative was proposed by Surjit Bhalla: he suggested universal cash transfers as an alternative to guaranteed employment. I leave it to the reader to guess whether this was a serious proposal, or just another stick to beat the Act with. Be that as it may, the proposal can easily be accommodated. All one has to do is to insert a clause in the Act stating that if the government prefers to pay the equivalent of 100 days' wages to every household in a particular district, instead of organizing public works, it is free to do so.

To avoid misunderstanding, let me clarify that I am not dismissing every critique of the Act as an act of propaganda or sabotage. Every version of the Act, from the first draft onwards (and including the final version), had major flaws, and there was much scope for substantive disagreement on many aspects of the proposed employment guarantee. What is striking, however, is that reasoned critiques of the Act were few and far between.[10] Instead, a plethora of shallow arguments were invoked to deride it, often by influential economists with PhDs from world-class universities. There is an interesting message here about the smooth integration of the economics profession with the structures of power.

EMPLOYMENT GUARANTEE ON THE GROUND

The NREGA came into force on 2 February 2006 in 200 districts, and was extended to the whole country on 1 April 2008.[11] The lively and often acrimonious debate that led to the enactment of NREGA continued thereafter in a different form. On one side, opponents of the Act (handsomely represented in the corporate-sponsored media) have continued their barrage of criticism.[12] 'Expensive gravy train', 'costly

[10] For examples of insightful critiques of the proposed Act, see Murgai and Ravallion (2005b), Patnaik (2005), Srinivasan (2005), Banerjee and Bardhan (2004), and Ramanathan (2004), among others.

[11] In between, the Act was extended from 200 to 330 districts (on 1 April 2007). The districts in the initial list of 200 were supposed to be the poorest in the country, based on an index of 'backwardness' devised by the Planning Commission.

[12] For a few examples, see Dasgupta (2008), Ghose (2008), Jain (2007), Acharya (2005, 2004a). Interestingly, opposition to NREGA in the corporate-sponsored media swiftly vanished, and even metamorphosed into guarded support, in late 2008, when the worldwide financial crisis led to a broad-based call for higher government expenditure as a means of 'pump-priming' the economy.

joke', 'corruption guarantee scheme', 'wonky idea', 'Sonia's pet project', and 'gargantuan guzzler of taxpayers' money' is just a small sample of the colourful terms that have been used to describe NREGA. On the other side, the government and its supporters have churned out a steady stream of upbeat reports. For instance, according to a recent note from the Press Information Bureau (released on 28 December 2007), NREGA is nothing short of a 'tremendous success'.

Thankfully, there have also been informative assessments of NREGA, on the sidelines of this propaganda war.[13] Findings of a number of field surveys are already available, and much has also been learnt from 'social audits' of NREGA across the country, notably in Dungarpur (Rajasthan), Ananthapur (Andhra Pradesh), Hardoi (Uttar Pradesh), Ranchi (Jharkhand), and Viluppuram (Tamil Nadu).[14] These reports suggest that, *where work is available*, NREGA is a new lifeline for the rural poor and is also quietly sowing the seeds of significant economic, social, and political change in rural areas.

To illustrate the point, Table 1.1 presents summary findings of a recent field survey of NREGA in six states of the Hindi-speaking region (Bihar, Chhattisgarh, Jharkhand, Madhya Pradesh, Rajasthan, and Uttar Pradesh).[15] The survey covered 100 randomly-selected worksites spread over 10 districts in these states, and a sample of about 1,000 workers currently employed at these worksites (see Chapter 3 for further details).

The table illustrates a number of interesting points that are also corroborated in other studies. First, NREGA is reaching the poorest of the poor, and is of particular significance for marginalized communities such as the Scheduled Castes (SCs) and Scheduled Tribes (STs). These make up 73 per cent of NREGA workers in this

[13] See, for example, Ambasta et al. (2008), Centre for Science and Environment (2008a), National Federation of Indian Women (2008), Shah (2007); also see National Council of Applied Economic Research (2009) and earlier studies cited there.

[14] Accounts of some of these social audits are posted at www.righttofoodindia.org.

[15] For a more detailed account of the findings, see Chapter 3.

sample, with a similar figure (about 60 per cent) for the national average based on official data (see Chapter 2).

Table 1.1 Perceptions of NREGA among Rural Workers

Socio-economic background of NREGA workers:	
Proportion (%) belonging to SC/ST households	73
Proportion (%) who live in a *kachcha* house	81
Proportion (%) who have no electricity at home	72
Average number of days of NREGA employment obtained by the respondent's household in the preceding 12 months	43
Proportion (%) of workers who felt that NREGA is 'very important' for them	71
Proportion (%) of workers who reported that NREGA had helped them to:	
avoid hunger	69
avoid distress migration	57
cope with illness in the family	47
avoid demeaning or hazardous work	35
Proportion (%) of workers who felt that NREGA had led to the creation of useful assets in the village	83
Proportion (%) of workers who had any complaint of 'harassment' at the worksite	10
Proportion (%) of female respondents who:	
had earned any cash income other than NREGA wages during the preceding three months	30
collect their own (NREGA) wages	79
keep their own wages	68
Proportion (%) of workers who wanted at least 100 days of NREGA employment over the year	98

Source: NREGA Survey 2008. For further details, see Chapter 3.

Second, NREGA is also of special significance for women, particularly in areas such as the 'Hindi heartland' (the location of this survey), where women have very limited opportunities for remunerated employment.[16] Only 30 per cent of women workers in the sample had earned any cash income, other than NREGA wages, during the three months preceding the survey. Further, most of them collected their own wages, and kept them too, confirming that NREGA is a genuine source of independent income for women, and not just an opportunity for other household members (for example, their husbands) to extract work and wages from them.

Third, NREGA workers have a positive view of the programme. A large majority (71 per cent) consider that NREGA is 'very important' for them, and there is also much evidence—from this and other studies—that the programme is helping them to avoid hunger, distress migration, demeaning work, and other hardships associated with unemployment. Another telling sign of their interest in NREGA is the fact that almost all the respondents wanted at least 100 days of NREGA employment over the year—the current 'ceiling' under the Act.

Fourth, the respondents also had a positive view of the productive value of NREGA works: an overwhelming majority (83 per cent) felt that the programme had led to the creation of useful assets in the village. It may be argued that this assessment is biased, in so far as NREGA workers are unlikely to disparage their own work. As it happens, however, the field investigators had similar views on this matter: at most of the sample worksites, the survey teams considered that the work being done was 'very useful' (70 per cent) or 'quite useful' (22 per cent). Tentative as they may be, these observations make interesting reading in contrast with the widely-held (but rather unsubstantiated) belief that NREGA works amount to little more than 'playing with mud', as one grumpy commentator recently put it (Ghose 2008).

Fifth, the transition to a rights-based framework appears to be leading (slowly but surely) to a major decline in the exploitation of labour on public works. As Table 1.1 indicates, there were few complaints of

[16] On this, see Chapter 7; also Ghosh (2009), Jandu (2008), and Bhatty (2008, 2006a).

'harassment' at NREGA worksites. From this and other studies, there is also much evidence of sustained progress towards assured payment of minimum wages. This is in sharp contrast with the situation that used to prevail before NREGA, when rural public works were under the control of highly exploitative contractors.[17]

Last but not least, NREGA has shown its potential as an organizational tool for rural workers. This feature, not evident from Table 1.1, came into sharp focus in the Pati block of Badwani district, where NREGA had been actively used as a means of public mobilization by Jagrut Adivasi Dalit Sangathan (JADS), a local organization of rural workers.[18] In this block, NREGA workers had been able to secure as many as 85 days of employment during the preceding 12 months, on average (compared with 43 days in the sample as a whole). The impact of the Sangathan's organizational work was also evident from high awareness levels among NREGA workers and their confidence in the power of collective action (Nayak 2008). Many of them had learnt to make written applications for work, insist on the payment of minimum wages, participate in vigilance committees, and even demand the unemployment allowance.[19]

Thus, in spite of all its shortcomings (also well documented, in this book and elsewhere), NREGA has already led to some major achievements. All these achievements, however, are conditional on work being available (Table 1.1 is based on a random sample of persons *currently employed at NREGA worksites*). This is a major qualification. Indeed, the basic principle of 'work on demand' is yet to be put into practice, and meanwhile, employment generation continues to happen on a top–down basis. As a result, the scale of employment generation has varied a great deal, depending on the political interest of different state governments in NREGA. The top performer in

[17] For further discussion, see Drèze (2007a).

[18] See Chapter 9; also Nayak (2008).

[19] After a long struggle, JADS secured the first-ever payment of the unemployment allowance under NREGA, in October 2006, for more than 1,500 workers.

this respect is Rajasthan, where NREGA generated as many as 77 days of employment per rural household during the first year of its implementation (2006–7), in the six districts where the Act applied at that time. This is an unprecedented achievement in the history of social security in India, or for that matter anywhere in the developing world. However, the general experience is that employment generation has lagged far behind the demand for work. In the 200 districts where the Act was in force in 2006–7, NREGA generated only 17 days of employment per rural household on average, with much lower figures in many states, for example, less than 10 days in Bihar, Gujarat, Haryana, Kerala, Maharashtra, Punjab, Tamil Nadu, and West Bengal.[20]

Even these figures are likely to be on the high side, based as they are on official statistics, inclusive of 'leakages'. There is, indeed, considerable evidence that the scale and impact of NREGA have been severely diminished (and even, in some states, comprehensively undermined) by major leakages. This problem is not specific to NREGA, but the fact that embezzled funds, in this case, are snatched away from people who live on the margin of subsistence makes it particularly critical. Also, the Act (and its Operational Guidelines) includes a range of 'transparency safeguards' that were aimed at preventing fraud, so that this has become something of a test case of the possibility of eradicating corruption from development programmes.[21] Positive experiences in several states, notably Rajasthan and Andhra Pradesh, suggest that strict enforcement of these safeguards can go a long way in preventing corruption. However, this requires a clear political choice to side with the workers in this matter, and not with the nexus of corrupt bureaucrats, politicians, and contractors who benefit from the embezzlement of

[20] See Chapter 2 for further details.

[21] These transparency safeguards include availability of the 'muster rolls' at the worksite, regular maintenance of 'job cards', formation of vigilance committees, social audits by the gram sabhas, proactive disclosure of essential records, and separation of payment agencies from implementing agencies. For further details, see Government of India (2008).

NREGA funds. In this unequal battle, vested interests still have the upper hand in many states.[22]

Further, there is still a very long way to go in protecting the basic entitlements of rural workers under NREGA: work on demand, minimum wages, payment of wages within 15 days, basic worksite facilities, and unemployment allowance, among others. While these entitlements have become legal rights under the law, the current grievance redressal provisions under NREGA are very weak, making it possible for government officials and gram panchayat functionaries to get away with gross violations of the Act on a routine basis. Effective implementation of NREGA requires much higher awareness levels among rural workers, more active organizational work, and—last but not least—stronger grievance redressal procedures.

This is a long haul, and the last few years are best seen as a learning phase in the difficult transition from top–down employment schemes to a rights-based approach. Whether this learning process will, ultimately, enable the vision of the Act to be realized, remains to be seen. Meanwhile, NREGA has at least led to a major refocusing of administrative energies, financial resources, and political attention towards the concerns of rural workers. That itself is a major achievement, as well as a significant step towards the realization of the right to work.

[22] Recent events in Jharkhand, including a spate of NREGA-related murders and suicides, illustrate the intensity of these tensions, and the sinister nature of the nexus of corruption and violence that surrounds NREGA in some states. For further discussion, see Drèze (2008b) and Vanaik (2008a).

2

NREGA

The Official Picture*

Jean Drèze and Christian Oldiges

The National Rural Employment Guarantee Act (NREGA) has been a subject of lively debate during the last few years. Unfortunately, the factual basis of this debate has been, so far, rather thin. This has made it possible for extremist positions to flourish, without being submitted to careful scrutiny. While the Act is regularly pilloried in the corporate-sponsored media as an 'expensive gravy train' (as a former Chief Economic Adviser described it), the government gets away with extravagant claims of success.

Fortunately, the scope for informed analysis is growing rapidly, as reports are beginning to pour in from various parts of the country. Some statistical evidence is also available, notably, on the NREGA website launched by the Ministry of Rural Development (www.nrega.nic.in). This website is not exactly a model of clarity and elegance, but nevertheless, there is much to learn here for those who have the patience to find their way through the maze. This note is a brief 'stock-taking' of NREGA based on official data from the Ministry's website. Since the 2008–9 figures were yet to be released at the time of writing, we focus specifically on 2006–7 and 2007–8—the first two years of implementation.

* This chapter is based on two articles originally published as 'Commendable Act', *Frontline*, 24 (14): 14–27, July 2007 and 'Work in Progress', *Frontline*, 26 (4): 14–27, February 2009.

All figures presented in this note are subject to the general qualifications applying to official data on NREGA. In some cases at least, there are serious credibility issues. For instance, the website presents impressive figures on the 'number of households who have demanded employment'. And as it happens, these figures are usually much the same (often exactly the same) as the 'number of households provided employment'. Yet, we know from numerous field reports that the work application process is simply not in place in most districts. The figures on 'employment demanded' are not worth the bytes they are made of.

The fact that at least some of the official figures are unreliable (to put it mildly) affects the credibility of the entire data set, since the accuracy of different variables is hard to guess. In this note, although we have tried to stay clear of 'toxic' data, some uncomfortable questions remain. For instance, while expenditure data are likely to be reasonably accurate, the corresponding employment figures may well be inflated, to the extent that there are 'leakages' in NREGA expenditure. The statistics presented in this note have to be read in this light, or rather, lack of light.

YEAR ONE: A SNAPSHOT

As a starter, Table 2.1 presents a simple 'factsheet' on NREGA based on official data from the Ministry's website. The data pertain to the financial year 2006–7, and should be interpreted bearing in mind that this was essentially a 'learning phase' for NREGA. The Act came into force on 2 February 2006 in 200 districts. Many districts were unable to put the required systems in place before the summer months (April to June), which tend to be the months of peak demand for employment on public works. The levels of NREGA expenditure and employment in these 200 districts were much higher in 2007–8 than in 2006–7 (see below). Nevertheless, it is useful to look at the record of NREGA in 'year one'.

Table 2.1 NREGA Factsheet, 2006–7

Person-days of employment generated	
Total	90 crore
Per rural household[a]	17 days
Per job card	24 days
Per household employed in NREGA	43 days
Share of marginalized groups in total NREGA employment (%)	
Women	40
Scheduled Tribes (STs)	36
Scheduled Castes (SCs)	26
Number of NREGA works	
Taken up	8.3 lakh
Completed	3.8 lakh
In progress	4.5 lakh
Expenditure on NREGA	
Total expenditure	Rs 8,813 crore
Average expenditure per district	Rs 44 crore
Average expenditure per person-day	Rs 98
Average wage cost per person-day[b]	Rs 65
Share of wages in total expenditure[b]	66%

Source: Calculated from official data posted on the NREGA website (www.nrega.nic.in). All figures pertain to the 200 districts where NREGA came into force on 2 February 2006. The reference period is the financial year, 2006–7.
Notes: [a] In the relevant districts; number of rural households was taken from the 2001 Census.
[b] Unskilled labour only.

As Table 2.1 indicates, NREGA generated 90 crore (nearly one billion) person-days of employment in 2006–7, at a cost of about Rs 9,000 crore. By any reasonable analysis, this is much below the employment and expenditure levels that would materialize if the Act were implemented in letter and in spirit. For instance, based on rather conservative assumptions, the National Advisory Council estimated (in 2004) that fair implementation of the Act in the country's poorest 200 districts would involve about 200 crore person-days of employment generation—more than twice the actual level of employment generation in 2006–7. Nevertheless, 90 crore person-days is a start of sorts, and certainly more—much more—than the amount of employment generated in these districts in earlier years under the National Food for Work Programme (NFFWP) and the Sampoorna Grameen Rozgar Yojana (SGRY).

Having said this, there are startling differences in the levels of NREGA employment between different states. This point is illustrated in Table 2.2, where states are ranked in descending order of employment generated *per rural household* (in the relevant districts). Some state governments have clearly decided to 'own' NREGA, and immediately seized this opportunity to provide large-scale employment to the rural poor at the cost of the Central Government (which foots about 90 per cent of the bill). In other states, the whole programme was yet to take off in 2006–7.

Looking first at the top of the scale, it is perhaps not surprising to find that Rajasthan was the best performer among all major states in 2006–7 (in terms of employment generation per rural household). Indeed, employment guarantee has been a lively political issue in Rajasthan for quite a few years, and the state also had a high level of preparedness for the Act, having organized massive public works programmes almost every year in living memory. Note, however, that the small state of Tripura in the North-East (not shown in the table) was doing even better than Rajasthan, with 87 days of NREGA employment per rural household in 2006–7. In both states, employment generation under NREGA is already quite close to the upper limit of '100 days per rural household'.

At the other end of the scale, there are some surprises. Kerala is at the rock bottom, but perhaps this is partly a reflection of the low demand for NREGA employment in Kerala, rather than of a failure to provide. The same interpretation, however, is unlikely to apply to Maharashtra and West Bengal. The fact that NREGA is—as of now—a flop in both states may seem surprising, but it is actually in line with recent policy priorities. Maharashtra has assiduously sabotaged its own Employment Guarantee Scheme from the early 1990s

Table 2.2 NREGA: State-specific Indicators, 2006–7

	Person-days of NREGA employment per rural household	Share of women in NREGA employment (%)	Share of wages in total expenditure[a] (%)	Average wage cost per person-day[b] (Rs)
Rajasthan	77	67	73	51
Assam	70	32	65	67
Madhya Pradesh	56	43	63	59
North-East[b]	45	49	63	73
Chhattisgarh	34	40	65	63
Orissa	21	36	58	53
Himachal Pradesh	20	12	52	69
Uttarakhand	20	30	61	72
Karnataka	17	51	60	67
Jharkhand	14	28	58	80
Jammu & Kashmir	13	4	65	69
Uttar Pradesh	11	17	59	56
Andhra Pradesh	10	55	86	86
Haryana	9	31	65	97
Tamil Nadu	9	81	96	80
Bihar	8	17	59	70
Gujarat	7	50	65	56
Punjab	7	38	59	94
West Bengal	6	18	78	70
Maharashtra	4	37	95	104
Kerala	3	66	89	121
INDIA	**17**	**40**	**66**	**65**

Source: See Table 2.1. All figures pertain to the districts where NREGA came into force on 2 February 2006. The states are ranked in descending order of 'person-days per rural household' (first column).
Notes: [a] Unskilled labour only.
[b] Excluding Assam (approximate figures, based on incomplete data).

onwards. The government of West Bengal, for its part, initially had an ambivalent attitude towards NREGA.[1]

[1] West Bengal had a Communist Party of India Marxist (CPI-M) government at that time. The Party strongly supported NREGA, but the Chief Minister of West Bengal was opposed to it (personal interview with Buddhadeb Bhattacharya, 20 November 2005).

There is another way of looking at the state ranking in Table 2.2. As is well known, the southern and western states (Andhra Pradesh, Gujarat, Karnataka, Kerala, Maharashtra, and Tamil Nadu) routinely do better than most of the northern and eastern states when it comes to social policy and rural development programmes. The large north Indian states, for their part, tend to lag far behind. But when it comes to NREGA, the pattern is altered: only one of the southern or western states (Karnataka) has generated more than 10 person-days of employment per rural household in 2006–7, while the eastern and northern states have done comparatively well in this respect. Of course, this pattern has to be read in the light of the fact that the need for fall-back employment may be greater in the eastern and northern regions. Nevertheless, it is encouraging to find that NREGA made an early start in these deprived regions (with the significant exceptions of Bihar and West Bengal).

The last three columns of Table 2.2 look at other features of the implementation of NREGA in different states, and enable us, in particular, to spot some important irregularities. Consider, for instance, the participation of women in NREGA. It is encouraging to note that women's share of NREGA employment is not far from half (40 per cent to be precise) at the all-India level, rising to a startling 81 per cent in Tamil Nadu. The economic dependence of women on men in rural India plays a major role in the subjugation of women, and in this respect, NREGA is an important tool of social change. However, many states are violating the Act by failing to ensure that the share of women in NREGA employment is at least one-third: Jammu and Kashmir (4 per cent share), Himachal Pradesh (12 per cent), Uttar Pradesh (17 per cent), among others. In this connection, it is also worth mentioning that the mandatory provision of crèche facilities at NREGA worksites has been brazenly ignored, so far, almost everywhere. Better arrangements for child care are urgently required to facilitate the participation of women in NREGA. Of course, it is not just a matter of child care. But the provision of crèche facilities at NREGA worksites would certainly help, and also have much value in terms of creating wider social acceptance of child care arrangements as a basic right of working women.

The labour component of NREGA is supposed to account for at least 60 per cent of the total expenditure. As Table 2.2 indicates, this requirement is comfortably met in most states, though some of them (for example, Bihar, Jharkhand, Orissa, and Uttar Pradesh) have marginally lower ratios, and Himachal Pradesh spends only 52 per cent of NREGA funds on the labour component. It would be interesting to know how states like Maharashtra and Tamil Nadu manage to implement NREGA works with virtually no expenditure other than wages. Of course, there is a strong incentive for states to adopt labour-intensive techniques under NREGA, since the labour component is entirely funded by the Central Government (unlike the material component, which is shared). The share of wages at the all-India level is 66 per cent, which seems like a satisfactory figure.

The last column in Table 2.2 presents average wage costs per person-day. This is, for practical purposes, the same as the average wage rate (in rupees per day). Here again, there are major inter-state variations, with, say, Kerala paying more than twice as much as Rajasthan. These large differences raise the question whether it is better to have state-specific wages, or a national norm. This complex matter is yet to be adequately debated. Indeed, wage payments raise a host of interesting and complex questions that have been lost in the din of arguments for and against the Act: how NREGA wages should be determined; whether there should be a national norm; whether piece-rate payments are better than daily-wage payments; how work should be measured; whether the 'Schedule of Rates' should be gender-specific; how to avoid long delays in the payment of wages; and so on. An informed debate on these issues is urgently needed.

Finally, it is alarming to find that some states are evidently paying less than the statutory minimum wage, in flagrant violation of the Act. The most glaring offender in this respect is none other than Rajasthan, where NREGA workers earned a meagre Rs 51 per day on average in 2006–7, even though the statutory minimum wage was Rs 73 per day. This is a trifle paradoxical, since workers' organizations in Rajasthan have been at the forefront of recent struggles for minimum wages. Also, it is in the context of relief works in Rajasthan that the Supreme

Court delivered a landmark judgement stating that employing labourers without paying the minimum wage is 'forced labour', in so far as it amounts to '[taking] advantage of the helpless condition of the affected persons' (*Sanjit Roy vs. State of Rajasthan 1983, SCC (1) 525*). More than 20 years after this indictment, the problem persists.

As one might expect, the contrasts discussed so far are even sharper at the district level. For instance, employment generation per rural household in 2006–7 was just about *one person-day* in Madhubani (Bihar), but as high as 111 days in Dungarpur (Rajasthan). Similarly, while women's share of NREGA employment is above 80 per cent in most districts of Tamil Nadu, it is *less than 1 per cent* in five districts of Uttar Pradesh. The inter-district contrasts are illustrated in Figure 2.1, with reference to the level of NREGA employment (measured, as before, in terms of person-days per rural household).

Behind these facts and figures is a simple yet powerful message about NREGA. Within a year of the Act coming into force, the programme was actively taken up in a small but significant number of districts (20 of them spent more than Rs 100 crore on NREGA in 2006–7). Further, field reports suggest that many of the anticipated benefits of employment guarantee are beginning to show in these pioneer districts: there is greater economic security, agricultural wages are rising, distress migration is declining, useful assets are being built, women have more economic independence, and so on. The need of the hour is to extend these positive experiences to other districts. If Surguja or Mandla or Banswara are able to spend more than Rs 100 crore on this programme in a single year, there is no reason why (say) Palamau or Kalahandi should not be able to do it.

Of course, it is also important to ensure that the reported expenditure levels actually correspond to 'real' work and wages. Earlier employment programmes have left a long trail of fake muster rolls and embezzled money. However, there is growing evidence that a firm enforcement of NREGA's extensive transparency safeguards can go a long way in preventing corruption. Success stories in this respect are no longer confined to Rajasthan—the stronghold of India's 'right to information movement'. In Andhra Pradesh, for instance,

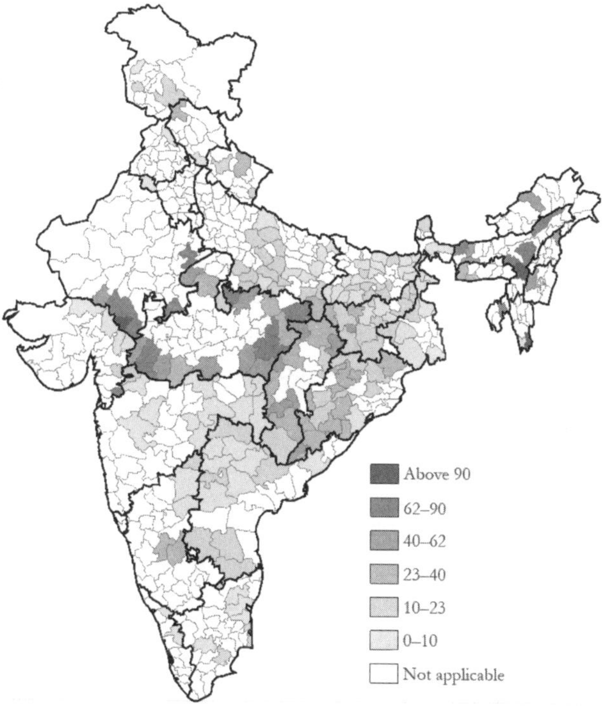

Figure 2.1 NREGA 2006–7: Person-days per Rural Household

institutionalized social audits and the separation of implementation agencies from payment agencies (in this case, the post offices) have imparted impressive levels of transparency in NREGA.[2] This is a major achievement, especially in contrast with the massive levels of fraud observed in the same state just a few years ago, under the NFFWP. The transition towards a more transparent and accountable system is also under way in many other states, even those that are notorious for endemic corruption.[3]

It would be naïve to think that the long history of fraud in public works programmes has already come to an end. But recent experience shows that it is possible to remove mass corruption from

[2] See, for example, Mathur (2009) and Shah and Ambasta (2008).
[3] For further discussion, see Drèze et al. (2008).

NREGA. This calls for strict implementation of the transparency safeguards, as well as firm action whenever corruption is exposed. In these simple steps lies the future of the Act.

YEAR TWO: CONTINUITY AND CHANGE

In the preceding section, we presented NREGA-related data for 2006–7, extracted from the official website of the Ministry of Rural Development. This section is essentially an 'update' along the same lines, including a brief comparison of the 2006–7 and 2007–8 figures.

An All-India Snapshot

An updated 'factsheet' on the all-India situation is presented in Table 2.3. As expected, there was a major expansion of the scale of NREGA works in the second year of implementation. In 2007–8, the programme generated 144 crore person-days of employment, according to official data. In other words, about 4 million persons were employed on an average day. Over the year, 34 million households participated in NREGA. Assuming an average household size of five, this is equivalent, say, to the entire population of Bangladesh. The scale of the programme is even larger today, with the NREGA budget shooting up to Rs 40,000 crore or so in 2009–10 (from around Rs 16,000 crore in 2007–8). Nothing comparable has been done before.

In Table 2.3, an attempt is also made to compare official figures for 2006–7 and 2007–8. Note that the comparison can be made in two ways: with or without restricting the focus to the 200 'Phase-I' districts where the Act came into force on 2 February 2006. Both comparisons are possible from Table 2.3. The 'unrestricted' comparison (first and last columns in Table 2.3) must be read bearing in mind that the number of districts covered by NREGA increased from 200 to 330 on 1 April 2007.

Table 2.3 NREGA Factsheet, 2006–7 and 2007–8

	2006–7	2007–8	
	Phase-I districts	Phase-I districts only	Phase-I + Phase-II districts
Number of districts under NREGA	200	200	330
Person-days of employment generated			
Total (crore)	90	108	144
Per rural household[a]	17	20	16
Per job card	24	25	22
Per household employed in NREGA	43	48	42
Share of marginalized groups in NREGA employment (%)			
Women	40	44	42
Scheduled Tribes (STs)	36	33	29
Scheduled Castes (SCs)	26	27	27
Expenditure on NREGA			
Total expenditure (Rs crore)	8,813	12,057	15,857
Average expenditure per district (Rs crore)	44	60	48
Average expenditure per person-day (Rs)	98	111	110
Average wage cost per person-day[b] (Rs)	65	75	75
Share of wages in total expenditure[b] (%)	66	67	68

Source: Calculated from official data posted on the NREGA website (www.nrega.nic.in). NREGA was launched in 200 (Phase-I) districts on 2 February 2006, and extended to another 130 (Phase-II) districts on 1 April 2007.

Notes: [a] In the relevant districts; number of rural households was taken from the 2001 Census.

[b] Unskilled labour only.

This unrestricted comparison suggests that the extension of NREGA from 200 to 330 districts was relatively 'smooth', in the sense that what was achieved in 2006–7 was achieved again in 2007–8 on a larger scale. Total expenditure increased more or less in proportion with the increased coverage, and most indicators remained much the same in both years. This applies, for instance, to 'employment per rural household' (and related indicators of the scale of works), as well to the share of women in the workforce, expenditure per district, and the share of wages in total expenditure.

Two minor changes can be noticed. First, the share of Scheduled Tribes (STs) in the NREGA workforce declined (from 36 per cent to 29 per cent) between 2006–7 and 2007–8, presumably due to the fact that the initial 200 districts had particularly high shares of ST households in the rural population. Second, there was an increase of about 15 per cent in the average wage rate ('wage cost per day' in the table), in nominal terms—from Rs 65 to Rs 75 per day. In real terms, this corresponds to an increase of about 8 per cent over one year. This is hardly 'hyper-inflation of wages', as some commentators (including the Minister for Rural Development, Raghuvansh Prasad Singh) described this pattern in the context of the alleged need to 'freeze' NREGA wages.

On closer inspection (that is, looking also at the restricted comparison, confined to Phase-I districts), this aggregate picture hides important differences between Phase-I and Phase-II districts. Specifically, employment levels were much higher in Phase-I districts than in Phase-II districts in 2007–8 (about 20 and 10 days per rural household, respectively). This is as expected, not only because Phase-I districts were able to build on the foundations they had laid the previous year, but also because the need for employment is greater in Phase-I districts, since they are poorer. Note that, consistent with this interpretation, employment levels in the first year of implementation (2006–7 in Phase-I districts and 2007–8 in Phase II districts) was considerably higher in Phase-I districts than in Phase-II districts. With these qualifications, the dominant pattern in Table 2.3 is one of relative continuity between 2006–7 and 2007–8.

State-specific Patterns

Table 2.4 presents a sample of state-specific indicators, much as in Table 2.2. In this table, the 'unrestricted' comparison (between Phase-I districts in 2006–7 and 'Phase-I + Phase-II' districts in

2007–8) is made state-wise. Here again, we find that the basic indicators for 2006–7 and 2007–8 are much the same, in most cases. However, there are interesting exceptions.

For instance, looking at the scale of NREGA works, as indicated by the number of person-days of employment per rural household, we find that the 'leaders' in this respect, in 2007–8, were Rajasthan, Madhya Pradesh, and Chhattisgarh (in that order) as well as the north-eastern region. In fact, the first three states alone accounted for more than half of total employment generation under NREGA in 2007–8. All three were already in a leading position in 2006–7, with similar levels of employment per rural household. On the other hand, Assam was also doing very well in this respect in 2006–7, but slipped back the next year.

Another state where there was a major setback is Orissa, where employment generation per rural household apparently declined from 21 days in 2006–7 to 8 days in 2007–8. Orissa was the focus of a wave of embezzlement reports in 2006–7, and there are at least two possible reasons for this employment crash the following year. One is that there was a substantial reduction in fudging of employment figures due to greater vigilance (there is some independent evidence of this from recent social audits initiated by the National Institute of Rural Development). This could bring down the official employment figures, even without any reduction in actual employment. The other possibility is that employment actually declined, perhaps because the corruption scandals (or the remedial measures that followed them) led to a loss of motivation on the part of implementing agencies. Quite likely, both factors played a role.

Looking at the other end of the scale, NREGA employment levels in 2006–7 were extremely low in Bihar, Gujarat, Haryana, Maharashtra, Punjab, and West Bengal; they remained abysmally low in these states in 2007–8, and even declined in several cases (for instance, Gujarat and Punjab). On the other hand, NREGA employment per rural household doubled in Andhra Pradesh, Kerala, and Tamil Nadu, three states where there have been active efforts to expand the programme

Table 2.4 Selected State-specific Indicators

	NREGA employment (person-days per rural household)[a]		Share of women in NREGA employment (%)		Share of SC/STs in NREGA employment (%)		Share of unskilled labour in NREGA expenditure (%)		Average wage (Rs/day)	
	2006–7	2007–8	2006–7	2007–8	2006–7	2007–8	2006–7	2007–8	2006–7	2007–8
Rajasthan	77	68	67	69	80	66	73	67	51	59
Madhya Pradesh	56	52	43	42	65	67	63	61	59	64
Chhattisgarh	34	43	40	42	58	56	65	64	63	68
North-East[b]	45	35	49	39	88	77	72	68	73	81
Assam	70	25	32	31	55	47	65	65	67	73
Tamil Nadu	9	21	81	82	58	60	96	97	80	77
Jharkhand	14	20	28	27	64	62	58	58	80	75
Andhra Pradesh	10	19	55	58	43	41	86	80	86	82
Himachal Pradesh	20	17	12	30	53	43	52	59	69	83
Uttarakhand	20	16	30	43	28	32	61	62	72	74
Uttar Pradesh	11	11	17	15	60	56	59	67	56	93
Haryana	9	10	31	34	60	54	65	85	97	124
Orissa	21	8	36	36	73	64	58	54	53	77
West Bengal	6	8	18	17	55	50	78	76	70	79
Bihar	8	7	17	27	50	48	59	65	70	80
Jammu & Kashmir	13	7	4	1	29	32	65	63	69	72
Karnataka	17	7	51	50	53	49	60	60	67	72
Kerala	3	6	66	71	33	34	89	86	121	118
Gujarat	7	5	50	47	71	72	65	71	56	64
Maharashtra	4	3	37	40	57	57	95	88	104	90
Punjab	7	2	38	16	69	76	59	65	94	101
India	**17**	**16**	**40**	**42**	**62**	**57**	**66**	**68**	**65**	**75**

Source: See Table 2.3. States are ranked in decreasing order of NREGA employment generation in 2007–8 (second column).

Notes: [a] In the relevant districts (Phase-I districts in 2006–7 and 'Phase-I + Phase-II' districts in 2007–8); number of rural households was taken from the 2001 Census. [b] Combined figures for Arunachal Pradesh, Manipur, Meghalaya, Mizoram, Nagaland, Sikkim, and Tripura (excluding districts with missing data).

in 2007–8 (starting from a relatively low base). The absence of a similar take-off in, say, Bihar and West Bengal is a matter of concern, given the high levels of rural poverty in those states.

It is a little ironic that the three NREGA 'leaders', in terms of scale of works, all had Bharatiya Janata Party (BJP) governments in 2007–8, considering that the Act is usually seen as the Congress Party's baby. If anything, the odd contrast between the BJP's activism in this regard, and the Congress' resilient inability to nurture its own baby, has become even sharper with Assam sliding back. Of course, it is not that every BJP government has done well in this respect—Gujarat is a prominent exception. But, on the whole, the BJP seems to have adopted the Congress' orphan with open arms. Whether this played a part in the BJP's recent return to power in two of these three states (Chhattisgarh and Madhya Pradesh), in spite of the anti-incumbency factor, is hard to guess.

Turning to other indicators, the share of women in the NREGA workforce was much the same in both years (around 40 per cent), though there was a noticeable increase (from 40 to 44 per cent) in Phase-I districts—a healthy indication of growing participation of women over time. The state-specific figures and rankings are fairly stable between 2006–7 and 2007–8, with, for instance, Tamil Nadu having the highest participation of women in NREGA in both years by a long margin (though Kerala was 'catching up' in the second year). One interesting development is a major increase in women's participation in Bihar and Himachal Pradesh. However, all the states where women's share of the NREGA workforce was below the statutory minimum of 33 per cent in 2006–7 were still below that cut-off in 2007–8, except for Haryana and Uttarakhand. Punjab, for its part, crossed the mark in the wrong direction. The share of SCs and STs in NREGA employment declined a little between 2006–7 and 2007–8, mainly on account of the decline in ST participation (mentioned earlier), with no major changes in state-specific figures.

As noted earlier, the labour component of NREGA accounts for almost 70 per cent of total expenditure, a significant achievement considering the relatively low labour-intensity of many earlier employment schemes (often due, in turn, to vested interests in favour of the material component). With the Central Government footing the entire wage bill, but only 75 per cent of the material costs, state governments have strong incentives to promote labour-intensive techniques under NREGA. Tamil Nadu went furthest in this direction, with virtually no material component, on the grounds that material expenditure attracts private contractors and breeds corruption. In 2007–8, Orissa was the only state where the labour component was substantially below the statutory minimum of 60 per cent of total expenditure.[4]

Finally, there have been substantial changes in wage rates (last two columns of Table 2.4) in several states, and also at the all-India level. The changes have been mainly upward, with a few exceptions. The largest upward jumps, in proportionate terms, have occurred in Uttar Pradesh (66 per cent), Orissa (45 per cent), and Haryana (28 per cent). In Uttar Pradesh, there have been successive increases in minimum wages, from Rs 58 per day to Rs 100 per day within a couple of years. The final hike to Rs 100 was due to a personal intervention by the Chief Minister and BSP leader, Mayawati. It was a shrewd political move, which created unprecedented interest in the programme among the rural poor and took the wind out of the sails of the Congress Party as far as taking credit for NREGA in Uttar Pradesh is concerned. This was also an interesting U-turn, considering that Mayawati (and her predecessor, Mulayam Singh) initially ignored and even disparaged NREGA as a hare-brained initiative of the Congress Party.

In Rajasthan, the increase in wages between 2006–7 and 2007–8 is likely to reflect the combination of an increase in minimum wages (from Rs 73 per day to Rs 84 per day), and higher productivity linked with improved worksite management. Indeed, the Government of

[4] Orissa also had an odd practice, at that time, of charging hefty 'royalties' (sometimes as high as 30 per cent of total expenditure on particular works) whenever digging is involved in NREGA works. Even digging of plain sand apparently attracted royalties. This anomaly was exposed in November 2007 by a delegation of the Central Employment Guarantee Council to Orissa.

Rajasthan has taken important initiatives in this field, including mass training of 'mates' (worksite supervisors) and 'group measurement' of NREGA work.[5] There is some evidence that this led to a significant increase in NREGA earnings under the piece-rate system. Even then, Rajasthan continues to have the lowest average NREGA wages in the country.

It is worth reflecting whether there is any causal link between low wages and high employment levels in Rajasthan. There is, in fact, something of a pattern in this respect across states: high levels of NREGA employment tend to be associated with relatively low wages (for example, in Chhattisgarh, Madhya Pradesh, and Rajasthan), and vice-versa (for example, in Bihar, Haryana, Kerala, Maharashtra, Punjab, and West Bengal). The association may be incidental, but it is also possible that low wages make it easier, in various ways, to implement NREGA on a large scale. Note, however, that the north-eastern region seems to be able to generate large-scale employment at relatively high wages.

Moving to more disaggregated data, Figure 2.2 displays district-specific employment levels (number of days of NREGA employment per rural household) in 2007–8, as with Figure 2.1 for 2006–7. From these maps, it is clear that NREGA, despite being a national programme, is still heavily concentrated in a small number of districts, mainly in the three leading states mentioned earlier (Chhattisgarh, Madhya Pradesh, and Rajasthan), where most of the NREGA districts have high levels of employment generation. Outside that region, very few districts have comparable levels of NREGA employment, except for pockets of the North-East. Except for Andhra Pradesh, employment levels are still very low throughout the southern and western regions, even in highly deprived areas such as northern Karnataka, eastern Maharashtra, or Nandurbar district. More importantly perhaps, the programme is yet to take off in most of the eastern region (Bihar, Jharkhand, Orissa, and West Bengal), where the incidence of poverty and hunger is very high and NREGA could make a big difference.

[5] For further discussion, see Chapter 8.

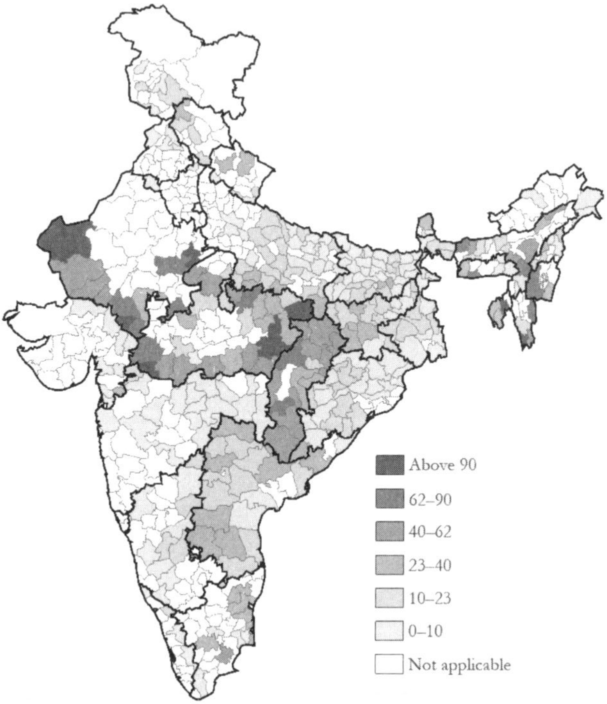

Figure 2.2 NREGA 2007–8: Person-days per Rural Household

CONCLUDING REMARKS

Such is the picture that emerges from official data. As mentioned earlier, the accuracy of the official figures is an open question, which calls for urgent scrutiny. In any case, independent large-scale surveys of NREGA (analogous to, say, the National Family Health Survey) would be very useful. It is not clear why a government that now spends about Rs 40,000 crore a year on NREGA is unable to spare a few crores for a comprehensive independent survey, to find out where the money is going and what the programme is achieving.

Last but not least, it is worth noting that there are crucial gaps in the present Monitoring and Information System (MIS). For instance, in our experience, most Programme Officers at the block level do not have a list of active worksites. All they know is that various sums of money were disbursed to various gram panchayats (or other implementing agencies) on various dates. Similarly, there is no systematic record of delays in wage payments. If labourers remain unpaid for weeks at a particular worksite, there is no trace of it in the MIS.[6] This is one reason why long delays in wage payments persist in many states, causing immense hardship to NREGA workers, and even inducing some of them to 'quit'. These and other gaping holes in the statistical system need urgent attention if NREGA is to achieve its ambitious transparency norms.

[6] The latest version of the MIS software attempts to plug this gap.

PART II

GROUND REALITIES

3

The Battle for Employment Guarantee*

Jean Drèze and Reetika Khera#

'The dream I have for my son is that he should get at least 15 days of casual labour every month.' Thus spoke an elderly agricultural worker at a public hearing held in Allahabad district five years ago, on the sidelines of the *Rozgar Adhikar Yatra*—an awareness drive launched as part of the campaign for a national Employment Guarantee Act. His dream was not that his son would earn the minimum wage, or become a skilled labourer—he only wanted 15 days of casual work every month. With local wages as low as 25 to 30 rupees a day at that time, it is not difficult to imagine the living conditions of a family that survives on 15 days' earnings.

Three years later, it may seem that this modest dream has come true. Under the National Rural Employment Guarantee Act (NREGA), anyone who is willing to do manual labour at the statutory minimum wage is entitled to being employed on local public works within 15 days, subject to a limit of 100 days per household per year. In reality, however, workers still have to fight at every step for their entitlements under the Act: to get employment, to be paid on time, to earn the minimum wage, to avoid harassment, and so on. This is the 'battle for employment guarantee'.

* Originally published as 'The Battle for Employment Guarantee', *Frontline*, 26 (1): 3–16, January 2009.

This chapter draws on collaborative work with Anish Vanaik, Ashish Ranjan, Kamayani Swami, Kartika Bhatia, Karuna Muthiah, Nandini Nayak, Navjyoti, Noor Zaheer, Siddhartha, Sunil Kumar, and Zia Khan.

The battle for employment guarantee is also a larger struggle, stretching from remote villages to the national capital, to ensure that the Act is implemented in letter and in spirit. At times, alas, the battle has turned violent. Whistle-blowers have been the main target. On 14 May 2008, Lalit Mehta was brutally murdered as he was about to initiate a social audit of NREGA in Palamau district, Jharkhand. About a month later, Kameshwar Yadav, an activist of CPI-ML (Liberation) working on NREGA and related issues in Giridih district—also in Jharkhand—was killed in circumstances that suggest a link with his political activities. In early July of the same year, Tapas Soren immolated himself in Hazaribagh to protest against harassment and corruption in the context of NREGA (a harrowing video of his last words is available at www.youtube.com). There have been violent incidents in other states, too, and while most of the deaths reported so far have occurred in Jharkhand, this wave of violence may well spread to other states in the near future, as the battle intensifies.

However, there is some good news too. Slowly but surely, the Act is making a difference to the lives of the rural poor. In Rajasthan, in the very first year of NREGA (2006–7), the average rural household worked for as many as 77 days under the programme. In most other states, the promise of 100 days of assured employment is still a distant dream, but employment generation is nevertheless much higher than under earlier public works programmes. And where employment is available, NREGA is having an impact: wages are rising, migration is slowing down, productive assets are being created, and the power equations are changing too.

These positive achievements have been lost in the wave of hostile reports and anti-NREGA editorials relayed by the corporate-sponsored media. A more informed and open-minded look at NREGA, warts and all, is long overdue—that is the main purpose of this essay.

SOCIAL BACKGROUND OF NREGA WORKERS

We begin by taking note of the perceptions of NREGA workers, who have rarely been heard in this noisy debate. This we do on the basis of a field survey conducted in May–June 2008 in six states of north India (see Box 3.1 for details). These account for about 40 per cent of India's population, and 62 per cent of NREGA expenditure in 2007–8. The survey involved unannounced visits to 100 randomly-selected worksites spread over these six states, and interviews with a random sample of about 1,000 workers employed at these worksites.

BOX 3.1 NREGA SURVEY 2008: IN BRIEF

The NREGA Survey 2008 was conducted in May–June 2008. It covered ten districts spread over six north Indian states (Bihar, Chhattisgarh, Jharkhand, Madhya Pradesh, Rajasthan, and Uttar Pradesh). The sample districts were Araria and Kaimur (Bihar), Surguja (Chhattisgarh), Koderma and Palamau (Jharkhand), Badwani and Sidhi (Madhya Pradesh), Dungarpur and Sirohi (Rajasthan), and Sitapur (Uttar Pradesh).

In each district, ten gram panchayats (five each in two different blocks) were selected for investigation. In each of the 100 sample gram panchayats, one active NREGA worksite was studied, and at each sample worksite, 10 workers were randomly selected for interview.

The survey teams consisted mainly of university students working with local volunteers. Each team spent two days in each sample gram panchayat, living either with the labourers themselves or in a public building such as the local school.

The survey was initiated by the G.B. Pant Social Science Institute, with joint support from Allahabad University and the National Commission for Enterprises in the Unorganized Sector (NCEUS). Pilot surveys were also conducted in association with the Centre for Development Economics (Delhi School of Economics) and the Institute for Human Development (Ranchi). This essay also draws on social audits and informal investigations of NREGA conducted in the sample states and elsewhere (including Himachal Pradesh, Orissa, and Tamil Nadu), before and after the survey.

Further details (including the survey instruments) are available at www.righttofoodindia.org.

PIW

The first point to note about NREGA workers is that most of them belong to the most disadvantaged sections of society. This should really go without saying; it is fairly obvious from casual observation at almost any worksite. Yet it is worth mentioning, because doubts have been raised about this feature of the programme (the 'self-selection' aspect). To illustrate the point, 81 per cent of the sample workers live in a *kaccha* house, 61 per cent are illiterate, and 72 per cent have no electricity at home (Table 3.1).

Table 3.1 NREGA Labourers: Rural India's 'Working Class'

Proportion (%) of sample workers who:	
Live in a kaccha house	81
Belong to SC/ST families	73
Are illiterate	61
Have no electricity at home	72

Source: NREGA Survey 2008.

Scheduled Caste (SC) and Scheduled Tribe (ST) families are also joining NREGA in large numbers. They account for 56 per cent of all workers at the all-India level, according to official data, and for 73 per cent of the workers in our sample. It is hard to think of any other development programme that involves SC/ST communities to this extent, without any reservation or quota. Clearly, NREGA is a powerful tool of economic redistribution and social equity.

MASSIVE DEMAND FOR NREGA WORK

Another 'obvious' point that bears mention is the fact that there is a massive demand for NREGA work. Among other myths floated some years ago to scuttle the enactment of NREGA was the notion that there is little demand for this sort of employment. One of India's leading economists even argued that NREGA was unnecessary because 'poor agricultural workers had an unemployment rate of only 1 per cent' (Bhalla 2004b). Contrary to this fairy tale, 98 per cent of the sample workers stated that they were ready to work for 100 days in the year—the 'upper limit' under the Act (Table 3.2).

Table 3.2 Massive Demand for NREGA Work

Proportion (%) of sample workers who:	
Want at least 100 days of NREGA work over the year	98
Have worked for at least 100 days on NREGA last year	13
Average days of NREGA employment in the last 12 months:	
Sample workers	31
Sample workers' households	43

Source: NREGA Survey 2008.

As things stand, NREGA meets a small fraction of this demand: only 13 per cent of the respondents had actually secured 100 days of NREGA work during the preceding 12 months. There were, of course, wide inter-state variations in this respect. While the proportion of sample workers who had completed 100 days of work was particularly low in Chhattisgarh (1 per cent), Bihar (2 per cent), Uttar Pradesh (3 per cent), and Jharkhand (7 per cent), it was considerably higher in Madhya Pradesh (17 per cent), and as high as 35 per cent in Rajasthan. This is one aspect, among others, of Rajasthan's impressive achievements in this field; the contrast between Rajasthan and other states is a recurring theme of this essay.

The survey does not tell us much about NREGA participation rates in the rural population as a whole. Some information on this is provided in Table 3.3, based on official data. A useful indicator here is 'number of days of NREGA employment per rural household' (second row). Among the sample states, this varied from 7 days in Bihar to 68 days in Rajasthan in 2007–8. The all-India average was 16 days, though that may be an over-estimate, bearing in mind that there are substantial 'leakages' in NREGA expenditure, not captured in official data (see Chapter 2).

Given the unimpressive scale of works so far, NREGA is bound to have a limited impact. Nevertheless, it is useful to examine its impact *where work is available*, as it ought to be everywhere under the

Table 3.3 NREGA Factsheet, 2007–8

	India 330 districts	Bihar 38 districts	Chhattisgarh 15 districts	Jharkhand 22 districts	Madhya Pradesh 31 districts	Rajasthan 12 districts	Uttar Pradesh 39 districts
Person-days of employment generated:							
Total (crore)	110	8.6	13.2	7.5	27.5	16.8	13.6
Per rural household[a]	16	7	43	20	52	68	11
Per household employed in NREGA	42	22	58	45	63	77	33
Expenditure on NREGA:							
Total expenditure (Rs crore)	15,857	1,052	1,041	1,062	2,891	1,477	1,898
Average expenditure per person-day (Rs)	110	123	107	142	105	88	139
Average wage cost per person-day[b] (Rs)	75	80	68	82	64	59	93

Source: Calculated by Christian Oldiges from official data posted on the NREGA website (www.nrega.nic.in). All figures pertain to the districts covered under NREGA in 2007–8. The states in this table are those covered by the field survey (see Box 3.1).

Notes: [a] In the relevant districts (number of rural households was taken from the 2001 Census).

[b] Unskilled labour only.

Act. The field survey throws some light on this, since it focuses on a sample of NREGA workers.

AWARENESS LEVELS

In contrast with earlier employment schemes, NREGA is a rights-based programme. The rights of NREGA workers include employment on demand, minimum wages, payment within 15 days, and basic worksite facilities, among others. The best guarantee of realization of these rights lies in organized demand on the part of well-informed workers. For instance, if workers insist on being paid the minimum wage, depriving them of it would be that much harder. For this to happen, of course, workers have to be aware of their rights.

The survey shows, however, that awareness levels among NREGA workers are still very low. Well into the third year of NREGA, less than half of the sample workers were aware of their entitlement to 100 days of work over the year—the starting point of the Act (Table 3.4). Similarly, barely half of them were aware of the minimum wage, or of their right to being paid within 15 days—with even lower awareness levels in the more deprived districts, where NREGA is needed most.

Table 3.4 People's Awareness of NREGA: Miles to Go

	Rajasthan	Other states[a]
Proportion (%) of sample workers who are aware of their entitlement to:		
One hundred days of work	90	42
Minimum wages	67	43
Payment within 15 days	64	54

Source: NREGA Survey 2008.
Note: [a] Bihar, Chhattisgarh, Jharkhand, Madhya Pradesh, and Uttar Pradesh.

Low levels of awareness play a major part in the lack of public pressure to make NREGA work. For instance, while there is a massive latent demand for work, very few workers in our sample had ever made a formal application for work (Table 3.5). The main reason is that they are not aware of the possibility of applying (not to speak of the application procedure). Instead, they passively wait for work to come their way.

Table 3.5 The Work Application Process is Not in Place

Proportion (%) of sample workers who:	
Never make an application for work	65
Made an individual written application	6
Made a collective written application	15
Made an informal demand	8
Main reasons for not applying (%):	
Not aware of the need to apply	71

Source: NREGA Survey 2008.

As Table 3.4 illustrates, awareness levels are much higher in Rajasthan than in other states. This is both a root and an outcome of the comparative success of NREGA there. Rajasthan has a long tradition of public mobilization for employment and wages in the context of drought relief. When NREGA came into force, it was quickly recognized as a crucial opportunity for the rural poor. Public interest in the Act quickly translated into serious pressure on the state government to act. The government itself foresaw the political value of NREGA and took major initiatives, including mass awareness campaigns. In other states, many awareness drives have also been launched, but in actual fact, government officials have often kept people in the dark, to avoid having to face their demands.

We found some evidence that awareness levels are higher in areas where some sort of a workers' organization has been built (discussed later). Even otherwise, awareness levels are definitely rising. For instance, the proportion of workers who know the minimum wage—around 50 per cent—does not look so bad when we remember that, before NREGA, the very notion of minimum wage was a mystery to most rural workers. Year after year, workers are likely to develop a better awareness of their rights as well as of their collective power. This is a key feature of the battle for employment guarantee: time is on the side of the workers.

A LIFELINE FOR THE RURAL POOR

In contrast with the scepticism of many economic advisers, most of the sample workers had a positive view of NREGA. This was especially the case where employment levels were relatively high. For instance, more than two-thirds of all sample workers felt that NREGA was 'very important' for them (Table 3.6), rising to 80 per among households that have worked for at least 60 days in the preceding 12 months. The proportion was also high among disadvantaged groups—for instance, it was 83 per cent among widows.

Table 3.6 A Lifeline for the Rural Poor

Proportion (%) of sample workers who stated that:	
NREGA is 'very important' for them	71
NREGA has helped them to avoid hunger	69
NREGA has helped them to avoid migration	57
NREGA has helped their family to cope with illness	47
NREGA has helped them to avoid demeaning or hazardous occupations	35

Source: NREGA Survey 2008.

The potential value of NREGA as a lifeline for the rural poor is also evident from other survey responses. To illustrate, about half of the respondents felt that NREGA had 'brought significant change in their lives', and 69 per cent said that it had helped them avoid hunger. There were also signs of NREGA having 'helped' in other ways, such as avoiding migration (59 per cent), sending children to school (38 per cent), coping with illness (47 per cent), repaying debts (32 per cent), and avoiding demeaning or hazardous work (35 per cent). Almost all the respondents reported *at least one* of these positive outcomes (on migration, see also Box 3.2).

Food and subsistence typically have the first call on NREGA earnings. Many respondents explained how NREGA had helped them to banish hunger from their homes, or to improve their frugal diet. Their earnings contribute to food security in a variety of ways: not only are incomes higher, cash in hand helps them to buy rations

BOX 3.2 'IN THE CITY WE HAD TO SLEEP WITH DOGS ON THE FOOTPATH'

'For us, getting work in our village is a big thing. Since I don't have any land, I am completely dependent on casual labour.'

—Gondi, a 45-year-old woman (Surguja district, Chhattisgarh)

'Because works have started opening, the idea of leaving the village doesn't enter our mind.'

—Dilsay (Surguja district)

'Migrating for work is very expensive. Half of our earnings are spent in commuting alone. When he [her husband] used to go to the bazaar to work, he had to face exploitation from his employer.'

—Sita Bai (Sirohi district, Rajasthan)

'Before NREGA we had to go far for work. There was no place to stay so we slept with our children on the footpath where dogs also slept with us.'

—Dinesh, 20 years (Badwani district, Madhya Pradesh)

These testimonies sum up the importance of NREGA in the lives of many migrant labourers. It is a valued source of local employment, if not, at times, the only source. In their minds, migration is associated with hardship and they resort to it only when there is no alternative.

Such is the outlook, for instance, of Baleshwar Mahto, a resident of Uttari Dehati (Araria district, Bihar). Baleshwar goes to Punjab every year in search of work to sustain his family. He had planned to go there this June as well. However, he got NREGA employment in his own village and so he decided to stay back. Comrades who accompanied him to Punjab had also got some NREGA work; he was in no hurry to head for distant lands. Baleshwar will definitely go to Punjab this year—the trip has only been postponed—but meanwhile he enjoys this respite. NREGA is a triple bonus for him: apart from providing local employment, it enabled him to combine this work with tending his own fields and spending more time with his family.

Baleshwar's story illustrates the situation faced by many in Araria. Large numbers of people there are forced to look for work in states like Punjab, Delhi, and Gujarat, as employment is hard to find locally. What is available is very poorly paid, with wages varying from 40 to 60 rupees per day during the harvest season, even less (Rs 25–50 per day) otherwise.

Baleshwar takes up such employment only when forced to stay back in his village due, for instance, to illness in the family.

In their survey responses, migrant workers often spoke about the hardships associated with migration. In the cities, they live in deplorable conditions, with no access to basic facilities such as shelter, sanitation, or even safe drinking water. Those working in quarries, mines, and construction sites are exposed to serious hazards, such as lung diseases. In the case of men-only migration, women and children face material and psychological insecurity, and family relations often suffer. NREGA is a potential liberation from these hardships. As Naresh Hirshi Dev from Palamau (Jharkhand) succinctly put it: 'To be with your family and get work in the village is a real relief.'

More than half (57 per cent) of the sample workers stated that NREGA had 'helped them to avoid migration', and a similar proportion (also 57 per cent) felt that migration had decreased in their village after NREGA was launched. As expected, these figures were even larger in areas with high levels of NREGA employment, or high rates of migration prior to the inception of the programme. For instance, in Pati block (Madhya Pradesh), a hub of out-migration, where NREGA has been deployed in a big way, 92 per cent of the sample workers felt that migration had gone down, and 88 per cent said that NREGA had helped them to avoid migration. The responses were similar in Dungarpur (Rajasthan), where some people had even returned from places like Mumbai and Gujarat on hearing that NREGA work was available in their villages.

What is interesting is that even in other areas, where the scale of NREGA is much smaller, there is some evidence of an impact on migration, for example, in Araria (Bihar) and Sitapur (Uttar Pradesh). One possible explanation is that a few days of assured employment in the lean season are enough to persuade some workers to 'stay back' for the entire period.

However, it is also possible that the promise of local employment is luring workers to stay back, and that if these hopes are dashed, migration will resume. Delays in wage payments are in danger of intensifying this potential 'discouragement effect', and pushing people back into the web of migration. If this setback is to be averted, NREGA employment must be expanded and made more predictable.

—Kartika Bhatia and Ashish Ranjan

in bulk at cheaper rates, or get credit from the local *bania* (trader). When many people in the same area work on NREGA, mutual support systems such as reciprocal credit also get a boost.

NREGA also seems to play a useful role as a 'health-line' for rural households. A majority (47 per cent) of the sample workers had used part of their wages to buy medicine or treat an illness in the family. For instance Babli Sopa, a tribal worker from Sirohi, used her earnings to buy medicines for her husband, who suffers from tuberculosis; NREGA also helped her to repay the loan she had taken for his treatment. School books and uniforms also ranked high among people's uses of NREGA earnings.

Some respondents had been able to go beyond subsistence expenditure and save or invest part of their wages. For instance, farmers in Rajasthan often mentioned that they had spent some of their NREGA earnings on seeds, fertilizers, or other agricultural inputs. And Sita (an 18-year-old girl in Sirohi district) used her wages to buy a sewing machine.

A UNIQUE OPPORTUNITY FOR WOMEN

In many areas, NREGA is a unique employment opportunity for rural women, who rarely get a chance to earn their own income (as opposed to working without wages at home). Only 30 per cent of the sample women had earned any cash income—other than their NREGA wages—during the three months preceding the survey. And even those who did earn some cash had been working for measly wages in most cases. What is more, women earn the same as men on NREGA—this impressed many of our respondents, both men and women.

It is also worth noting that a large majority of women workers collect their own wages (79 per cent), and also keep them (68 per cent) (see Table 3.7). Thus, women are not just sent to NREGA worksites to earn money on behalf of other, male family members; they are individual workers in their own right. For many women, however, participating in NREGA is a major challenge, for reasons ranging from hostile social norms to the lack of child care facilities (Box 3.3).

Table 3.7 A Job of One's Own

Proportion (%) of female sample workers who:	
Collect their own wages	79
Keep their own wages	68
Earned any cash income (other than NREGA wages) during the last 3 months	30

Source: NREGA Survey 2008.

BOX 3.3 A BATTLE OF ONE'S OWN

Kamla Das, a 25-year-old NREGA worker from Salba gram panchayat (Surguja district, Chhattisgarh) belongs to a landless family. Her husband does not earn anything, so she is especially appreciative of this opportunity to earn in her own village: 'Now women can also earn, so the family's earnings increase. NREGA is very important because women get the same wage as men.' NREGA has enabled her to stop working for a local landlord, who pays women less than men. She has used her NREGA earnings to buy rice to feed her family, books and clothes for her children, fertilizers (they are share-croppers), and also to celebrate Holi. However, she has faced some harassment from the mate who pressurizes them to work harder. She is also worried about her four-year-old child, who stays alone at home when she goes to work. She would like to bring her child to the worksite, but this depends on a child care facility being made available there.

In spite of the vital importance of this new work opportunity, the participation of women in NREGA was below the stipulated minimum of 33 per cent in our sample, and in many of the survey areas it was abysmally low. Uttar Pradesh and Bihar were at the bottom, with women accounting for only 5 per cent and 13 per cent of the NREGA workforce, respectively; the situation was only marginally better in Jharkhand (18 per cent) and Chhattisgarh (25 per cent). The only states where women were well represented were Madhya Pradesh (44 per cent) and Rajasthan (71 per cent).

What prevents women from joining NREGA in larger numbers in the other states? We were often told by gram panchayat functionaries that women are not interested in NREGA work. But when the field investigators spoke to women directly, most of them expressed a keen desire to work. The interviews with women revealed five important barriers to their participation in NREGA.

First, there are, in many areas, tenacious social norms against women working outside the home. In Uttar Pradesh and Bihar, we met women who said that they had not been able to register and were told that this programme was 'not for them'. Women in Sitapur also reported that when there are more applicants than can be accommodated at a worksite, they are turned away to make way for men. Some of them also faced verbal sexual harassment—they were teased, ridiculed, or verbally abused by male labourers and other villagers.

Another big hurdle is the lack of child care facilities. The Act requires that when there are more than five children under the age of six at the worksite, a female worker should be spared to take care of them. But we did not find child care facilities anywhere (except at two or three worksites, that too possibly due to 'window dressing'). The lack of these facilities can be crippling for women, especially those with breastfed babies who cannot be left behind for long hours.

Third, the continued illegal presence of contractors at many worksites also affects the availability of work and its benefits for women. In some places, the presence of contractors actively impacted women's participation in NREGA work. At some sites in Madhya Pradesh, contractors were offering work only to young, able-bodied men. On worksites where contractors were involved, 35 per cent of women workers said that they had faced some harassment, as compared to only 8 per cent on contractor-free worksites.

Fourth, in some states productivity norms are too exacting, because the Schedule of Rates is yet to be revised in line with NREGA norms. To illustrate, in Jharkhand the standard task for a day's work at the time of the survey was digging 110 cubic feet (in soft soil), which is far too much. Certain types of NREGA work also limit the participation of women. This applies, for instance, to the construction of wells on private land. The nature of this work is such that women stop being employed as soon as digging has reached a certain depth.

Fifth, delayed payments also come in the way of participation of poor women. Delays in wage payments make things particularly difficult for single women, who cannot afford to wait as they are the sole earners in the family. When the wages do not come on time, they are often forced to return to previous, less preferred forms of employment.

Women's battle to be full participants in NREGA goes beyond being able to get their names on the job cards and getting work. An important part of NREGA is participatory planning, where the list of NREGA works is to be decided. Only a small proportion of women workers in our sample had attended a gram sabha, and even fewer had spoken at one. Many do not go to gram sabhas because they do not feel welcome, or because they believe these meetings are not for women.

Over time, much of this is changing, and the participation of women in NREGA is certainly improving. But there are also new challenges. One of them is the introduction of wage payments through banks. When a single account is opened per job card (as happened in some of the sample villages), the account is generally opened in the name of a male member of the family. This means that women have to rely on men to withdraw their wages. Ideally, there should be one account per registered NREGA worker, or at least joint bank accounts instead of men-only accounts. Even better would be for every individual worker (man or woman) to have his or her own job card, bank account, and entitlement to 100 days of work.

—Reetika Khera and Nandini Nayak

The special value of NREGA for women often came through in their personal testimonies. For instance, Lungibai (Sirohi district, Rajasthan) said that she was working outside the house for the first time; her husband allowed her to work because employment was available within the village. Bejni Devi (Araria district, Bihar) is also glad to have a chance to work on NREGA. She earns Rs 75 per day on NREGA, which is less than the minimum wage (Rs 82 per day in Bihar), but much higher than what she earns as an agricultural labourer—as little as Rs 15 per day at times. Bejni Devi had not earned any income in the preceding three months. 'Without NREGA,' she said, 'I would have had to migrate with my four-month-old child.'

Widows and single women were especially appreciative of this opportunity to earn close to their homes. Often, social norms do not permit them to migrate, and paid work is hard to find in the vicinity of their homes, except possibly for abysmal wages. Takdiri, a Muslim widow who lives in Sitapur district (Uttar Pradesh), said that NREGA had changed her life because it enables her to earn Rs 100 per day at her doorstep, whereas earlier she worked for Rs 35 per day, that is, when she found any work at all.

The interviews also revealed that for many rural women (and especially for single and widowed women), feeding the family is not just an economic burden but also a source of enormous mental strain. In that respect, too, NREGA makes an important contribution to women's well being.

WORK WITH DIGNITY

Among NREGA's early achievements is a major reduction in the exploitation of labour on public works. Just a few years ago, we found that labourers working on schemes like the National Food for Work Programme (NFFWP) were mercilessly exploited. They worked hard, earned a pittance, and were not paid for weeks or even months. For instance, in May 2005 we found that NFFWP workers employed in Padrikala (Sonebhadra district, Uttar Pradesh) had been paid as little as Rs 2 to Rs 4 per day, along with 200 grams of rice. One worker (Lal Bahadur) and his wife earned Rs 48 for 19 days of work!

In this respect, NREGA is bringing about radical change. For instance, wages today are much closer to the minimum wage, and minimum wages themselves have risen sharply. The average wage earned by NREGA workers in our sample was around Rs 85 per day, compared with about Rs 50 per day, on average, for local agricultural labour. And at half of the sample worksites, all workers were paid the minimum wage (Table 3.8)—this is a big step forward.

Table 3.8 The 'Minimum Wage Revolution'

Proportion (%) of sample workers who knew the minimum wage	48
Proportion (%) of sample worksites where all workers earned the minimum wage	46

Source: NREGA Survey 2008.
Note: Last figure refers to the most recent wage payments.

NREGA is also seen by many rural labourers as an opportunity for dignified employment. The work conditions tend to be better than in the private sector, for example, in terms of hours of work and productivity norms. Only a small minority (10 per cent) of respondents had any complaint of harassment at the worksite (Table 3.9).

Table 3.9 The Retreat of Exploitation at the Worksite

	Rajasthan	Other states
Proportion (%) of sample workers who reported that:		
Machines had been used at the worksite	2	8
A contractor was involved	0	35
They had faced harassment at the worksite	6	12

Source: NREGA Survey 2008.

The improvement of work conditions partly reflects the gradual exit of private contractors (see Box 3.4). Three years ago, contractors ran the show, and labourers—especially women—were at their mercy. Often they had no idea whether, when, and how much they would be paid. Under NREGA, contractors are banned and gram panchayats are the main implementing agencies. The ban is not without loopholes (28 per cent of the sample worksites were managed by a contractor), but it has certainly dislodged many contractors, with more on the move. And in our sample, we found that contractor-free worksites were less exploitative than contractor-driven worksites. For instance, the incidence of worksite harassment was much lower where contractors were absent (Table 3.10).

Table 3.10 Contractors: A View from the Worksite

	Contractor-managed worksites	Contractor-free worksites
Proportion (%) of sample workers who faced harassment at the worksite:	17	8
Proportion (%) of sample workers who reported that:		
Attendance is taken on the official muster roll at the worksite	5	35
They signed the muster roll last time they were paid	29	53
Job card entries were made last time they were paid	10	32
Proportion (%) of sample workers whose job cards were blank:	48	23

Source: NREGA Survey 2008.

BOX 3.4 WHAT'S WRONG WITH CONTRACTORS?

Contractors are banned under NREGA, but the survey found that contractors were, in fact, involved at 27 per cent of the sample worksites. The worst state in this respect was Jharkhand, where contractors were found at more than half (57 per cent) of sample worksites. A common excuse for this is the shortage of staff: gram panchayats, the main implementing agencies under NREGA, do not exist in Jharkhand (the only state that had not held elections to Panchayati Raj Institutions since the 73th and 74th amendments to the Constitution).

However, contractors are a more widespread phenomenon. Except in Rajasthan, the survey teams encountered contractors to varying extents in all the sample states. Often, the way they get a foot in the door is on account of delays in the flow of funds. When funds are delayed, contractors step in to ensure timely payments to labourers and suppliers. In exchange for easing the flow of funds, they are given a free hand in forging muster rolls, job cards, and other NREGA documents.

Why is the involvement of contractors such a big issue? This question has to be seen in the light of the unscrupulous character of most contractors in rural India. Their job is to make money, in a highly competitive environment where cheating and exploiting is the way to get ahead. The semi-criminal petty contractor, roaming around on a motorbike with dark glasses and a *gamchha* (scarf), chewing paan, is not a fictitious Bollywood character—it is a familiar figure in many Indian villages. On a more serious note, the survey findings amply confirm that private contractors are best kept at bay. This is so for at least three reasons.

1. *Corruption*: Corruption levels tend to be higher where contractors are involved. For instance, in an earlier survey in Orissa in October 2007, we found higher rates of embezzlement of wages on worksites managed by contractors. Worksites with contractors were more likely to have muster rolls with fake names. More than half (55 per cent) of the wages did not reach the concerned labourers, with a lower figure (25 per cent) for contractor-free worksites.
2. *Exploitation*: Contractors typically thrive by exploiting labourers—making them work hard and paying them as little as possible. This often goes hand-in-hand with harassment. For instance, 35 per cent of women working at contractor-managed worksites reported being harassed.

The figures are much lower (only 8 per cent) for contractor-free worksites. At one worksite in Surguja district (Chhattisgarh), women were verbally abused for working too slowly; the contractor made them work for 10 hours a day and turned away those who came late. At another worksite, also in Surguja, the survey team noted: 'The women who complained about these work conditions were verbally abused by the contractor who also threatened to replace them with workers from other gram panchayats. Our team learned from a worker that these workers from other gram panchayats were paid at the rate of Rs 50/day.'

3. *Accountability*: It is easier to keep gram panchayats' or line departments' employees on their toes than to hold private contractors accountable. In fact, in our experience, contractors are very difficult to 'catch' even when there is proof of their mischief. For instance, in Masmohna (Koderma district), we found conclusive evidence that a private contractor, Vasudev Mahto, had brazenly cheated NREGA workers and embezzled their wages. This evidence was presented at a massive public hearing attended by three members of the Central Employment Guarantee Council (on 18 June 2008), and confirmed again in a detailed follow-up report by the local Sub-Divisional Officer (SDO). Yet, in the First Information Report (FIR) lodged against the culprits, which is supposed to be based on this very enquiry, Vasudev Mahto's name is quietly missing! Reason: he is 'protected' by the local MLA (Member of Legislative Assembly).

As Vasudev Mahto's story illustrates, many contractors enjoy the patronage of political leaders (and return this favour by funding election campaigns). This nexus of corruption and crime, which also involves corrupt bureaucrats, has been the bane of public works programmes for many years. NREGA seeks to break this nexus and replace it with a transparent and accountable system where Panchayati Raj Institutions are in charge. If this new system is to see the light of day, contractors have to be kept at bay.

—Jean Drèze and Reetika Khera

These developments are of special relevance to women. Even the fact that NREGA is considered 'government work' is associated, for many of them, with a certain sort of dignity (especially in areas where social norms prevent them from participating in the labour market). Sometimes, NREGA also enables labourers to give up undesirable occupations: as noted earlier, about one-third of the respondents said that NREGA had helped them avoid demeaning or hazardous work.

PLAYING WITH MUD?

The productive value of NREGA works is something of a mystery. Through sheer repetition, an impression has been created that they are mostly useless. To illustrate, one influential commentator (or 'opinion-maker') recently dismissed them as a futile attempt 'to play with mud, to create a road that goes from nowhere to nowhere, to dig ditches that will be washed away in the next monsoon' (Ghose 2008). This verdict, however, has not been substantiated.

The productive value of NREGA works was not a major focus of our survey. Still, it is interesting to note that, according to a large majority (83 per cent) of the respondents, NREGA had led to the creation of useful assets in the village (Table 3.11). Similarly, 70 per cent of the sample workers felt that the work being done at the worksite was 'very useful', and another 22 per cent felt that it was 'quite useful'. Only 3 per cent considered it 'useless'—quite a contrast with the accepted refrain in urban circles.

Table 3.11 Playing with Mud?

Proportion (%) of sample workers who felt that:	
NREGA had led to the creation of useful assets in their village	83
The work they were doing on NREGA was useful	92
Proportion (%) of sample worksites where the survey team felt that:*	
The asset being created or repaired was useful	87 (32)
The work being done was useful	81 (29)

Source: NREGA Survey 2008.
Note: * Figures in brackets refer to 'very useful'.

It may be argued that these responses are self-serving and, therefore, suspect. However, they are corroborated by the assessments of field investigators: at most of the sample worksites, the survey team felt that the work being done was 'very useful' (70 per cent) or 'quite useful' (22 per cent). Informal as they are, these observations debunk the myth that NREGA works are useless. It is, in fact, possible that economic returns on NREGA works compare quite favourably with those of many industrial projects.

One of the best examples of productive NREGA works we encountered was the construction of a kaccha road in Kope panchayat (Latehar district, Jharkhand), where the villagers had creatively planned and self-managed the entire project. The road led to a previously inaccessible tribal hamlet. 'If someone fell ill, the existing path was not enough for people to place him on a bicycle to take to the hospital for medical care,' said Bhukhan Singh. The construction of the road was combined with levelling of the adjoining land, so that where there used to be wild bushes, we now saw paddy fields. An inventive culvert had also been built (to avoid disrupting the natural flow of water), using wood and other local material instead of expensive cement or bricks. The road was a concrete proof of people's ability to plan valuable NREGA works.

Having said this, the general quality of assets created under NREGA left much to be desired. For instance, kaccha structures were often incomplete as the monsoon arrived; many check dams were left without 'dressing', making them vulnerable to soil erosion; roads did not have an adequate top layer; and the location of many of these assets was often inappropriate. In one extreme case of poor planning (in Gurdah gram panchayat of Sonebhadra district), we found that a large pond had been dug at the top of a hill, with little scope for water harvesting!

The productive value of NREGA works could be much enhanced with moderate doses of scientific or technical inputs. For instance, it is possible to build relatively good roads through labour-intensive techniques. But this requires technical inputs of a sort that has not been encouraged in the traditional, contractor-based approach. It is also important to activate the process of participatory planning through gram panchayats and gram sabhas, which is mandatory under the Act but rarely visible in the field.

THE GHOST OF CORRUPTION

The survey clearly brings out that *where work is available*, NREGA has many positive effects on the quality of life in rural areas. This does not mean that NREGA is in the pink of health—far from it. In all the sample districts, the provisions and guidelines of the Act were routinely violated, causing much frustration (if not anger) among NREGA workers. For instance, the scale of works was inadequate, delays in wage payments were rife, and basic worksite facilities (water, shade, first-aid, and child care) were missing in most cases (Table 3.12). Behind these failures were deep structural problems including poor flow of funds, staff shortages, flawed record-keeping, and lack of grievance redressal, to cite a few.

Table 3.12 Worksite Facilities: A Gaping Hole

	Rajasthan	Other states
Proportion (%) of sample worksites that had:		
Drinking water	95	52
Shade for periods of rest	37	45
First-aid kit	60	20
Child care facility	17	0

Source: NREGA Survey 2008.

Just to illustrate the first issue, the haphazard flow of funds has often caused havoc with people's entitlements. In May 2008, there was no NREGA work anywhere in Sonebhadra district (initially part of our sample), forcing us to select another district for the survey. The same problem occurred in Chainpur block of Palamau district: not only had work come to a standstill, there were also huge arrears in wage payments. The Block Development Officer did not expect to be able to start any new works for another six months or so.

The positive impact of NREGA has also been undermined by rampant corruption (Box 3.5). The chief method of embezzlement is fudging of muster rolls. For instance, in Khendra Khurd (Palamau district), we found that 100 out of 108 names listed in the muster rolls for one particular week were fake. The wages of the 100 fictitious workers had been happily siphoned off by corrupt officials and middlemen. Had this money been well used, the scale of employment in Khendra Khurd would have been much larger. This is an extreme example, but fudging of muster rolls was observed to varying extents in most of the sample districts (with the notable exception of Rajasthan).

BOX 3.5 ALL IS NOT WELL WITH THE WELLS

October 2008. The fields of Mahua Tand (Deogarh district, Jharkhand) are full of rice. Farmers and field hands are busy irrigating their lands. The rains have not been very helpful this year and pump-sets and wells are the saviours of crops. Our social audit team is inspecting two NREGA projects in Mahua Tand, both involving the construction of a well on private land—a common type of NREGA work in Jharkhand.

The well constructed by Taufique Zarra reminds the team of the tragic Tapas Soren episode. In the short video recording of his last words (available at www.youtube.com), Tapas Soren testifies that a corrupt government machinery had driven him to take his own life. He had tried to construct a well on his own land under NREGA, but was unable to cope with constant demands for bribes. A helpless and distraught Tapas set himself ablaze at the Collector's office in Hazaribagh, to highlight his plight and warn others about this trap. But Taufique, unaware of Tapas' fate, did fall into the same trap.

Hailing from a BPL (below poverty line) family, Taufique's sole source of income is the little agricultural land he owns. In the absence of a reliable source of irrigation, he is often at the mercy of unpredictable rains. Having heard that wells can be constructed on the land of BPL families under NREGA, Taufique applied. Soon enough the Gram Sevak (Panchayat Secretary) informed Taufique that if he could pay Rs 2,500 a well would be allotted to him. NREGA mandates that a shelf of works be prepared in the gram sabha, but no such attempt was made in Mahua Tand. Taufique paid the bribe and the well was sanctioned.

Once the well was sanctioned in Taufique's name, he became both the beneficiary and *abhikarta* (manager) of the project. As an abhikarta, Taufique signed an agreement with the government and was in charge of executing the work. He was to fill the muster rolls, purchase materials, and oversee the worksite. He also had to pay for workers' wages and construction materials as the work progressed, but the funds were often delayed depending on his ability to pay the 'PC' (percentage, a common term for illegal commissions) to government functionaries like the Gram Sevak and Junior Engineer. The PC was fixed at 10 per cent for the Gram Sevak and 13 per cent for the Junior Engineer, and the PC had to be given in cash before a bill was passed. Taufique had to take a loan of Rs 20,000, sell a buffalo, and mortgage his land to arrange for the PC as well as construction costs.

For Taufique, this well was a chance to escape poverty, but today he is an impoverished farmer struggling to make ends meet and pay off the loan. In addition, due to the heavy PC, the work done by him and his brothers remains unpaid. Luckily, Taufique was not driven to commit suicide as did Tapas Soren. But the whole PC system did push him into the web of indebtedness. Maybe for every Taufique who survives this gamble, there is a Tapas Soren who may not!

—Kamayani Swami

To address this problem, the Central Government recently instructed state governments to pay all NREGA wages through banks or post offices. This is, in principle, a good idea. It is an example of the 'separation of payment agencies from implementation agencies', one of the key transparency safeguards. However, the transition to bank payments is being made in an abrupt and careless manner, making matters worse in some cases (Box 3.6). For instance, during a follow-up social audit in Deogarh district (Jharkhand), we found that middlemen were operating bank accounts in the names of NREGA workers, and using them to siphon off funds in collusion with bank managers. As discussed in Chapter 6, bank payments are not a 'magic bullet' against corruption—other transparency safeguards remain as important as ever.

BOX 3.6 A STAMPEDE OF ACCOUNT-OPENING

From mid-2008 onwards, the Central Government has insisted that NREGA wages be paid exclusively through savings accounts opened for workers in nearby banks and post offices. A major public relations campaign has tried to present this as the solution to corruption. So much so that the progress of NREGA is being measured in terms of the number of accounts opened—an impressive 42 million according to a recent statement by the Rural Development Minister. This extraordinary investment of energies, however, must be viewed with caution. A recent social audit of NREGA in Karon block (Deogarh district, Jharkhand) shows that corruption persists, at times with the collusion of the banks themselves.

The Deogarh Scam

Manchan Rajwar of Ranidih panchayat had no reason to suspect that his NREGA account at the Deoghar-Jamtara Cooperative Bank had been activated. Severely crippled, he had not worked at the site where his name figured, nor signed any withdrawal slips. His passbook was blank. However, inspection of bank records (during a social audit in October 2008) revealed that many transactions—deposits and withdrawals—had been made, over a whole year. It turned out that middlemen were siphoning off NREGA funds through his account, in collusion with bank officials. Similar tricks were played on many other workers in Ranidih, and also in Ganjebari panchayat where they were paid through the Madankatta post office. The amounts moving through these accounts could add up to as much as Rs 9,000 within 14 months for a single account. In Deogarh, banks and post offices have been smoothly integrated in the system of corruption within a few months.

Aggravating Old Vulnerabilities

Even where collusion is not as blatant as in Ranidih, the rush to bank payments has been associated with serious vulnerabilities. First, little effort has been made to integrate bank payments with other transparency safeguards, such as payment of wages in public and regular updating of job cards. In fact, there is a dangerous tendency to assume that these safeguards are redundant when wages are paid through banks or post offices. In Dungarpur district (Rajasthan), the traditional safeguards used to work, and bank payments were—at least initially—a step back!

Where bank payments were in place, we found (in our May–June 2008 survey) that job cards were not updated and that muster rolls were no longer read out in public at the time of wage payments. The situation is worse where these transparency safeguards were being ignored to begin with, as we found in many other districts.

Second, bank payments have often increased delays in wage payments. In Rajasthan, for instance, where wages used to be paid regularly, teething problems with bank payments this summer were causing delays of up to 50 days. Such delays cannot be tided over by NREGA workers, often leading to cycles of debt. They must be treated as a serious violation of the Act.

The combination of opaque procedures and delayed payments has created new opportunities for middlemen. Many middlemen have privileged access to panchayat and block officials and are often the first to find out that wages have been credited. They then collect workers (both real and fake) and escort them to the bank. There, a combination of loans, coercion, and (sometimes) monetary enticements induces workers to hand over the money that they have withdrawn. In Karon, workers from Mahuatand, Tekra, and Ganjebari panchayats stated publicly that this had happened. They had been paid in cash at the rate of Rs 60–70 per day while the stipulated minimum wage was Rs 86.40—the difference went to middlemen. In some cases, middlemen collude with the Panchayat Sevak to inflate the muster rolls, steer inflated payments through people's bank accounts, collect the difference, and share the gravy.

New Complications

The introduction of bank payments has also resulted in new complications. For instance, banking procedures have not been publicized at all. Most NREGA workers are using bank accounts for the first time and do not know how to operate them. This, in turn, increases their dependence on intermediaries.

Another serious irregularity in many places is the opening of accounts solely in the name of the male head of the family. This makes it very hard for women to collect and keep their own wages, as they usually do otherwise. Other problems associated with the hasty introduction of bank payments include: bribes being taken from workers to open accounts; people without bank accounts being turned away from worksites; workers having to spend time and money to withdraw their wages, when banks are far away; and staff shortages in banks and post offices.

So far, the introduction of bank payments has been little more than a stampede of account-opening. Crucial guidelines and safeguards have been ignored. Consequently, the aim of ending corruption in wage payments has not been achieved. This can only happen when bank payments are combined with other transparency safeguards, as has happened to some extent (with post office payments) in Andhra Pradesh. Otherwise, as is already happening, new vulnerabilities will get entrenched. On the brighter side, this experience has demonstrated the Centre's ability to enforce critical guidelines. This power could be used to put in place a more comprehensive structure of vigilance and transparency.

—Anish Vanaik

IS TRANSPARENCY POSSIBLE?

This is not to say that corruption is an immutable feature of NREGA. Some states (notably Rajasthan and Andhra Pradesh) have made considerable progress towards a transparent and accountable system. And even in the more corrupt states, there is evidence of the possibility of curbing corruption. For instance, recent social audits initiated in Orissa by the National Institute for Rural Development suggest that leakages in wage payments declined from 66 per cent in 2006–7 to 33 per cent in 2007–8 in the sample areas; the proportion of fake names in the muster rolls (the most 'blatant' form of corruption) declined from 42 per cent to 7 per cent. Further progress in this direction is possible.

The best weapon against corruption is strict enforcement of the transparency safeguards. These include keeping muster rolls at the worksite, regular maintenance of job cards, payment of wages in public, separation of payment agencies from implementation agencies, vigilance committees, social audits, and much more. In Rajasthan, we found that these safeguards were taken seriously; for instance, muster rolls were generally available at the worksite and job cards were well maintained (Table 3.13). And, in line with earlier social audits in Rajasthan, we found little evidence of major fraud, at least in the labour component of NREGA. A few other states, such as Tamil Nadu, have also taken creative measures to eradicate corruption (see Box 3.7 and Chapter 13).

Table 3.13 Transparency is Possible

	Rajasthan	Other states
Proportion (%) of sample worksites where:		
Muster roll was available at the site	86	11
Workers had signed muster roll at the time of payment	100	45
Job cards were being maintained	100	25
Wages were paid in public space	100	56

Source: NREGA Survey 2008.

Notes: Payment-related figures refer to the most recent round of wage payments. Data for Rajasthan are indicative as they are based on data from seven worksites only where payment had been made recently. However, recent social audits conducted elsewhere in Rajasthan broadly corroborate these findings.

In other states, however, the transparency safeguards were grossly neglected. For instance, muster rolls were rarely kept at the worksite and job cards were poorly maintained (Table 3.14). The main problem is that those who are supposed to implement these safeguards (for example, the Panchayat *Sevak* and the Block Development Officer) are often part of the nexus of corruption in the first place. To make things worse, the Central Government takes the view that the transparency safeguards are 'advisory' only, and violating them attracts no sanction. For instance, a Panchayat Sevak who fails to maintain job cards has nothing to fear.

Table 3.14 Job Cards or Joke Cards?

	Rajasthan	Other states
Proportion (%) of NREGA workers who:		
Did not have a job card	0	11
Had to pay for their job card	10	22
Were not in possession of their job card at the time of the survey	57	44
Proportion (%) of job cards where the following irregularities were found:		
No entries have been made	9	37
Fake entries	8	20

Source: NREGA Survey 2008.

BOX 3.7 NREGA: A VIEW FROM THE SOUTH

A social audit of the NREGA in Viluppuram district in Tamil Nadu in July 2007 and a field survey in Surguja district in Chhattisgarh in June 2008, conducted as part of the six-states survey presented in this chapter, brought out to this writer the contrasts between Chhattisgarh and Tamil Nadu.

In Chhattisgarh there were many lapses in implementation, including the involvement of contractors, the fudging of muster rolls, corruption in material usage, low scale of work, and delays in wage payment. Tamil Nadu, on the other hand, has taken measures to address these problems. It has successfully kept out machines and contractors through close monitoring and strict action against any breach of the ban on both under the NREGA.

Another reason for Tamil Nadu's success is the stipulation (under Tamil Nadu's Employment Guarantee Scheme) that only works devoid of any material component be taken up. (The Act allows up to 40 per cent expenditure on material costs.) The material component tends to give private contractors a foothold as they provide engineering expertise the gram panchayats may not have. The possibility of doing away with the material component arises partly from the fact that Tamil Nadu has a vast network of canals and other traditional water-harvesting structures. The repair and maintenance of these structures is a vast source of useful, labour-intensive work.

If the Act requires that at least 50 per cent of the works be taken up by gram panchayats, the Tamil Nadu scheme stresses that *all* NREGA works be managed by gram panchayats. In Chhattisgarh, there is more reliance on the line departments (for example, the Irrigation Department or the Forest Department), which tend to be less accountable than gram panchayats. Tamil Nadu also avoids delays in wage payment by a well-rehearsed routine of payment on a fixed day every week. In Chhattisgarh, by contrast, delays in wage payments cause great hardship to workers, to the extent that some of them have given up NREGA work. In one work implemented by the Forest Department in Udaipur block, people had not been paid for almost a year.

Tamil Nadu has put in place a good monitoring system. For instance, every worker is required to put his signature or thumb impression on the muster roll every day (by way of marking attendance), making it difficult to fudge muster rolls. The employment guarantee assistant (*Makkal Nalla*

Panniyalar) in each gram panchayat is expected to phone the block office every day before 10 AM to report worksite attendance figures. This information is immediately collated at the district level and officials from different departments do random checks the same day to verify these reports.

In Chhattisgarh, there was no regular monitoring of muster rolls or worksite attendance. At many worksites, the official muster rolls were not available. In Kedma panchayat of Udaipur block, our survey found that more than half of all entries in one set of muster rolls of a completed worksite were fake.

Most importantly, in Tamil Nadu, a strong message has been sent from the top that NREGA works are unlike other schemes and that corruption will not be tolerated. This has been done by taking strict action against panchayat presidents, employment guarantee assistants, and Block Development Officers who have been found guilty of major fraud. The seeds of such a change could be seen in Chhattisgarh: on the basis of a social audit in Mareya panchayat (Udaipur block) in June 2008, a complaint was lodged with the district authorities and strict action was taken.

To be sure, Tamil Nadu has its own set of problems, including politicization and some corruption in NREGA works, conflicts over non-payment of minimum wages, low worker productivity, lack of worksite facilities, unmet demand for work, and lack of community monitoring. Nevertheless, Tamil Nadu has achieved some success in providing employment on a large scale, paying wages on time and avoiding mass corruption.

W

Another special feature of the NREGA in Tamil Nadu is that an overwhelming majority (about 80 per cent) of NREGA workers are women. Most of them have no comparable work opportunities in the private sector.

Indeed, Tamil Nadu's strong tradition of active involvement in the social sector is finding a new expression through the NREGA. There is much to learn from this experience, just as Tamil Nadu itself has much to learn from pioneering experiences elsewhere.

—Karuna Muthiah

This situation calls for the creation of a strong system of mandatory grievance redressal, so that complaints are heard and culprits punished. For instance, rules should be framed to activate Section 25 of NREGA, which provides for penalties on those who fail to do their duty under the Act. The Central Government has been beating around this bush for a long time, without getting anywhere (see also Box 3.8). Is it an accident that there is so much resistance to greater accountability?

EDUCATE, ORGANIZE, AND AGITATE

'It is only after getting organized that we were able to make good use of NREGA. The Sangathan fought for this at every step.' In these simple words, Dinesh sums up years of struggle in Pati block (Badwani district), under the banner of Jagrut Adivasi Dalit Sangathan (JADS). Initially focused on land rights, JADS started organizing NREGA workers as soon as the Act came into force. The results are impressive. Workers' awareness of their rights is very high in Pati, and so is their confidence in their collective strength. They generally make joint applications for work in writing, and many of them are able to secure a full 100 days of NREGA work over the year (Table 3.15). In November 2006, JADS won the first-ever payment of unemployment allowances under NREGA, to hundreds of men and women who had been denied work. The Sangathan has also formed its own vigilance committees, to prevent corruption (see Chapter 9).

The experience of JADS illustrates the power of organized action in enabling workers to secure their entitlements under the Act. And NREGA, in turn, facilitates this organizational work. As one of the field investigators observed: 'NREGA is useful for the Sangathan as well because it has brought a sense of solidarity to all its members'. Thus, the implementation of NREGA and the empowerment of rural labourers are complementary processes, mutually reinforcing each other.

BOX 3.8 NREGA: RIGHT WITHOUT MIGHT?

The NREGA is a new age legislation which invokes the framework of legal rights to provide employment in rural areas. The rights framework should, ideally, provide an antidote to government irresponsibility in the form of accountability under the law.

In practice, however, this transition towards an accountable system has not occurred—far from it. In our survey, we found that NREGA workers had to put up with numerous infringements of their rights without being able to do much about it: lack of work, delays in wage payment, non-payment of minimum wages, absence of worksite facilities, to cite a few. Most of these irregularities remain unaddressed, often even unnoticed. The persistence of corruption is another aspect of this lack of accountability.

Three related problems have contributed to this state of affairs: confusion about the operational requirements of the Act; absence of any grievance redressal system; and lack of independent monitoring of NREGA.

Ship without Rudder

To start with, there is a troubling lack of clarity about various actors' basic responsibilities under NREGA. The Act directs each state government to notify an Employment Guarantee Scheme to give effect to the work guarantee. The combination of a central Act with state-specific schemes (and generally, the complex Centre–state relations behind NREGA) calls for rigorous coordination between the Central Government and state governments. This is not happening; to illustrate, the Ministry of Rural Development does not even have a copy of each of the state schemes. The result is a confusing duality in the source of norms.

Schedules I and II of NREGA spell out mandatory features of the schemes, for example, the minimum entitlements to be guaranteed. However, most of the state schemes fall short of these norms and fail to define an adequate operational framework to fulfil the work guarantee. In many states, schemes have been notified as a mere formality, and the programme is actually run through oral or written instructions issued from time to time.

The Central Government, for its part, has issued Operational Guidelines on various functional matters such as selection of works, worksite management, payment procedures, and record keeping. Unfortunately, the status of these Guidelines is ambiguous. In response to the Comptroller and Auditor General's (CAG) widely publicized report of widespread non-compliance with the operational guidelines (see Chapter 5), the Ministry of Rural Development clarified that these Guidelines are not binding. With Operational Guidelines reduced to a 'best practice' template, NREGA is being implemented in a dangerous vacuum.

Lack of Grievance Redressal

One aspect of this vacuum is the absence of clear remedies against infringements of the Act. Curiously, NREGA talks the language of rights but there is virtual silence on available remedies when rights are violated. So far, the Central Government and state governments have failed to put in place any system to respond to people's complaints. Interesting ideas have been floated, such as the involvement of Ombudsmen or the activation of Lok Adalats, but they are yet to see the light of day.

Transparency and Accountability Rules have been drafted and discussed in New Delhi for years without getting anywhere. According to the Ministry of Rural Development, the Law Ministry now takes the view that the Central Government has no mandate to make such rules under NREGA—an illiterate reading of the Act. Meanwhile, essential transparency safeguards (including job card maintenance, proactive disclosure of muster rolls, and regular social audits) are languishing in the Operational Guidelines. Since the Guidelines are now treated as 'advisory', these safeguards have no teeth.

Dogs who Failed to Bark

A third issue is the lack of independent monitoring of NREGA, whether at the state or central level. The Central Employment Guarantee Council (CEGC) was intended as an active, powerful, independent monitoring body for NREGA at the national level. However, the Council is virtually non-functional. The performance of the State Employment Guarantee Councils is no better—in fact it is worse in most cases. These watchdogs, too, have no teeth—they are not even barking.

Similarly, no independent survey has been conducted so far, on a national scale, to evaluate the implementation of the Act. It would just take a few crores (out of NREGA's annual budget of Rs 40,000 crore or so) to conduct or commission an independent evaluation of the programme, and find out what is happening on the ground in different states. Yet the government, for mysterious reasons, seems to be unable to take this simple step towards transparency and accountability.

The Buck Stops in Delhi

The Central Government bears a heavy responsibility for this state of affairs. NREGA is a national Act, and about 90 per cent of the funds come from the Central Government. If only for that reason, the Central Government should take the lead in creating an effective system of checks and balances. It has wide-ranging powers to do so under the Act.

Meanwhile, some state governments have taken useful initiatives in this regard. Rajasthan, with its unerring focus on maintenance of job cards and muster rolls, is a case in point. Similarly, Tamil Nadu has developed impressive monitoring arrangements, while Andhra Pradesh has put in place a full-fledged system of institutionalized social audits. These initiatives combine learning from the grassroots with building systems of accountability. The Central Government, too, is duty bound under the Act to put in place mandatory operational norms to protect labourers' entitlements. Failing that, the new hopes that have been kindled by NREGA in rural India are likely to be dashed.

—Jean Drèze and Siddhartha

(R)
(TN)

Table 3.15 Educate, Organize, and Agitate

	Pati block	Other sample blocks
Average days of NREGA work in the past 12 months	85	41
Proportion (%) of sample workers who:		
Worked for 100 days during the last 12 months	47	11
Got employed in response to a written application	92	19
Proportion (%) of sample workers who were aware of their entitlement to:		
One hundred days of work	88	50
Minimum wages	74	47
Payment within 15 days	76	55

Source: NREGA Survey 2008.

This experience also gives a sense of the vast possibilities that lie ahead if NREGA workers are able to organize. Aside from helping them to get employment and wages, this would also facilitate their active involvement in the entire NREGA process. For instance, informed and empowered workers could give a new life to gram sabhas, vigilance committees, and social audits. Workers' organizations could also add new dimensions to the whole programme, for instance, by linking employment guarantee with social security schemes. Even demanding the provision of child care facilities at NREGA worksites could be a major action point, with a potential wider impact on workers' perceptions of what is due to them at the workplace. Last but not least, greater bargaining power would help rural workers in other domains, including the realization of other social and economic rights (for example, the right to food or the right to education).

In the course of our survey, and related activities (such as social audits), we came across other organizations that have done impressive work with NREGA workers, such as the Mazdoor Kisan Shakti Sangathan (MKSS) and the All India Agricultural Labourers' Association (AIALA). The reach of these organizations is still quite limited. Indeed, except in Pati block, it is only on rare occasions that we met NREGA workers who had been helped by a local organization, in any way, to secure their entitlements. The process of organization building has been much slower, so far, than was anticipated a few years ago. But this state of affairs is not immutable.

While NREGA has done quite well in both Pati and Rajasthan, there is an instructive contrast between the two approaches. In Pati, this achievement is based primarily on popular mobilization and organizational work. The government has acted mainly in response to people's demands, rather than on its own initiative. In Rajasthan, on the other hand, the government has actively tried to make NREGA work, as soon as the Act came into force (Box 3.9). This is not to say that Rajasthan's achievements are unrelated to popular mobilization. The right to information movement, for one, has strong roots in Rajasthan and made its mark on NREGA at every step. It also had an important influence on state priorities. But the decisive factor, ultimately, was a strong political backing for NREGA at the top, across party lines.

BOX 3.9 'ZORDAR GUARANTEE' IN RAJASTHAN

'*Rozgar* Guarantee, *Zordar* Guarantee' (employment guarantee, powerful guarantee)—for Lalubhai of Obri panchayat in Dungarpur district, this upbeat slogan sums up what NREGA means to him and others in his village. Our field survey, too, puts Rajasthan in a fairly good light. Most sample workers there had spent at least 60 days on NREGA worksites during the preceding 12 months, the main transparency safeguards were in place, and the administration was working overtime to implement the Act.

Preparedness

The seeds of these achievements go back a long way: public employment programmes have a long history in Rajasthan. Basic systems are in place and there is a wealth of administrative experience to draw upon. A good illustration of this preparedness was the launch of the Act on 2 February 2006. In many other states, this was 'just another day'—but not in Rajasthan. One of us was witness, in Dungarpur, to the unprecedented enthusiasm among villagers on that historic occasion. In many villages, the atmosphere resembled that of a fair. Loudspeakers blared out the main provisions of the Act from cassettes provided by the government. Armed with their ration cards (as an identity document), men and women had been queuing up since early morning to apply for job cards. Arrangements to issue job cards on the spot were in place. Many already had a fair idea of what NREGA was about. In fact, in Thana panchayat, when a group of villagers was asked what was happening, they said that they had been given the right to work!

Scale of Works

Perhaps the most impressive aspect of NREGA in Rajasthan is the staggering scale of works. During the survey it was not uncommon to find entire hamlets empty until 2.30 PM, when NREGA work ends (during the summer). In many gram panchayats, muster rolls for over 2,000 workers were being issued every fortnight. In our sample, 36 per cent of households had worked for a full 100 days of work in the preceding 12 months. The scale and predictability of NREGA employment have brought Rajasthan much closer to the goal of a 'work guarantee' than any other state.

Participation of Women

In a state where prevalent social norms militate against women having independent incomes, it is particularly heartening that the NREGA workforce consists overwhelmingly of women: 71 per cent of the workers in our Rajasthan sample were women. Only one-fifth of these women had earned any cash income other than NREGA wages in the preceding 12 months. For them, NREGA is a new-found source of economic independence and freedom. 'I am the head of the household,' said Haski, a married adivasi woman from Sirohi.

Transparency Norms

Few states, if any, have taken transparency norms as seriously as Rajasthan (see Table 3.13). Muster rolls are usually available at the worksite and daily attendance is taken on them in front of the workers. This makes it much harder to fudge muster rolls and siphon off NREGA funds. Further, wages are paid in a public space (as per guidelines), and job cards are updated at the time of payment. These and other safeguards have considerably narrowed the scope for embezzlement, at least in the wage component of NREGA (though there have been reports of continued cheating in the material component, such as inflated technical estimates).

Worksite Management

Worksite management has been an important area of innovation in Rajasthan. Mates (worksite supervisors), both men and women, have been trained in large numbers to maintain muster rolls, assign tasks to the workers, record their output, and ensure that worksite facilities are available. This experiment is still at an early stage, but there are good prospects of it leading to better worksite supervision, higher productivity, an improved work environment, and—last but not least—further improvement of the transparency norms.

These are some distinctive features of the Rajasthan experience, among others. Challenges do remain: for instance, Rajasthan has a very poor record of payment of minimum wages on NREGA. Nevertheless, this experience is an impressive demonstration of the possibility of implementing the Act. It also shows how skilful public mobilization can be brought to bear on state politics. Indeed, these achievements also owe much to citizens' organizations such as Mazdoor Kisan Shakti Sangathan. Aside from acting as watchdogs (for example, by conducting social audits), these organizations have also been involved in constructive work such as mass training of mates. Recently, they have been charting out an ambitious programme of unionizing NREGA workers.

—Reetika Khera and Anish Vanaik

It is worth reflecting on what would happen if every block in the country had an active workers' organization (as in Pati) and every state government had a strong commitment to NREGA (as in Rajasthan). This may seem like a pipe dream, but as noted earlier, time is on the side of this process. Political parties are already vying with each other to take credit for NREGA and proclaim their commitment to it; while some of this is just posturing, political support for NREGA is likely to consolidate over time. Similarly, the collective strength of NREGA workers is likely to grow in the future—there are signs of it already. If adequate energy is invested in this process, the battle for employment guarantee may just be won.

4

Women Workers and Perceptions of the NREGA*

Reetika Khera and Nandini Nayak#

INTRODUCTION

Women workers receive special attention in the National Rural Employment Guarantee Act (NREGA) in several ways. To start with, the Act mandates that at least one-third of the workers should be women. This, combined with the fact that the Act places no restriction on how each household's quota of 100 days is shared within the household, means that there is ample scope for women's participation in NREGA works. The Act also provides for equal wages for men and women, in contrast with the private sector where women often earn less. Besides this, child care facilities at the worksite are

* Originally published as 'Women Workers and Perceptions of the National Rural Employment Guarantee Act', *Economic and Political Weekly*, 44 (43): 49–57, 24 October 2009.

We would like to thank Ritambara Mehta who did much of the research on the qualitative data used in this paper. She was also helped by Mary Abhraham, Ankita Agarwal, Kartika Bhatia, Ketaki Jaywant, Megha Kalia, Bharat Rastogi, and Eklavya Vasudev. Besides, we would like to thank all the enumerators who worked in a voluntary capacity and took meticulous notes. We would also like to thank all the participants at a workshop on Gender and Rural Employment organized by FAO–ILO–IFAD in April 2009, where an earlier version of this paper was presented. The authors would also like to thank Jean Drèze and Subir Sinha for helpful comments.

mandatory when more than five children under six years of age are present. This is an important provision, given that, in large parts of the country, there are no child care arrangements (for example, functional *anganwadis*) for working women.

This essay attempts to understand the perceptions of this legislation as reported by women workers currently working under the Act. The NREGA's potential in empowering women by providing them with work opportunities has been commented on by others as well (see Pankaj and Tankha 2010, Jandu 2008, Institute of Social Studies Trust 2006).[1] Women's participation in NREGA rose steadily during the last few years from 40 per cent of total NREGA employment in 2006–7 (the first year of implementation) to 50 per cent or so today. Large inter-state variations in the participation of women could be observed in 2007–8: women constitute more than two-thirds of NREGA workers in states such as Kerala (71 per cent), Rajasthan (69 per cent) and Tamil Nadu (82 per cent) and less than the mandatory one-third in states like Assam (31 per cent), Bihar (27 per cent), Himachal Pradesh (30 per cent), Jharkhand (27 per cent), Uttar Pradesh (15 per cent), and West Bengal (17 per cent). The purpose of this essay is twofold: one, to highlight the importance of NREGA, as perceived by women workers, and two, to show that the full potential of this legislation is far from being realized.

This essay is based on testimonies of women NREGA workers from the NREGA Survey 2008, conducted in May–June 2008 in six north Indian states: Bihar, Chhattisgarh, Jharkhand, Madhya Pradesh, Rajasthan, and Uttar Pradesh (see Box 3.1 in Chapter 3 for details of the survey). The 10 sample districts are all Phase-I districts, where the Act came into force in February 2006.

[1] Interestingly, even in the Maharasthra Employment Guarantee Scheme (an Act similar to the NREGA, enacted in Maharashtra in the 1970s), the importance of the programme for women had been highlighted in many studies, to the extent that one describes it as a 'women's programme' (Mahendra Dev 1995). See also Krishnaraj et al. (2004a, 2004b), Sathe (1991), and Dandekar (1983).

The survey was aimed at understanding the impact of NREGA on the lives of workers who are currently employed under the Act. The survey was not focused on women specifically, however, 32 per cent of sample workers were women. The interviews with women workers provided insights into the significance of NREGA for these women and highlighted the 'transformative' potential of NREGA in enhancing economic and social security. In a mosaic of chequered implementation, however, many narratives from women workers tell a significant story about the benefits of NREGA. We highlight this significance of NREGA work for women workers and make the case that attention must be paid by the government towards effective implementation to ensure that these important benefits are not scuttled.

WOMEN'S ACCESS TO CASUAL WAGE WORK

Using qualitative and quantitative data from the survey, this section highlights the significance of NREGA work in light of the fact that women in rural India have limited access to wage work.[2]

As expected, there are large variations in women's participation in NREGA across sample areas. Overall, 32 per cent of the sample workers are women (see Table 4.1). In Rajasthan, 71 per cent of sample workers were women. In Madhya Pradesh, the proportion of women among sample workers was 44 per cent. However, the corresponding figures for Chhattisgarh (25 per cent), Jharkhand (18 per cent), Bihar (13 per cent), and Uttar Pradesh (5 per cent) are very low—lower than the minimum female participation rate prescribed by the law (33 per cent).

[2] The random sample of workers was drawn from lists of workers on NREGA sites. As a result, some categories of 'potential workers', such as women unable to participate in NREGA for lack of child care facilities, are actually excluded from the sample. The focus of the survey was the implementation of NREGA and the perceived benefits, if any, to the workers actually engaged under the Act.

Table 4.1 Profile of Sample Workers

	Women	Men
Proportion (%) of NREGA workers who are		
Scheduled Castes (SC)/Scheduled Tribes (ST)	75	71
Illiterate	82	52
Proportion (%) of NREGA workers who		
Had other sources of cash income in the past 3 months	30	55
Collect their own wages	78	92
Keep their own wages	69	51
Prefer payments through banks	53	44
Average wage (Rs/day)		
Statutory minimum wage	88*	88*
Agricultural work	47	53
Other casual labour	58	71
NREGA	85	85

Source: NREGA Survey 2008.
Note: * Unweighted average of state minimum wages in the six survey states.

It is interesting to note that the figures on women's share in NREGA employment according to our survey, are broadly in line with the official data (available on www.nrega.nic.in) for 2007–8. For instance, if we rank states based on women's participation rates, both sources give us the same ranking with Rajasthan and Madhya Pradesh at the top and Uttar Pradesh at the bottom (see Table 4.2). Possible reasons for the low participation rates of women in these states are explored in the last section.

Low Workforce Participation Rates

In the study areas, NREGA has provided income-earning opportunities to women where hardly any existed before. Table 4.2 reports the female labour/workforce participation rates (based on 2000–1 and 2004–5 NSSO data). Again, Madhya Pradesh and Rajasthan (in that order) significantly outperform Bihar and Uttar Pradesh, yet, not more than 40 per cent of women were part of the workforce even in these states.

Table 4.2 Women's Share of Employment

	Women's share in NREGA employment according to		**Women's participation rate (rural)**	
	NREGA Survey, 2008 (sample districts only)	Official NREGA data, 2007–8 (all districts)	Labour force (2000–1)	Workforce (2004–5)
Bihar	12	27	12.3	13.8
Chhattisgarh	25	42	44.7	–
Jharkhand	18	27	24.6	31.3
Madhya Pradesh	44	42	37.0	36.6
Rajasthan	71	69	32.5	40.7
Uttar Pradesh	5	15	17.9	24.0

Sources: Drèze and Oldiges (2009) for official NREGA figures, 2007–8. Female labour force participation rate and female workforce participation rates are from www.indiastat.com and based on National Sample Survey data.

The reasons for the low availability of wage labour for rural women are complex and vary across regions. Women are primary providers of care roles for the sick and the elderly. Outside of unpaid housework, women have some opportunities for paid agricultural work. The combination of a labour surplus economy and sharp gender divisions of labour implies that these opportunities tend to be seasonal in nature.[3] There are even fewer opportunities for non-agricultural wage work in areas where the rural economy is predominantly agricultural. The limited access to wage work for women in these areas is captured by the fact that only 30 per cent of the female respondents reported earning a cash income other than NREGA in the three months preceding the survey (see Table 4.1). In fact, even among men just over half (55 per cent) said that they had earned cash from sources other than the NREGA.

The women who reported wage work other than NREGA were performing agricultural labour in their own village or in other villages, working in the construction industry in towns and cities,

[3] See, for instance, Drèze and Sharma (1998), Breman, (1996), and Chen (1989). On this see also Harriss-White (2003).

working at stone quarries, and collecting and selling forest produce such as *tendu* leaves, *mohua* flowers, grass, and wood.

These employment opportunities, however, are not without problems. The earnings from them were limited or seasonal or insecure. Much of this work is irregular (for example, agricultural work, collection of tendu leaves, and mohua flowers are all seasonal in nature) and consequently, women find themselves in a vulnerable position. Migration for work in the construction industry exposes workers to a range of vulnerabilities (for example, exploitation, illness) to add to which gender biases are consistently faced in the availability of work.[4] Many of these occupations (construction, factory, mining work, and stone crushing) are replete with hazards and the possibility of injury. Even respondents engaged in the collection of forest produce often pointed out that they feared attacks from wild animals.

Half of the women in the sample said that had they not worked on the NREGA worksites, they would have worked at home or would have remained unemployed. This could be either because they have few other employment opportunities (locally, and even otherwise in some cases) or because women workers are, 'as a rule', paid less than their male counterparts in casual wage work (see Table 4.1).[5] When women do have other employment opportunities, they often face 'invisible' social constraints: some respondents might have considered working only on the fields owned by farmers from their own community or at a place where other persons from their community are working. Similar constraints and limitations prevail when migrating for work to cities.[6] On top of this, the harsh work conditions in the private labour market may also deter women from participating in it.

[4] See, for instance, Breman (1996).

[5] See, for instance, National Commission for Enterprises in the Unorganized Sector (2007), Olsen and Mehta (2006), and Chen (1989). With regard to agricultural wage work, Chen points out that 'generally, across regions, women are paid less than men for the same agricultural operations...In all regions, the lower-paid off-peak season operations (weeding, preservation, processing) are dominated by women.'

[6] Mosse et. al. (2007) and Breman (1996), for instance, mention the physical and sexual vulnerabilities faced by women migrants.

To summarize, employment opportunities for women in the private labour market are limited, irregular, poorly paid, and often hazardous. They often involve migration which raises a whole range of issues of its own. In additional to 'invisible' social barriers, working conditions in the private labour market are often very demanding and exploitative.

Attractiveness of NREGA Employment for Women

Many female respondents said the work provided under NREGA opens up a new opportunity for them. The wider acceptability of NREGA work derives from several factors: it is locally available; being government work there is regularity and predictability of working hours; work conditions are less exploitative; and work is considered socially acceptable and 'dignified'. Last but not least, NREGA work is better paid than other work. These attractive features of NREGA for women are discussed here.

The Act stipulates that work be provided locally, within 5 km of the residence. This greatly facilitates women's participation in NREGA work. Since they continue to bear the main responsibility for household work, travelling any distance for paid work is difficult for them. Apart from the fact that NREGA work is provided in the village itself, the fact that women work in groups and that work is provided by the government helps to make NREGA work 'socially acceptable'.[7]

Other reasons why NREGA work was considered 'acceptable' are pertinent. NREGA promises the statutory minimum wage. Even in cases where the minimum wage is not paid (as is often the case,

[7] Lungibai (Sirohi district, Rajasthan) said that this was the first time she was working for a wage and that her husband had 'allowed' her to work since work was available within the village. Similarly, Maina (Aant panchayat, Sitapur district) stated that she had never worked for a wage earlier. Interestingly enough, she felt that NREGA employment 'has not changed her life substantially' but went on to state that she had started sending her daughter to school as a result of this work.

especially in Rajasthan),[8] NREGA earnings are substantially higher than the earnings from the private labour market (see Table 4.1). As per survey data, the average wage earned by women in the private labour market ranged between Rs 47 and Rs 58 per day, for agricultural and other casual labour, respectively. On NREGA, the average wage earned was Rs 85, clearly a large increase over other wage opportunities. Some women stated they did not engage themselves in agricultural wage labour earlier because they would have been paid too little and it was not worth their while to go out and work for a pittance. The prospect of earning a substantial wage within the village in some cases might swing 'acceptability' in favour of women.

The fact that NREGA work is offered by the local government rather than by a private employer in some ways frees potential women workers from caste and community based strictures related to who they can and cannot work with.[9]

Further, being government work, the hours of work are clearly stated (and are limited to 8 hours in a day in the case of daily-wage work). Fixed working hours often cannot be expected in the case of other work. This is of special concern for women who combine any paid work with household work. NREGA employment is therefore considered relatively 'safe', in the sense that it is thought that there are some checks and balances in place to prevent harassment of workers.

Moreover, NREGA employment offers a new sense of independence: for instance, Gita (Sirohi district, Rajasthan) said she would have stayed at home or worked on her own fields had NREGA work not been available. She considered working on the NREGA worksite

[8] NREGA allows wage to be calculated on a time rate or piece rate basis. Since the wage is often calculated on a piece rate rather than a time rate basis, as is typically the case in Rajasthan, workers get less than the statutory minimum wage. The calculation of wage on a piece rate basis is dependent on a 'schedule of rates' for specific tasks done by workers.

[9] Barbara Harriss-White (2003: 31), for instance, states, 'caste ideology … affects whether women work at all, what work they can do and how far from home they may move.' Also, with regard to migrant labour, Breman comments on restrictions faced by women migrant workers—they are likely to travel with male relatives (1996: 45–53).

because she did not have to go through a potentially embarrassing and humiliating conversation to ask anyone in the village for work.

SOCIAL AND ECONOMIC BENEFITS

This section focuses on the impact of NREGA earnings as reported by female NREGA workers in our sample. It is worth noting that NREGA workers (men and women alike) belong to the most disadvantaged groups. As Table 4.1 shows, a large majority (over 70 per cent) of sample workers belonged to the Scheduled Castes (SCs) and the Scheduled Tribes (STs), and most NREGA labourers were illiterate (80 per cent in the case of women).

We begin by looking at the scale of NREGA employment. Average days of NREGA employment, in the 12 months preceding the survey, have been reported in Table 4.3. Again, Rajasthan tops the chart with an average of 46 days per female worker. Apart from Rajasthan and Madhya Pradesh, the days of NREGA employment reported in the other states are very low (less than 20 days in each case).

Yet, in the overall sample, NREGA was considered 'very important' by 68 per cent of the respondents.[10] This figure increases to 81 per cent in the households that have worked for at least 60 days in the last 12 months (here responses for male and female workers are taken together). Looking at the response from widows separately, NREGA was also considered 'very important by 82 per cent of widows in the sample. Of the total sample, more than two-thirds (69 per cent) of the sample workers stated that NREGA had helped them avoid hunger, while 57 per cent stated that NREGA had helped them avoid migration and about half also said that they had used NREGA wages to buy medicines in the last 12 months.[11]

[10] The terms 'very important', 'somewhat important', and 'unimportant' used in the survey questionnaire need to be interpreted broadly. The use of these terms aims at emphasizing perceived benefits by workers under NREGA. This and other supplementary questions on access to healthcare, nutrition, and education were intended to capture the essence of the discussion with labourers.

[11] Preliminary results from a survey of 320 households in one district of Andhra Pradesh report similar results (see Ravi and Engler 2009).

Table 4.3 Participation of Women in NREGA

	Bihar	Chhattisgarh	Jharkhand	Madhya Pradesh	Rajasthan	Uttar Pradesh	All survey states
Number of women in the sample	28	23	37	90	154	6	338
Participation of women (%)	13	25	18	44	71	5	32
Days of NREGA employment in the past 12 months	15	16	14	23	46	18	30
Proportion of women workers who							
Collect their own wages	75	74	63	71	100	0	78
Keep their own wages	67	74	59	71	74	0	69
Had other sources of cash income in the past 3 months	61	22	41	29	22	83	30
Prefer payments through banks	56	73	13	39	64	67	53

Source: NREGA Survey 2008.

A large majority (79 per cent) of women workers collect their own wages, and generally they also keep their wages. In fact, as Table 4.3 shows, the proportion of workers who keep their own wages is higher for female workers (69 per cent) than for male workers (51 per cent). One may argue that what really matters is not only who keeps the money, but also who has control over it. Interviews with women suggest that in a large number of cases, they have substantial say in deciding how the money is spent.[12]

Two-thirds of the female respondents reported having to face less hunger as a result of NREGA employment (Table 4.4). These earnings bring improved food security in a variety of ways: cash in hand allows households to buy food in larger quantities, which is generally cheaper than buying on a daily basis; women reported easier access to credit from local moneylenders to meet food expenditures; there were also some indications of a diversification of diets, even if only marginally, away from a cereal-dominated diet.

Table 4.4 Social and Economic Benefits to Women

	Proportion (%) of female NREGA workers who said that NREGA helped them:					
	avoid hunger	avoid migration	avoid illness	avoid hazardous work	repay debts	with child's schooling
Bihar	74	14	57	7	7	25
Chhattisgarh	78	39	35	39	39	26
Jharkhand	57	40	31	45	17	12
Madhya Pradesh	57	39	33	17	24	27
Rajasthan	69	26	56	30	29	39
Uttar Pradesh	100	17	17	20	67	50
All sample states	**67**	**31**	**46**	**27**	**26**	**31**

Source: NREGA Survey 2008.

12 As Haski, a tribal woman in Chanar panchayat (Sirohi district), put it: '*Main ghar ki mukhiya hoon*' (I am the head of the household). That women have some measure of control over savings can also be seen later in this section, where women state they spent the money on their personal needs, including medical problems and to travel to their parents' village.

NREGA also seems to be functioning as a 'healthline' for many rural households. Across states, NREGA workers (men and women alike) reported using their wages to treat an illness in the family or for their own medical expenses. Nearly half of the female respondents said that NREGA helped them cope with an illness in the family (see Table 4.4). Much of the economic uncertainty which afflicts the lives of the rural poor stems from sudden illnesses and chronic ailments. To that extent, NREGA seems to have enhanced economic security.

Interview after interview provides insights into how NREGA employment is helping women take charge of their lives, in little (and not so little) ways. Where NREGA is implemented well, it has provided predictable and regular employment to women. In their fragile existence, NREGA has brought respite from the anxieties associated with fulfilling their basic needs. These signs of relief emerge clearly through their statements regarding 'improved creditworthiness'; from knowing that they won't have to sleep hungry; from not having to migrate in search of work which they are not sure of getting; from not having to spend money on travelling in cases where they work in nearby areas as labourers; from the assurance that there will be some money to pay for small and large medical bills should someone in the family fall ill; from being protected from very strenuous and poorly paid work (for example, collecting forest produce and bringing it to the market for amounts as little as Rs 10 per day) as well as from exploitative work conditions (including sexual exploitation and harsh productivity norms). In this sense, NREGA has made a significant contribution to the well-being of women. Some examples from Rajasthan are given below.

In Rajasthan, where the scale of NREGA employment has been substantial, women reported purchasing productive assets with their earnings: Leela Ajma (Sirohi district, Rajasthan) spent some money buying agricultural inputs; Sumiri Jogira (Sirohi district, Rajasthan) said she and her family were able to hire a tractor to plough their fields; Sita said she bought a sewing machine with her earnings.

For some women, NREGA work has allowed them to spend money on their own needs, while earlier they might not have had the liberty to do so. Keyo, a 45-year-old widow (Sirohi district, Rajasthan), states she has been able to take care of medical bills to treat a respiratory problem that was contracted earlier while working a stone quarry. Had NREGA work not been available to her, she would have been unemployed, since other wage work is hazardous and too strenuous for her. She was also dependent on a wage-earning daughter who is married—because of the number of people dependent on her daughter, Keyo might not have had the option to treat the medical problem earlier, but her own NREGA earnings enabled her to do this. Santosh, a 22-year-old respondent, also from Sirohi (Rajasthan), said she is happy to have money she can spend. Since she is earning money herself, she does not feel answerable to her husband or parents-in-law as to how she spends her money and she can now travel to her parents' house when she wants. In a society with strict norms of patrilocality, where often significant exclusion from natal homes prevails, this is a remarkable statement in itself.

Significance for Single Women

We have seen that NREGA offers the relatively high (compared to the private market) statutory minimum wage and women workers are paid the same as men. Work conditions on NREGA worksites are better and there is perceived dignity in doing NREGA work. Social barriers in the case of NREGA employment are lower. In the case of single women, these benefits are magnified. In this short section we use testimonies gathered during the survey to highlight the benefits to some single women in the sample.

The extremely vulnerable position of widows is brought out by the case of Timmo Kuwar, a 40-year-old widow from Palamau district, Jharkhand. She has hardly any land (only 0.05 acres) and even that, she said, her brother was trying to usurp. NREGA work was very important for her because earlier she had to migrate in search of work, whereas now she got work locally. Earlier she worked at breaking stones, which she said was very dangerous, and if she does not get NREGA work, she would have to go back to that.

In Sitapur (Uttar Pradesh), Takdiri, a widow said that NREGA had 'changed her life' because earlier she was able to get work at Rs 35 per day, whereas now she earns Rs 100 per day. Bejni Devi (Araria district, Bihar) said that she was glad to have access to NREGA employment since the wage she can now earn in the village has increased significantly. The wage she would get for locally available work was Rs 15 per day, whereas she gets Rs 75 for NREGA work (as opposed to the statutory minimum wage of Rs 82 per day in Bihar). If she had not got this work, she would have had to migrate with her four-month-old child, since she had not been able to get any other local employment in the past three months.[13]

NREGA work provides some measure of protection from having to migrate in search of work, or, given the small amount of work currently available, at least allows women to postpone migration. This protection from migration is a significant improvement in the quality of life because of the costs and risks associated with migration. Tejki Dhira's (a widow from Sirohi district, Rajasthan) case illustrates this: she is 61 years old and migrating to Ambaji to sell wood would be very difficult for her. This is what Tejki would have done if NREGA employment had not been available. The money she earned by working under NREGA helped her repay the loan she took to treat her husband's illness and to perform the death ceremonies.

Access to work in the village is also critically important for those who are coping with illness of a family member. Kali Bai (from Sirohi district, Rajasthan) had a constant source of income when her husband was alive. Now, it is her NREGA wages that allow her to sustain herself and her son who has a mental health problem. In the same district, another widow, Jamnabai Galbaji said that NREGA wages were crucial for her child's heart treatment.

[13] Similarly, Nani Bai (Badwani district, Madhya Pradesh) said she now earns Rs 85 (the minimum wage in Madhya Pradesh) instead of Rs 20–25 that she earned earlier as an agricultural labourer.

For those widows who do not get widow pensions, NREGA employment offers relief and confidence.[14] Keshi (a Rajput widow from Sirohi, Rajasthan) is one such woman.[15] While earlier there was uncertainty as to whether she would have enough food to eat, she is now in a position to contribute to the family expenses by paying for her grandchildren's education. Like many others, she reports improved creditworthiness (getting small advances from the local moneylender is now easier because moneylenders seem to be assured that they will get their money back). Importantly, for some women, and especially for women heading households, NREGA has made loans more easily available and, in some cases, women say they have been able to repay at least part of their loan.

The dignity associated with doing government work and not having to seek work from private landlords or contractors is also a very significant benefit for single women. Baby Pusaji Rawal (Sirohi district, Rajasthan) said that NREGA employment suited her because she does not have to go out and find work, and she does not need to wait for work. Government work opened under the NREGA has allowed her to leave work with private landlords and contractors, which is often replete with an underlying threat or possibility of sexual abuse and exploitation.[16]

Many widows also spoke of the harsh working conditions in the private labour market. Aansi Bai (Sirohi district, Rajasthan) said that at the private contractor's worksite she used to get Rs 50 for 12 hours of work. NREGA pays her more (Rs 100/day) for 8 hours of work.

[14] The Government of India has a widow pension scheme which pays Rs 200 per month; some states supplement this amount with contributions from the state budget.

[15] The Rajput community is particularly conservative, and for Rajput women, access to wage work is difficult and often looked down upon.

[16] These very same issues are highlighted by Herring and Edwards in their study of the Employment Guarantee Scheme implemented since the 1970s in Maharashtra. Women heads of households who Herring and Edwards spoke with stated that they consider government work under the Maharashtra EGS 'safer' and that EGS work provided by the government has led to a reduction in subtle forms of coercion and overt sexual exploitation faced by women workers (1983: 583).

Several respondents (27 per cent of the female respondents) stated that NREGA work has allowed them to stop doing hazardous work or work they did not want to do (for example, working at quarries, going to the forest to cut wood, etc.) (see Table 4.4). Rina Devi (Koderma district, Jharkhand) said she no longer needs to go the jungle to cut wood where wild animals were a constant threat. Several female respondents in Palamau district (Jharkhand) and Sirohi district (Rajasthan) said that NREGA employment has allowed them to avoid working at a stone quarry, which was hazardous.

Before moving on, it is worth noting that although we have focused only on widows in this section, the category of single women is not restricted to widows. Further, many women in the sample, who were primary wage earners (that is, not necessarily single women), found themselves facing the same vulnerabilities as single women and presented very similar testimonies.

AREAS OF CONCERN

This section focuses on two areas of concern with respect to women and their access to work under NREGA. First, in spite of the relative accessibility of NREGA for women, major barriers remain. Second, there has been a thrust (from the government) towards payment of wages through banks. Some issues related to bank payments are discussed here.

Barriers to Women's Participation

We begin with a discussion of the persistent barriers to women's participation in NREGA works. The low participation rates in four out of six sample states bears witness to the existence of such barriers.

First, there are, in many areas, tenacious social norms against women working outside the home. In Uttar Pradesh and Bihar, we met women who said that they had not been able to register as workers under the NREGA and were told that this programme was 'not for them'.[17] In Sitapur district (Uttar Pradesh), there was a significant amount of hostility to female participation in NREGA, both from gram panchayat functionaries and male relatives. Names of adult women were excluded from job cards and it was commonly stated that women 'cannot' work on worksites, that they are 'too weak', and that it is 'socially unacceptable' for them to undertake this work. The widespread prevalence of these opinions related to female labour was reflected in the fact that only 5 per cent of the sample workers in Sitapur district were women.

The reason for this bias seems to be partly related to the difference in the statutory minimum wage earned under NREGA, and the local market wage rate (especially for women). This, combined with the fact that men and women earn the same wage, has created resistance to the participation of women by men who want to maintain privileged access to this (relatively high paid) work.

Takdiri (Sitapur district, Uttar Pradesh) pointed out that she has been turned away from several worksites—and that when there is an 'excess of workers' women are the ones who are turned away. It may be pointed out that barriers in accessing work highlighted by Takdiri are 'illegal'—in that all workers who seek work have a right to work and must be provided work by the government as per law. Moreover, as against the legal provisions of the NREGA, work in most places is not 'demand driven'. Instead, in most places work is started at the initiative of the local government[18] and can be in limited supply at any given time. This is also the case for many respondents to the current survey. For many people facing difficult economic circumstances, the certainty of accessing work when

[17] Under NREGA, work is provided to workers who are listed on the 'job cards' issued in the name of the head of the household. All adults in the family may register for work. One job card is provided per household—which, according to Operational Guidelines for the Act, is supposed to be a nuclear family.

[18] The incentive to do this, for the state government, is that the funds to be spent under NREGA are provided by the Central (federal) Government. Therefore, the state government is effectively using Central funds for local area development without dipping into the state exchequer.

sought is critical, as is regularity of payment.[19] However, women being turned away from work, especially in these circumstances, is a matter of concern.

Second, the continued illegal presence of contractors is a significant negative factor affecting the availability of work and its benefits for women. On worksites where contractors were involved, 35 per cent of women workers said that they were harassed, as compared to only 8 per cent on contractor-free worksites.[20] Besides, as mentioned earlier, the conditions of work at worksites run by contractors tend to be more exploitative (see Table 4.5). It is quite likely that the complete absence of contractors is one of the factors that contributes to the high participation of women in Rajasthan.

Table 4.5 Barriers to Women's Participation

	Proportion (%) of female workers in the sample	Proportion (%) of female workers reporting		
		harassment at the worksite	contractor-managed worksites	delays in payment of wages*
Bihar	13	15	15	12
Chhattisgarh	25	35	30	70
Jharkhand	18	3	38	20
Madhya Pradesh	44	28	46	7
Rajasthan	71	5	0	7
Uttar Pradesh	5	0	0	100
All sample states	**32**	**14**	**19**	**16**

Source: NREGA Survey 2008.
Note: * Proportion who reported that wages were not paid within 15 days among those women workers who had been paid at the sample worksite.

In Rajpur block (Badwani district, Madhya Pradesh), for instance, work was being implemented by contractors in four out of five works

[19] See Khera (2006).

[20] The proportion of male NREGA workers reporting harassment is much lower—only 9 per cent. On worksites where contractors were involved, it is slightly higher (11 per cent).

visited. Women workers said that the contractor would come to the village and ask for names of able-bodied men to work on the site. If women asked for work, their pleas were ignored. Importantly, since the legal entitlement to get work on demand is not understood by many, this turning away of women workers does not meet with opposition from the village community—in fact, male workers engaged by the contractors thought the turning away of women was perfectly justified. In Udaipur block (Surguja district, Chhattisgarh), Bodhsai from Marya panchayat said that women and girls are subjected to verbal abuse by the contractor and women workers are often told that they do not work fast enough.

Another big hurdle inhibiting the participation of women is the lack of child care facilities. The Act requires that when there are more than five children under the age of six at the worksite, a female worker be appointed to take care of them. We did not find child care facilities being provided anywhere. (Only 3 per cent of the worksites had child care facilities, and even these need to be taken with a pinch of salt because at least two were cases of 'window dressing' in anticipation of the investigator's visit.) The lack of these facilities can be crippling for women, especially for those with breastfeeding infants who cannot be left behind for long hours.[21] Most women who have young children do not bring them to the worksite as it is not seen as a safe place for them: apart from the dangers of babies being left untended in the open, women are also worried about the heat and sometimes they are harassed when they spend time with the child (for example, to breastfeed). However, leaving the child at home is not without its problems: sometimes the child is left unsupervised, or breastfed children are fed once in the morning and left alone until evening when the mother returns, which has a significant adverse impact on the health of the child and the mother. Meanwhile, the mothers spend their day in anxiety worrying about the child's safety at home. What is encouraging is that four out of every five women

[21] See Chapter 7 for further discussion.

said that if child care facilities were provided they would bring their child to the worksite.[22]

Fourth, in some states productivity norms are too exacting, because the Schedule of Rates is yet to be revised in line with NREGA norms. To illustrate, in Jharkhand, the standard task for a day's work at the time of the survey was digging 110 cubic feet (in soft soil), which is far too much. Certain types of NREGA work also limit the participation of women.[23] This applies, for instance, to the construction of wells on private land. The nature of this work is such that women stop being employed as soon as digging has reached a certain depth.

Fifth, delayed payments also come in the way of participation of poor women. Delays in wage payments make things particularly difficult for single women, who cannot afford to wait for work and wages as they are the sole earners in the family. When the wages do not come on time, they are often forced to return to previous, less preferred forms of employment. For example, Shanti Devi (Koderma, Jharkhand) said that at the mine where she worked before, she was paid on a daily basis whereas she has to wait for a month for her NREGA wages. As Table 4.5 shows, in Uttar Pradesh, where only 5 per cent of the sample workers were women, all of them reported that wages had not been paid within the stipulated 15-day period.

Bank Payments of NREGA Wages

Another area of concern relates to the *en masse* switch over to bank payments of NREGA wages since September 2008. This is a

[22] It might be reiterated here that the sample was drawn from lists of workers at worksites. If anything, concerns related to child care are, therefore, underemphasized in the survey findings, since there are likely to have been many women who would not have been on the muster rolls because of the lack of child care facilities.

[23] The Schedule of Rates have been revised downwards in almost all the sample states after the survey concluded.

relatively recent administrative innovation, which is perceived by the government as a 'magic pill' for ending corruption.[24]

Respondents were asked whether they preferred to be paid in cash, or through banks and/or post offices. The introduction of bank payments could benefit women in several ways. In the survey, roughly 53 per cent of women in the sample wanted payments through banks and/or post offices.[25] The main reasons in favour of bank payments include the perception that payment through banks will increase the possibility of saving and reduce the risk of being cheated by those who distribute wages in the village. Other reasons why people want bank payments include the perception that this will lead to a reduction in delays (in payments), or that a lump-sum of money will be available in one instalment (stated by respondents especially in Uttar Pradesh and Bihar). Interestingly, for women, it is also seen as an effective tool for increasing their control over the use of this money (for example, some women said that when wages are paid in cash, it is easier for husbands to take control over it).

However, if payments through banks are introduced without consciously taking into account women's concerns, this change could end up hurting them. For instance, in the event when bank accounts are opened in the name of one job card holder (as has happened in many of the survey areas), women might be denied rightful direct access to their own earnings. The case for cash payments is sometimes made on the grounds that banks are often at a distance from the place of residence, in some cases, in distant (larger) villages or towns, and getting there involves additional costs, and that it would lead to some loss of liquidity.

What has emerged from the survey is that if banks are close to the worker's residence, if women have their own accounts and are able to operate their own accounts, then the introduction of wage payments through banks/post offices may turn out to be a good development for women.

[24] See Chapter 6 of this book; also Kar (2009), Drèze and Khera (2008b), and Vanaik and Siddhartha (2008).

[25] Interestingly the figures for women are higher than those for men (44 per cent)—see Table 4.2.

NREGA AND GENDER EQUALITY

As noted at the beginning of this essay, NREGA has several provisions aimed at improving the participation of women. We have seen that these have met with varying degrees of success in different parts of the country. In the case of women, it is important to note that even relatively small levels of NREGA employment have resulted in significant perceived benefits. Serious problems remain in implementation across states (such as the lack of crèches for mothers of young children and the continued illegal presence of contractors). Given the critical gains made by women workers—in accessing work and an income, food and healthcare for themselves and their families, and in leaving potentially hazardous work—it needs to be ensured that the problems in implementation do not derail the gains.

More importantly, NREGA has the potential to have a wider impact (over time) on gender relations. This can happen in several ways. For instance, NREGA employment can enhance women's economic independence by providing them access to cash earnings. Moreover, NREGA earnings can bring about a sense of equality fostered by earning, for the first time, the same wage as men. Gender relations will also be impacted through the effect of NREGA on the gender division of labour. This could happen because women are seen to be contributing 'actively' (in the conventional sense) to the economy and their contribution to economic activity becomes more directly visible. Further, in keeping with similar provisions under Panchayati Raj legislation, NREGA Guidelines have provisions for female participation in vigilance committees. Over time, it is hoped that women will be able to take advantage of such provisions, making their own space in public and social life (more on this later).

However, for effective participation of women, it is important for NREGA to go beyond the initial gender related provisions such as fixing the minimum share of women workers and equal wages. A more comprehensive perspective on gender equality needs to be built in all aspects of the Act. One of the first steps in this direction is to move from the household entitlement of 100 days to individual entitlements, which will assure women 100 days of work in their own right, without having to negotiate within the household. In order to ensure direct access to NREGA earnings, instead of having joint bank accounts (or worse, accounts in the name of the male member of the household), there should be separate bank accounts for women. This has already been done in some states (for example, in Tamil Nadu, men and women have separate job cards and separate bank accounts). Increasing the share of women in NREGA staff appointments would also contribute to the agenda of gender equality and sensitivity. One encouraging example of this is the move, in Rajasthan, towards appointing trained female mates.[26]

That gender equality remains a distant goal is evident when we look at women's participation in gram sabhas. Only 33 per cent of sample workers (both men and women) stated that they had attended a gram sabha during the preceding 12 months.[27] A large number of women respondents said that they do not go to gram sabhas either because they are not welcome there or because they think that 'it is not a meeting that women can attend'. Since decisions related to the implementation of NREGA works are supposed to take place in gram sabhas, it is significant that most women look at these as meetings that they 'should not attend'.

However, there are also heartening departures from this pattern, which suggest that NREGA is an important opportunity for improving gender relations in some areas. For instance, in Pati block (Badwani district, Madhya Pradesh), women were among the most vocal members of the vigilance committees and also participated actively in gram sabhas. This also raises the question as to why women have been able to gain so much out of NREGA in Pati block. In this context, it is appropriate to mention the role of the Jagrut Adivasi Dalit Sangathan, a small organization of peasants and labourers, working in the area towards helping workers claim their entitlements under

[26] Mates are worksite supervisors, selected from among NREGA labourers. See Chapter 8 for more details of this experiment.

[27] It is important to qualify this, however, with the fact that at the moment, in many places, gram sabha meetings tend not to be held.

NREGA. The emphasis of the work of the Sangathan has been on making the local government answerable to gram sabhas and to the people. In several pockets in Pati block, NREGA is implemented as a demand driven employment programme, as is intended by law. Sangathan members submit applications for work and work is opened by the government in response to work demanded. Members of the Sangathan, women and men, have collectively participated in NREGA planning and implementation by way of participation in gram sabhas and in supervision committees for NREGA sites, so that engagement with NREGA is not just in terms of getting employment. Rallying around NREGA has also strengthened the Sangathan and encouraged higher female participation in vigilance committees.

To reiterate the main benefits from NREGA for women: work is available at the statutory minimum wage; workers get work in their village; and migration and hazardous work can be avoided. These benefits should be adequately recognized and efforts should be made to strengthen these gains. Ensuring the establishment of crèches for women workers, abolition of contractors, effective implementation of transparency mechanisms, and the establishment of a Schedule of Rates more favourable to women will go a long way in removing the short-term barriers to women's participation in NREGA. For the longer-term goals of gender equality to be realized, attention also needs to be paid to ensuring greater participation of women at all levels (for example, as labourers, in NREGA worksite management, and staff appointments), and in all spheres (for example, participatory planning through participation in gram sabhas and social audits). These measures can simultaneously impact gender relations and improve the implementation of NREGA.

5

CAG Report on NREGA

Facts and Fiction*

Siddhartha and Anish Vanaik#

The debate sparked off in January 2008 by the leak of an interim report of the Comptroller and Auditor General on the National Rural Employment Guarantee Act (hereafter, CAG report on NREGA) came at a critical moment.[1] Two years after NREGA came into force in selected districts, balanced and careful stock-taking of the performance of the Act was certainly the order of the day. Indeed, the exercise could have proved a useful signpost to the changes that ought to have been introduced in the context of the imminent extension of the programme across the country in April 2008. Unfortunately, the controversy over the CAG report, as it unfolded in the media, precluded any constructive effort of this sort. Instead, the report was, by and large, used to dismiss the Act as a failure.

* Orginally published as 'CAG Report on NREGA: Facts and Fiction', *Economic and Political Weekly*, 43(25): 39–45, 21 June 2008.

Acknowledgements are due to Nikhil Dey, Jean Dréze, Reetika Khera, and Amitabh Mukhopadhyay.

[1] This essay is based on the interim report of the CAG, which was leaked in January 2008 through a series of four articles in *Indian Express*. In August 2008, a final version of the report was released (with much less media attention), which took into account the clarifications of various state governments as well as the response of the MoRD to the interim report. All references in the text, however, are to the leaked January 2008 report unless indicated otherwise.

OVERVIEW

The CAG audit covered a quarter of the 200 'first phase' districts where NREGA came into effect in February 2006. The range of records audited included the relevant records of the Ministry of Rural Development (MoRD), State Rural Development offices, and block and gram panchayat level offices for the duration of February 2006 to March 2007. It was, therefore, the first extensive assessment of NREGA.[2] As such, there was a temptation to view the report as the last word on NREGA implementation. However, given this massive scale of operations, the CAG report focused on certain aspects of implementation at the expense of others and ought not to have been seen as a comprehensive assessment.[3]

It is also important to recall the context in which the CAG undertook this 'performance audit' of NREGA. This was an audit initiated at the request of the MoRD and not in the routine course of the CAG's operations. The intention, at least to begin with, seems to have been commendable, even courageous: to commission an independent body to identify problems in the programme as they were emerging.[4]

[2] In each state, the CAG selected 25 per cent of NREGA districts. In each district two blocks were selected, and in each block, four gram panchayats were short-listed for detailed examination. Finally, four work-sites (preferably three completed and one ongoing) were selected for audit in each gram panchayat. In all, the CAG studied records relating to 68 districts in 26 states, 128 blocks within the selected districts, and 513 gram panchayats in the selected blocks. See CAG (2007).

[3] Numerous examples of the use of CAG findings as an authoritative statement on the state of NREGA implementation have circulated in the press. They found their way into research papers as well. For examples see Ambasta et al. (2008) and Mahapatra et al. (2008). Indira Hirway (2008) warns against using the report in such a manner: 'The CAG has taken a very simplistic and sweeping approach in analysing the weaknesses as well as in making recommendations for improving the working of NREGA.'

[4] Vinod Rai, the Comptroller and Auditor General, points out: 'This is a case in which the government invited the auditors to do the study. Under normal circumstances we would have done this at a later stage. The government took a positive view saying that it would like to do mid-course corrections if corrections are required' (Chikermane 2008).

This aim, however, can only be served by a careful assessment of what the CAG report can (and cannot) be interpreted to say. Such an exercise is necessary, we argue in the first section, because of the ways in which the media coverage unfolded. Much of the coverage was sensationalist and many of the opinions expressed would not be borne out by a plain reading of the report. For instance, the reportage and initial controversy centred on three aspects—the national average estimates (including the figure of 3.2 per cent of households availing 100 days of employment), the alleged violations of Operational Guidelines, and claims about corruption. We demonstrate that the report is far more circumspect and measured in its treatment of each of these.

However, the confusion is not merely media-driven. Part of the blame for this must also be laid at the doors of the CAG, for what was effectively a half-hearted 'performance audit'. Auditing 'performance' must surely include some sense of the actual impact of the programme, along with issues of compliance with prescribed requirements. For a variety of reasons that we explore, the CAG is deafeningly silent on the former—the impact on the lives of workers and the quality of the assets created.[5] The report has little to say about actual socio-economic outcomes, whether it is the impact of NREGA on poverty, or on women's empowerment, or agricultural productivity. The main benchmark of performance is a procedural one: conformity with the Operational Guidelines of NREGA (including the main provisions of the Act itself).[6] Indeed, even this benchmark, on a strict reading of the NREGA stipulations, is a mistaken one, since the Guidelines—rightly or wrongly—are not binding on the states. Further, precisely because the main focus is procedural, the report has relatively little to say about corruption. Some of the procedural irregularities identified by the CAG, of course, do make the programme vulnerable to

[5] In an interesting addition, the final report from August 2008 does identify aspects of 'good practices' that they found in various states. Nevertheless, these were mainly instances of procedural innovation, rather than outcomes.

[6] See Government of India (2006).

corruption, and the report also mentions specific instances of embezzlement. But nothing in the report substantiates sweeping claims that 'NREGA funds do not reach the poor'.[7]

The loaded media coverage did more damage than simply propagate misinformation about the report. The MoRD, largely as a result of such coverage, went into denial mode—the concerned minister even terming the report 'totally false'.[8] Therefore, we present some findings of the CAG report that can help in providing direction to the mid-term course-correction, which was the stated objective of the MoRD in inviting the CAG in the first place. Rather than outright dismissal, a constructive response was called for. Indeed, many of these recommendations continue to have resonance as the NREGA enters its fifth year of implementation.

MEDIA COVERAGE

The CAG episode was, perhaps, the first occasion when NREGA received sustained negative media attention since its enactment in mid-2005. Up until then, reportage about social audits and Central Employment Guarantee Council visits had highlighted instances of corruption within a framework of overall optimism about the Act. The wave of media coverage that took off from the initial story on

[7] Perhaps the most misleading headline in this regard was, 'It's official: In poorest states, job funds don't reach the poor' (Tiwari and Pandey 2008b). This headline stretched the limits of ethical journalism. As Jean Drèze points out about this headline: 'This statement, and variants of it printed in this article and elsewhere, give a very misleading picture of the CAG report. Indeed, the report does not present any evidence of massive leakages in the NREGA, nor was this the objective of the investigation' (Drèze 2008a).

[8] 'Bharat Nirman becomes Cong's latest theme song' (*Business Standard*, 15 January 2007). Such a reaction is not altogether unexpected. Sustained negative media attention, a looming budget session, and an opposition looking for political mileage in a year of major assembly elections were just three of the factors that must have fed into the furious back-pedalling of the MoRD on the report.

the CAG report was marked by a negative outlook about the Act. Is this outlook corroborated by the CAG report?[9]

The tone set by the initial reportage on the matter vitiated the possibility of a dispassionate reading of the CAG report.[10] Consider the headlines of the four-part article series (published in *Indian Express*), which broke the story on the issue:

> 'UPA guaranteed 100 days of work to poor, over 96% didn't get it, says first audit'[11]
> 'It's official: In poorest states, job funds don't reach the poor'[12]
> 'Cong ka haath kiske saath?'[13]
> 'In opposition camp too, delays, mismanagement'[14]

This mix of dramatic numbers and well-worn clichès, in evidence here, was characteristic of the stories as well. The articles consistently distorted the findings of the report by stringing them together, out of context, into exaggerated conclusions.[15]

Controversies

As pointed out earlier, 'performance' in the report has meant compliance rather than outcomes. Contrary to the impression given in many

[9] To quote Vinod Rai again: 'Now, it is not that the government or those managing the schemes have only made mistakes. There are a large number of good points that have emerged. A large number of success stories have unfortunately been ignored, only the inadequacies have been discussed' (Chikermane 2008).

[10] See Ghosh (2008).

[11] See Tiwari and Pandey (2008a).

[12] See Tiwari and Pandey (2008b).

[13] See Tiwari and Pandey (2008c).

[14] See Tiwari and Pandey (2008d).

[15] The Centre for Science and Environment policy paper also takes note of the biases of the media coverage of the CAG report: 'The recent CAG assessment of NREGA performance has been making headlines. Media coverage has mostly projected the CAG report as a failure of the NREGA. Instead, a closer analysis of the findings shows that the NREGA has performed badly due to absence of right implementation framework as well as obsessive focus on employment creation only' (Mahapatra et al. 2008). See also Roy and Dey (2008).

media reports, the report has not investigated the veracity of documents (for example, by speaking to labourers), except in a section on works and muster rolls. This prevents the CAG from making a conclusive statement on many of the suspected irregularities that it has uncovered. For the most part, the CAG has carefully refrained from making any categorical claim about these irregularities, but the media has harped upon them as concrete evidence to damn the Act.[16] In this section, we try to understand some aspects that have generated much heat, but little light, during the course of the media coverage.

Estimates of Employment Generation

Many initial media reports focused on a particular set of figures mentioned in the CAG report, according to which each registered household received 18 days of employment on average (over a period of one year), and only 3.2 per cent of registered households worked for the full 100 days.[17] In response to this, the MoRD came out with an alternative calculation, suggesting an average of 44 days of employment per household, with 10 per cent of households getting 100 days of employment (Table 5.1).

These two sets of figures were reported by the media as competing claims. Ironically, what was overlooked in this false controversy was that both sets of figures were valid and that the difference reflected distinct approaches employed by the CAG and the MoRD in their calculations. To arrive at these figures of average employment and percentage of households completing 100 days of work, the

[16] Interestingly, Vinod Rai, when asked his perspective on the CAG report, put it in the following terms: '…[T]he government is not the executor all the way down. The central government allots the money, state government agencies implement the scheme. When the central government looks at it, it looks at it piecemeal. So do state governments. When audit did it, it did so holistically. And found the lacunae. And *we're not saying this is all mala-fide*' (Chikermane 2008, emphasis added).

[17] This was the basis of the 96 per cent figure cited in Tiwari and Pandey (2008a).

CAG took *registered households* as the base, while the MoRD's calculations focused on *households employed* under NREGA.

Table 5.1 Different Approaches

	Registered households (CAG report)	Households employed under NREGA (MoRD figure)
Average days of employment (per household)	18	44 (approximately)
Proportion (%) of households accessing 100 days	3.2	10 (approximately)

Sources: CAG data are from CAG (2007: 44). The MoRD figures are from Drèze and Oldiges (2007).

As a first step towards getting employment under the Act, a rural household has to get registered with the gram panchayat and obtain a job card. Registration serves as an expression of potential interest in applying for employment. But, in many instances, government servants, shop owners, and others who are unlikely to engage in manual labour have got registered without ever actually accessing employment under NREGA. The official Monthly Progress Reports (MPRs)[18] suggest that only around 55 per cent of all registered households have actually ever worked under NREGA. There is, thus, a gap between total 'registered households' and total 'households employed'.

The CAG used 'registered households' as the base to calculate average employment, whereas the MoRD used 'households employed'. It is entirely understandable, then, that the CAG's figure for average number of days of employment per household was considerably lower than that of the MoRD.

Each of these figures is important. On a strictly technical basis, the total number of days ought to be calculated without considering those who have registered but did not demand employment. One of the

[18] MPRs consist of the basic statistics reported by each district to the MoRD (District Implementation Reports). They are available at www.nrega.nic.in (the official NREGA portal).

innovations of the Act was precisely that it was to be 'demand-driven', and self-targeting. These people, it might be suggested, 'selected' themselves out of the programme. However, the extent of the gap between the households registered and those actually employed suggests that there are barriers to accessing work. Many of those who have registered are, for some reason, prevented from actually working. Field visits lend support to both propositions—that some people select themselves out and that there are barriers to getting work.[19] The latter is probably the more dominant aspect. At most NREGA worksites the authors have visited, work is accessed as and when a project is initiated by the authorities. Indeed, the procedures for demanding work are among the least clearly understood aspects of the Act—among officials as well as workers.

In either case, the figures, when carefully understood, can serve as a useful starting point for further investigation, rather than a simple condemnation or celebration. The sensationalized figure of 3.2 per cent could only serve to obscure the more crucial issue of what the figures represent.

Finally, it must also be kept in mind that these are average, national-level figures that reflect data from very different regions. An uneven performance of states in the implementation of NREGA in the first few years, while troubling and unacceptable in the long term, is also a realistic initial forecast. As such, an average figure would not reflect NREGA's potential. In other words, these averages ought not to be treated as the benchmarks for judging the viability of the programme at this stage. The fact that this was among the only real measures of performance (in the sense of achievements and outcomes) deployed by the CAG is a major lapse.[20]

[19] The authors have been involved in surveys of the implementation of NREGA in Chhattisgarh, Orissa, Himachal Pradesh, and Rajasthan. Some reports from these surveys are included in the present volume.

[20] 'It has neglected the variations in the performance in different districts. For example, there are at least 30 districts where about 90 per cent of allotted funds are spent, 100 days of work has been generated per participant, about 60 per cent workers are women and the average wage rate paid is more than Rs 70 per day. Instead of calculating all-India averages, the CAG should have tried to understand why the NREGA has succeeded in these districts' (Hirway 2008).

Statement of Non-compliance

In assessing compliance, the CAG has compared actual practices with the stipulations from three sources: the Act, the Operational Guidelines, and the MoRD communications. A significant chunk of the report consists of lists of states that have not complied with some norm or the other stipulated in any of these three. Lists have been compiled for over 45 such norms. Not all of these are equally significant. The fact that '...(21 States) had not prepared exhaustive lists of all tasks to be taken up under REGS in different geo-morphological conditions' can hardly be considered as significant as delays in the payment of wages, for instance (CAG 2007: 41). However, the investigation of the core stipulations of the NREGA is certainly a valuable part of the report. We have selected nine of the more significant of these criteria and arranged them into a table showing the compliance status of the 10 states with the maximum districts under NREGA in the year 2006–7 (Table 5.2). If treated as the starting point for analysing the reasons for non-compliance, this is a useful exercise. However, compliance tests are in many ways very blunt instruments of assessment: a stipulation is either complied with in its entirety, or not. The fact that Bihar, for instance, seems to be the most compliant state on these criteria should point towards some of the dangers of mindlessly using compliance with stipulations as an index of the success, or otherwise, of a programme.[21]

Findings on Irregularities Having Financial Implications

Instances identified by the CAG as possibly involving financial irregularities have been splashed across media articles and news bulletins. Financial irregularities are not the main focus of the report. However, it does mention specific cases from which corruption can be inferred. In contrast to their presentation in the media, careful scrutiny of such instances does not lead to the inference of wide-

[21] Reports we have received from some districts in Bihar, while admittedly anecdotal, suggest that this assessment is highly exaggerated.

Table 5.2 Statement of Non-compliance in 10 States with the Highest Number of NREGA Districts

	Non-appointment of employment guarantee assistants[a]	Job cards not issued within the prescribed time frame[b]	Lack of worksite facilities[c]	No district Schedule of Rates	Non-payment of minimum wages	Delay in payment of wages[d]	Non-payment of unemployment allowance[e]	Expenditure without administrative approval and technical sanction	Monthly squaring of accounts not done[f]
Spread in total sample →	**268 GPs in 18 states**	**162 GPs in 15 states**	**202 GPs in 15 states**	**23 states**	**90 GPs in 11 states**	**200 GPs in 18 states**	**53 blocks in 17 states**	**24 GPs in 7 states**	**131 GPs in 10 states**
Andhra Pradesh	x	x	x	x	x	x			x
Assam	x	x	x	x			x		
Bihar					x				
Chhattisgarh	x	x	x	x	x	x	x		x
Jharkhand	x	x	x	x	x	x	x	x	x
Madhya Pradesh	x			x	x	x		x	x
Maharashtra		x			x				
Orissa	x	x	x	x	x	x	x		x
Uttar Pradesh	x	x	x	x		x	x	x	x
West Bengal	x	x	x	x		x			x

Source: Compiled from CAG (2007).

Notes: GP—gram panchayat.

[a] These are supposed to be staff dedicated to NREGA present at every gram panchayat. They are the most important operational unit at this level. [b] Job cards have to be issued within 15 days of application for registration. [c] Shade, drinking water, first aid, and provision for child care. [d] Beyond 15 days of the date on which the work was done. [e] Labourers are due unemployment allowance if 15 days have elapsed since the date of application for work and no work has been provided. [f] Monthly squaring of accounts is to be done under three heads, viz., money held in bank accounts at various levels, advances to implementing or payment agencies, and vouchers of actual expenses.

spread corruption. At any rate, the methodology of the audit does not permit any extrapolation from these instances.

In a small number of cases, the CAG has reported clear-cut financial irregularities. These are based largely on desk audits and, only in Orissa, on cross-verification of records with the concerned labourers. An instance of this from Bihar is quoted here.

> Rs 8.99 lakh was paid as wages to fictitious labourers in respect of 7 works, as the name of the same labourer was recorded twice or thrice for the same period in the same or other MRs [muster rolls]. (CAG 2007: 59)

Tallying up such examples reveals that the scale and the number of these clearly stated financial irregularities are not particularly significant in the CAG report.

It would not, however, be unfair to add to these clear cut instances others like the following from Andhra Pradesh.

> Tampering of muster rolls by using white fluid and marking absent as present and also overwriting the number of days worked was noticed in general during examination of muster rolls pertaining to the works selected in certain selected GPs [gram panchayats]. (Ibid.)

In a case like this, while the description of the practice suggests that funds have been siphoned off, the CAG provides no numbers by which we can gauge the extent of the fraud. Even adding these, evidence of corruption forms a very small part of the report.

The fact that such meagre findings about corruption have been unearthed is more a testimony to the limitations of the approach of the CAG to this audit, than an accurate picture of the extent of corruption. Indeed, processes like social audits and detailed muster roll verifications (of the kind that have been pioneered by Mazdoor Kisan Shakti Sangathan in Rajasthan) are far more effective as ways of quantifying corruption. The fundamental point, which bears repetition, is that the draft CAG report is not an assessment of the extent of corruption in NREGA.

At the same time, there are a number of other formulations in the report that, prima facie, ought not to be understood as instances of financial irregularities but could easily pass for one to a layman. Part of the reason why this has happened relates to the sensationalist nature of the media coverage. However, the aphoristic style of the draft CAG report has also provided grist to the mill.

The use of the term 'ineligible labourers' is a case in point:

> In 13 muster rolls (Bhawanipatna block), 64 ineligible labourers (30 unregistered labourers and 34 labourers belonging to the households already provided with 100 days employment in a year) were engaged on work and paid Rs 0.77 lakh as wages. (Ibid.: 51)[22]

As is (inadequately) clarified in the report, 'ineligible labourers' are those who are either unregistered (that is, labourers without a job cards) or those who had already received 100 days of employment. Those who do not have job cards and come to work on NREGA worksites are entitled to have job cards made for them. It is laxity on the part of the panchayat administration that it failed to facilitate the registration process. However, it is not evidence of corruption.[23]

Corruption in NREGA is a real problem, and other reports, of varying quality, have pointed to its existence. But it must also be appreciated that NREGA, when placed in the context of the past experience of public works in India, is a step forward. It would be unrealistic to expect corruption to disappear overnight, particularly from states where the structures for it have been deeply entrenched for some time. However, even when inadequately implemented, the NREGA transparency safeguards have had some effect.

Given the fact that it evokes diverse reactions, corruption is an issue that requires sensitive handling. By harping on average figures and sweeping statements, rather than steady reportage based on concrete situations, the media coverage has reinforced a prevailing

[22] This instance is also used in Tiwari and Pandey (2008b).

[23] Roy and Dey (2008) extend this point to a number of the other findings of the CAG. 'Many of the shortcomings brought out by the CAG report like low registration, insufficient employment provided, delayed payments to workers, low payments are not really because of corruption. They are because of apathy and the lack of a structure to implement the Act.'

article of faith that public works are irrevocably shackled by corrupt implementers. In effect, this ignores the task of unearthing corruption where it exists in favour of an easy and dubious *a priori* line of argumentation. The key tasks before us are to uncover corruption aggressively, analyse it constructively, and present it responsibly. The CAG report is only a partial success on the second of these and the media a complete failure on all three.

CAG'S PERFORMANCE AUDIT METHODOLOGY: A WORK IN PROGRESS

The 'performance audit' is a specialized and relatively new form of audit being taken up by the CAG.[24] It seeks to go beyond the more usual kinds of audits which simply check the account books or look at compliance with stipulations. The guidelines for performance audit suggest that the CAG is ideally expected to opine on three facets: the effectiveness of a programme/department in achieving its objectives (outcomes), the levels of economy achieved, and the efficiency displayed. Beyond these three basic elements, it also has a number of subsidiary aims: to understand the unintended consequences (both negative and positive) of the operation of the programme, assess the fitness of the built-in control and audit functions, and address issues relating to equity. This is a vast brief, and could, potentially, enable a wholesome and comprehensive examination of any programme. In practice, however, the methodology of the CAG seems to have been inadequately geared to opine authoritatively even on the first three let alone the subsidiary aims.

Economy and Efficiency

Judging economy and efficiency in public spending entails both minimizing the cost of inputs for a given quality of services

[24] CAG lays down an elaborate framework for the performance audit. See CAG (n.d.). Much of the information about auditing guidelines in this section is sourced from that document.

('spending less'), and maximizing the utilization of the resources at hand ('spending well').[25]

It is difficult to see how an assessment of avoidable expenditure (or, as has been pointed out earlier, levels of corruption) can be done in the absence of a full-fledged survey including interactions with workers. Other evidence within this category of investigation would include instances of duplication of labourers' names in muster rolls, fraudulent payments, diversion of NREGA money for non-NREGA purposes, and so on. However, here too, the lack of investigation of the situation on the ground has meant that these findings cannot definitively conclude how 'well' the money has been spent.

The CAG report would also have been more informed and reasonable had it compared the levels of economy and efficiency achieved in NREGA with comparable schemes, such as the National Food for Work Programme and the Employment Assurance Scheme. Absence of such a comparative framework may prevent the findings from being placed in proper perspective.

Effectiveness

Assessing the effectiveness of any programme would entail comparison of actual impact with the intended impact. The CAG itself terms it 'goal attainment analysis' and considers it a vital part of the performance audit process.[26] Judging effectiveness requires auditors to comment on outcomes. Given the complexity of NREGA, as well as its anticipated outcomes, it would have required creative thinking on the part of the CAG to come up with performance benchmarks against which to judge the early implementation of the programme. With reference to NREGA, effectiveness would include delivery of entitlements, socio-economic impact, and usefulness of assets created.

On this count, the report is an almost unmitigated failure. For the most part, it avoids the question altogether. Where it has stepped

[25] See CAG (n.d.).
[26] CAG (n.d.).

into an overall assessment, the CAG has chosen to use either national averages of employment generated, or existing poverty lines to pronounce on the impact of NREGA. The complexity of the employment figures and the inadequacies of the national average have been discussed already. Using the Below Poverty Line (BPL) status as a marker of access (coverage of the scheme among the rural population) is not a holistic indicator of distribution; it might at best serve as a rough guide to the same.[27]

NREGA outcomes ought to be assessed in terms of socio-economic impact in the lives of people. Only an intensive field-based interaction with the labourers will suffice as methodology for fulfilling this objective. A performance audit dedicated mainly to finding contradictions within the records must be an incomplete one *ab initio*.

Having not even assessed outcomes satisfactorily, the supplementary aim of identifying additional ones has not even been attempted. For instance, there is scattered evidence from many places that NREGA is empowering women, encouraging rural savings, helping with schooling, activating Panchayati Raj Institutions, and so on. It would have been invaluable if some of these had been investigated by the CAG.

Compliance Appraisal

We have mentioned earlier that compliance is one of the major concerns of the CAG report. While assessing the performance of implementing agencies, the CAG has chosen to check the compliance of administrative practice with the Operational Guidelines and the norms mentioned under the Act. In a technical sense, however, while the stipulations of the Act have to be followed by all states, they are not bound to comply with the Operational Guidelines.

It will be helpful to briefly recount the status and hierarchy of these documents. The Act lays down the broad operational design, financing arrangements, and rights framework for the workers. It stipulates,

[27] See Jha et al. (2008) for an approach to judge the determinants of participation in NREGA.

however, that the specifics of the operational practices and principles are to be left to the state governments. Thus, the Act enjoins responsibility on the state governments (under Section 4) to develop *sui generis* Employment Guarantee Schemes subject to the provisions of the Act. Rules (Central and State) are the next level of norms envisaged under the Act.[28] In addition to the schemes and rules, the Central Government is also empowered under Section 27 to pass directions. It is to be noted here that the Operational Guidelines issued by the MoRD do not belong to any level in the hierarchy of binding norms mentioned earlier. In essence, the Guidelines were originally formulated only to guide the design of state schemes.[29] Administrative practice is bound to comply with the Act, the state schemes, and the rules and directions formulated, but not the Guidelines.

In the aforementioned backdrop of the norm architecture of NREGA, it is clear that the Guidelines, by their very nature and origin, are formulated to have persuasive value: a model of what a good state scheme might be. Now, many state schemes fall short of the high threshold prescribed under the Guidelines, which gives rise to a state of confusion and conflict. But practices which are a result of such confusion cannot be treated as outright procedural irregularities or instances of non-compliance. The CAG has termed state-wide faulty practices (which may have their origin in the state schemes) as irregularities, which, technically speaking, they are not.[30] Once again, the information generated is useful (since we get some sense of where best practices are being followed). Terming it a compliance check, however, is misleading.

[28] The Central Government is empowered under Section 31 to make rules, whereas, state governments can make rules with respect to selected issues under Section 32. According to Section 37, Central Rules would override State Rules, in case any conflict arises between the two.

[29] Curiously, the introductory section (entitled 'Context') explaining the character of, and need for, Operational Guidelines, inserted in the 2006 edition, is missing in the 2008 edition.

[30] Following explanation is offered in the final report of the CAG on this aspect: '[I]t holds the view that though the guidelines and advisories were suggestive, these needed to be followed in spirit as these were intended to facilitate the effective and efficient implementation of NREGA and achievement of its intended objectives (CAG 2008b).

Ironically, exclusive reliance on compliance with the Guidelines has meant that the CAG has failed to audit the implementation of the programme against binding norms other than the provisions of the Act. In effect, while, on the one hand, the CAG has assessed the performance of implementing agencies against a non-binding standard (the Operational Guidelines), on the other hand, it has done an incomplete job in examining the compliance with binding norms (Central Government directions, circulars, and rules, as well as state government schemes, circulars, and rules).

Another oversight on the part of the CAG in terms of compliance appraisal was the failure to assess fitness of these additional binding norms against the express provisions of the Act. Some of these additional norms are in conflict with the provisions of the Act, and thus, an audit to assess these additional norms against the Act was the need of the hour.

Methodological Oversights and Their Fallout

Those aspects that the CAG has omitted to consider have proved to be just as significant as the ones it has examined. Omissions in the report have become an important issue, given the high expectations of a performance audit report and the weight it carries.[31] For instance, silence on effectiveness of the programme in the CAG report has been taken as evidence of absence of any impact of NREGA in rural areas. Yet, there is considerable independent evidence of NREGA making a significant difference to the lives of people.[32] The absence of this kind of analysis in the CAG report has done

[31] The status of the CAG as a constitutional body and, therefore, an 'official' and final arbiter on public spending has had its impact on the credence that has been lent to the performance audit. Immediately after the leak of the report, the MoRD swung into damage control mode. Just 10 days after the story broke it called a meeting of all states to seek responses on the findings of the report.

[32] See the many findings of reports such as Ambasta et al. (2008), Jha et al. (2008), Mahapatra et al. (2008), and Mathur (2008); also see various chapters of this book.

immense disservice to the cause of the people to whom NREGA has given a measure of control over their lives.

In other instances, the unduly narrow terms of investigation have precluded bringing out the 'teething problems' that are responsible for the shortcomings mentioned in the report. For instance, in some states, an ill-drafted scheme (failing to provide an effective framework to the implementing agencies in the field) is responsible for many of the violations of the Act or the Operational Guidelines, or the lack of a centralized monitoring system has allowed Central Government to sleep over most of the instances of mis-utilization, diversion, and under-utilization. The CAG has successfully pointed out the symptoms and violations that can be made out by comparison with the Guidelines, but analysis of the underlying systems (internal control structures, IT backbone, and so on) and review of procedural framework (adequacy and fitness of administrative norms and rules) has not been attended to.

Simply terming it a 'performance audit' ought not to serve as a gloss for what has been, in the case of NREGA at least, a far more limited exercise. It is high time that the CAG shifts to a more intensive and organized system of collecting evidence, leading to a report which is not merely a checklist of non-compliance but a substantial, transparent, and conclusive report.

RECOMMENDATIONS OF THE CAG REPORT

The CAG report points to a number of issues in the implementation of NREGA. Despite methodological problems, the section on recommendations is the most valuable part of the report. Some of them are novel. Others have been advocated for some time, but are likely to receive more attention now that they have been endorsed by the CAG. Given the way the debate has unfolded, there is a genuine danger of the recommendations getting lost in the din of exaggerated opinions. This is particularly tragic as many of them could have made a positive contribution in the run-up to NREGA's extension to the whole of rural India. More so as this seems to have been part of the original intention of the MoRD in inviting the CAG to conduct a performance audit.

Staffing

The CAG singled out lack of dedicated administrative and technical staff for NREGA as the key constraint responsible for procedural lapses. For instance, according to the Operational Guidelines, the Programme Officer at the block level is supposed to be a full-time, dedicated post of rank equivalent to the Block Development Officer (BDO). Similarly, the Guidelines recommend the appointment of a full-time *Gram Rozgar Sevak* (employment assistant) in each gram panchayat. The lack of these staff has come to be a standard excuse among officials for non-compliance with prescribed stipulations.

Transparency Measures

Quite correctly, the CAG has chosen to highlight shortcomings in the maintenance of job cards and muster rolls. Among other things, they have recommended that the state governments must ensure that job cards are not retained by gram panchayat or departmental officials under any circumstances.

Another major problem that the CAG identifies is that in many places the mandatory biannual social audits are not taking place. Here too, the CAG's findings lend important support to a demand that others have raised—that the social audit process must be taken far more seriously by the administration.

Works

The CAG has pointed out that a number of projects not on the list of permissible works (such as *shamshan ghat*s, *panchayat ghar*s, community entres, school buildings, and playgrounds) are being executed.

It has recommended that state governments should be empowered to expand the list of permissible works in the light of local conditions, after keeping the MoRD informed.

Employment and Wages

According to the Guidelines, district-wise Schedules of Rates (SORs) must be prepared, after undertaking careful 'time and motion studies', for the NREGA workforce. On NREGA works, as the CAG points out, anyone above the age of 18 years can come to work, including first-time workers, women, and elderly persons who may not be as productive as an able-bodied experienced worker. As such, it is important that new SORs be formulated for NREGA with carefully calibrated and realistically stipulated tasks so as to ensure a fair payment of wages. The CAG makes a pointed observation to the effect that the state governments should ensure payment of minimum wages, 'notwithstanding any other conditions', which is possible only if tasks have been carefully configured to take into account the specificities of NREGA works and the composition of the NREGA workforce.

Unemployment Allowance

The reluctance of state governments to disburse unemployment allowances has been noted by many. The CAG has indicted a number of state governments for effectively scuttling the unemployment allowance. Noting the aforementioned, the CAG has advised the Central Government to consider amending NREGA rules to allow the Centre to pay part of the unemployment allowance, while instituting controls to minimize chances of persons drawing unemployment allowance without demanding employment or working.[33]

[33] Under the stipulations of the Act, the state governments will be responsible for the payment of the unemployment allowance. The provision is intended as incentive to the states to provide employment since the Central Government provides the entire amount spent on labour.

A CONSTRUCTIVE RESPONSE

As we have reflected in this chapter, the CAG report is a mix of constructive elements interspersed with easily mis-representable facts. Nevertheless, it is an independent look into the NREGA and as such, an extremely important exercise. The report's major shortcoming has been that it fails to match up to the comprehensive terms of reference of a performance audit. Against its own stated brief, the report often breaks into a random assortment of facts, and the media has used this as an opportunity to amplify and extrapolate from the negative findings (CAG n.d.: 9). The silence of the CAG on the overall impact of the NREGA (apart from the two figures discussed earlier—on average employment and households completing 100 days) was an outcome of these failings. Had the CAG methodology incorporated more interaction with NREGA workers, its own purposes might have been better served.

Nevertheless, it is imperative that the government respond constructively to the report, instead of simply discarding it or dismissing it as false. One immediate step in this direction would be to comb through the report and take firm action in cases where labourers' entitlements have been denied. To illustrate, over 12 cases involving delayed payment of wages have been presented in the report. This is a growing problem in various parts of the country. For those who come to NREGA worksites, often, the poorest in areas where alternative employment is not easily available, the consequences of not receiving wages on time are often cycles of debt or migration. These are the very hardships that the Act is designed to prevent. Delays in wage payments should be addressed with utmost seriousness, through prompt and exemplary administrative action. This would also send the salutary signal that the fair and timely payment of NREGA wages is a government priority. Immediate action could have far-reaching demonstration effects, with relatively little effort. In the longer term, obviously, much more sustained effort will have to be put in to ensure continued compliance with norms.

On many of the longer-term questions we have presented some of the CAG's useful recommendations. A constructive response, however, would also look beyond the report and attempt to deal with a number of other administrative systems that need to be in place. There is urgent need to clarify issues like the Centre–state relationship within the Act. States have considerable autonomy under the Act, enabling them to formulate their own schemes and rules. The disadvantage of this is that there are no minimal best practices that every state is compelled to follow. As states move towards clarifying and finalizing their rules and schemes, it is important that some space for these minimal procedures be created.

At the same time, the diversity of administrative practices has also been an advantage. In many places, innovative solutions to specific problems are being implemented. A substantial pool of administrative experiences has been built up over two years, which can be drawn upon to anticipate challenges that lie ahead.[34]

In many ways, the CAG report has been superseded by more recent assessments (some included in this volume) of the failures and successes of the NREGA. Nonetheless, the report still carries considerable authority. Its inadequacies have been discussed here at length and should temper the force of its criticism of NREGA. More worryingly, however, little progress seems to have been made on most of its key recommendations. One would have hoped that, today, the 'teething troubles' identified by the CAG would be over. Tragically enough, three years down the line many of them threaten to become lasting problems.

[34] Helpfully, the revised and updated final report of the CAG does carry a list of such 'good practices' (CAG 2008).

6

Wage Payments

Can We Bank on the Banks?*

Anindita Adhikari and Kartika Bhatia#

INTRODUCTION AND BACKGROUND

The recent switch from cash payments to bank payments of wages under the National Rural Employment Guarantee Act (NREGA) has been acclaimed by the Government of India as the 'world's largest ever financial inclusion scheme'.[1] But has this switch really served as an effective check against the embezzlement of NREGA wages? Has the siphoning of funds by intermediaries ceased? Have workers really gained greater control over their wages? This essay probes these questions on the basis of findings from a survey conducted in December 2008.

* Originally published as 'NREGA Wage Payments: Can we Bank on the Banks?', *Economic and Political Weekly*, 45 (1): 30–7, 2 January 2010.

This essay has benefited from useful inputs from survey coordinators (Sunil, Kalyani, Shiva, and Umashankar) and the entire survey team. We value Jean Drèze's guidance and suggestions, which have given shape to this research. Special thanks are also due to Reetika Khera, Anish Vanaik, and Siddhartha for helpful comments. The fieldwork was conducted under the auspices of the Krishna Raj Summer Programme at the Centre for Development Economics (Delhi School of Economics), initiated in memory of Krishna Raj, former editor of *Economic and Political Weekly*.

[1] Raghuvansh Prasad Singh, Minister of Rural Development, October 2008 (see www.commodityonline.com/news/NREGA-to-help-in-largest-financial-inclusion-ever-11409-3-1.html).

Rationale for Wage Payments through Banks

Critics have often decried public works programmes on grounds that they are easy prey to corruption. The NREGA, before and after its inception, has also been a target of such criticisms in spite of various transparency safeguards being built into the Act.

Prior to the introduction of bank payments, NREGA wages were paid in cash, based on the entries made in the 'muster roll' (or attendance sheet) by the implementing agency—in most cases, the gram panchayat. The muster roll is a record of the number of days worked and wages due to each labourer. After the muster roll is submitted to the block office, funds are transferred to the gram panchayat account. The money is then withdrawn by the implementing agency to make cash payments to the labourers. Under this system of cash payments, the implementing and payment agencies are the same, that is, wages are paid by the same agency that maintains the record of attendance and dues. This makes embezzlement of funds easier, as the money from inflated or fake muster roll entries made by a corrupt official will come into his own hands. In order to monitor wage payments under this system, the NREGA includes a range of transparency measures to maximize vigilance of public funds by workers themselves. These include public disbursal of wages (which also creates an opportunity for the public scrutiny of muster rolls), maintenance of workers' job cards (enabling them to check their payment details at any time), and regular social audits.

Despite being mandated by the Act, these checks have often been flouted and irregularities in wage payments have been widespread. Investigating these irregularities has given rise to a widely-held view that the vulnerability of the programme to diversion of wage funds is born from a system where the implementing agency and payment agency are the same. Also, a system where cash passes through different hands before it reaches the workers made it easy for contractors and middlemen to collude with gram panchayat officials to divert wage funds.

Against this backdrop, the main reasons for introducing bank payments (or, in some areas, post office payments) of NREGA wages were presented as follows. First, by making an independent financial institution, which is not involved in the actual implementation of the NREGA, responsible for paying wages to workers, there is a distinct separation of the implementing and payment agencies. It is believed that this will de-incentivize the implementing agencies from fudging muster roll entries, as they no longer have access to funds at the time of the payment of wages. Second, by paying workers directly through their bank accounts, the possibility of middlemen laying their hands on the wages of workers will also be made more difficult. Third, workers will be initiated into the organized banking system which will then pave the way for developing a habit of saving in the future. Fourth, this new system was also expected to lead to more transparency in record-keeping, as banks generally maintain fairly good records.

Motivation for a Survey of Bank Payments

Despite these seemingly clear advantages of the system of bank payments, it is important to recognize that the banking system does not function in a vacuum and is vulnerable, in some respects, to the same pressures as the system that preceded it. Social hierarchies that bind workers in a feudal and exploitative relationship with gram panchayat officials and contractors are deep-rooted rural realities, which are bound to exert their influence on the system of bank payments as well. Findings from previous surveys and social audits in Orissa in 2007, as well as in Deogarh (Jharkhand) in October 2008, have shown that even wage payments through banks are not free of the maladies which afflicted the previous system of payments: corruption, fraud, and misconduct.[2]

The most disturbing findings have emerged from a recent social audit of five gram panchayats in Karon block of Jharkhand's Deogarh district, where the earlier nexus of corruption between contractors

[2] See Kar (2009), Drèze and Khera (2008a), and Vanaik and Siddhartha (2008).

and gram panchayat officials now includes banks as well.[3] In a case of blatant collusion, in Ranidih gram panchayat, it was found that contractors had been siphoning off funds from the accounts of NREGA workers in connivance with the officials of a local cooperative bank. The workers' accounts were brazenly manipulated by the contractors; in fact, many workers were completely unaware that an account had been opened in their name! Other irregularities included asking NREGA workers to sign withdrawal slips in bulk (for the purpose of 'proxy withdrawals' in their name), and extorting money from workers after they withdrew money from the bank. For instance, in Ganjebari gram panchayat of the same district, the local post master had taken signatures of NREGA workers on blank withdrawal slips, in collusion with a contractor, making it possible for them to extract money from post office accounts.

As this experience illustrates, the system of bank payments is not a fool-proof protection against corruption, and the ground realities can be quite different from what one might expect from the positive arguments presented earlier. However, bank payments certainly offer useful opportunities for tightening the noose. In order to explore these issues more deeply, to determine whether Deogarh was an isolated case or the manifestation of a more widespread problem, and more generally to evaluate this new system of NREGA wage payments, a survey focusing specifically on bank payments was undertaken.

Survey Method

Our survey covered two blocks each in Allahabad district (Uttar Pradesh) and Ranchi district (Jharkhand). In Allahabad, the sample blocks were Karchana and Shankargarh. Karchana is well connected to Allahabad city and, being close to the Ganga, is predominantly agricultural land. In comparison, Shankargarh is relatively remote and has a primarily rocky terrain, with silica mining and stone-breaking as

[3] Private contractors are banned under the NREGA but continue to survive in some areas.

the main activities. In Ranchi district, both sample blocks (Mander and Angara) are relatively accessible from the city of Ranchi. Mander lies in the plains, with most land under agriculture. Angara on the other hand has a hilly terrain, and some Maoist activity is palpable here.

As mentioned earlier, gram panchayats are the main implementing agency under the NREGA. In Allahabad district, the implementation of the NREGA is largely carried out by the *Sarpanch* and the Panchayat Secretary on behalf of the gram panchayat. In Jharkhand, however, there are no gram panchayats (elections had not yet taken place), and the NREGA is primarily implemented by the block administration with the Panchayat Secretary and the *abhikarta* (de facto entrepreneur).[4] The absence of gram panchayats and other grassroots institutions in Jharkhand has given space to private contractors and middlemen. The block administration and Panchayat Secretary, incapable of implementing and monitoring NREGA works on their own, often contract them out (in effect) to private parties. Since private contractors are banned under NREGA, these private players can only make a profit through swindling.

Two payment agencies (that is, specific banks, or post offices where applicable) were selected in each block (see Table 6.1). From these, five 'payment orders' (the most recent) for worksites in different gram panchayats were chosen for verification.[5] Thus, the survey covered five gram panchayats in each block.[6] Twenty workers were randomly selected from each payment order, and banks were asked to furnish their account details.

[4] The abhikarta (implementing agency) is supposed to be a committee, with president (*adhyaksh*) and secretary (*sachiv*), constituted by the gram sabha. In practice, it tends to be a *de facto* entrepreneur acting in the name of the committee—often, the owner of the land on which work is being done (most NREGA works in the sample blocks were executed on private land), or the puppet of a private contractor, or even just a contractor.

[5] A payment order is a letter of instruction from the implementing agency to the payment agency (that is, bank or post office), ordering the payment of wages into the accounts of NREGA workers. This is explained in greater detail later in the paper.

[6] In Shankargarh block, the survey team could only cover four gram panchayats.

Table 6.1 Sample Payment Agencies

District	Block	Sample payment agencies
Allahabad	Karchana	(1) Bank of Baroda Eastern Uttar Pradesh Grameen Bank (Panchdeora, Bhaderwa, and Bharaon branches)
Allahabad	Shankargarh	(1) Bank of Baroda (2) Bank of Baroda Eastern Uttar Pradesh Grameen Bank (Lohgarh and Bashara Uperhar branches)
Ranchi	Angara	(1) Jharkhand Grameen Bank (2) Post office (Jonha and Tati Silway branches)
Ranchi	Mander	(1) Ranchi-Khunti Central Cooperative Bank (2) United Bank of India

Source: NREGA Field Survey, December 2008.

Banks were also asked to share the details of the gram panchayat accounts for the sample gram panchayats. The verification process involved interviewing as many as possible of the 20 workers selected in each gram panchayat, followed by a public verification of all the entries in the payment order. Awareness generation around the system of bank payments was carried out simultaneously.

Socio-economic Background of Respondents

We interviewed a total of 259 workers, of which 201 (78 per cent) were men and 58 (22 per cent) were women. This male-dominated sample reflects the fact that the sample payment orders had a high proportion of males. That, in turn, is partly due to the relatively low participation of women in NREGA in the sample districts. Another reason, however, is that the NREGA workers listed on the payment orders are those who have a bank (or post office) account. We often found that women workers did not have an account in their name and received their wages through their husband's accounts. To that extent, there is an under-representation of women workers in our sample.

As one might expect, education levels among NREGA workers were relatively low. Almost half (45 per cent) of the sample workers were illiterate, with only 21 per cent having completed class 10. In Allahabad district, caste divisions were palpable, with spatial segregation also clearly visible. Members of the upper castes were economically better off, with the Sarpanch and Panchayat Secretary also belonging to this group. The blocks surveyed in Ranchi district had a predominantly tribal population.

BANKING SYSTEM IN THE SURVEY DISTRICTS

In both survey districts (Allahabad and Ranchi), accounts have been opened in a variety of banks, such as *grameen* banks, cooperative banks, nationalized banks, and in some cases even in post offices (see Table 6.1). Most (87 per cent) of our survey respondents were bank account holders, while 13 per cent (all in Angara block) had their accounts in a post office. In Allahabad there has been a recent trend towards shifting accounts of NREGA workers from post offices to banks due to a charge levied by post offices for transfer of NREGA funds.[7]

Opening of Accounts

In the survey districts, the accounts were being opened proactively by gram panchayats and bank officials, but in a haphazard way, resulting in many workers being left out. The common practice is for gram panchayat officials or contractors to take groups of NREGA workers to the bank to get their accounts opened. We found that 44 per cent of our sample workers were accompanied by a gram panchayat official at the time of opening an account, and 16 per cent had been accompanied by a contractor. Only 28 per cent of the sample workers had opened their accounts on their own. Thus, close to

[7] Personal communication, Chief Development Officer, Allahabad district.

90 per cent of sample workers were present at the bank at the time of opening of their accounts, and the rest were not. Many (40 per cent) of the workers had opened their accounts over six months prior to the survey, and had developed some familiarity with banking procedures. In the worst cases, they had no knowledge that there was an account in their name. For instance, in Mandro gram panchayat of Mander block, many people were unaware that their accounts had been opened. These irregularities reflect the absence of strict norms and guidelines for the account opening process, as well as a lackadaisical attitude on the part of gram panchayat and bank officials.

Type of Accounts

Ideally, there should be a separate account for each person listed on the job card, and in the case of joint accounts, all members—including women—should be included. In the absence of this, women workers may be deprived of the opportunity to collect and keep their own wages. In our survey, a large majority (89 per cent) of workers had individual bank or post office accounts, and the rest (11 per cent) had joint accounts, which included the names of female members of the household. However, this is not a confirmation that women were always properly included in the banking system (as individual or joint account holders), since anyone listed in a payment order is necessarily an account holder. As mentioned earlier, some women are paid through their husbands' accounts. An instance of the 'exclusion' of women workers was found in Bhaderwa gram panchayat, Karchana block, where some women workers complained of being shooed away from the bank when they went to open their accounts. As if this was not enough, they were asked to be satisfied that accounts were being opened in the name of their husbands.

In a clear breach of the Reserve Bank of India's directive that banks should open zero balance, 'no frills' accounts for NREGA workers, we found that about half of our sample workers had to pay for opening their accounts. In most cases, this amount was reflected in the passbooks as the opening balance. In Mander block, however, there were cases where money was taken from the workers in the name of opening of their accounts but was not credited in their accounts at all.[8] Interestingly, most of the sample workers could not tell whether the money given to the bank at the time of opening the account was deposited in their account, or just a bribe. It was only after looking at their passbooks or account statements that the survey teams were able to make the distinction.

Pattern of Withdrawal

One of the widely-cited benefits of the bank payments system is that wages directly reach the hands of NREGA workers. The pattern of withdrawal is a preliminary indicator of whether this benefit is truly being realized. In our survey, we found that at the time of withdrawal of wages, 41 per cent of workers went unaccompanied to the bank and withdrew the money themselves while 50 per cent went and withdrew the money with someone's help. The rest did not go—someone else went on their behalf. In extreme cases, they had no idea about the existence of a bank account in their name.

In Angara, and to a lesser extent Karchana, a relatively positive picture emerged whereby a majority of workers went to the bank (or post office) on their own. In Mander and Shankargarh, most workers went with someone else, and withdrew their wages with the help of that person (see Table 6.2). In Shankargarh, it was mostly the Sarpanch who accompanied the workers, whereas in Mander, the contractor or abhikarta usually went with the workers at the time of withdrawal. This is a matter of concern, considering the exploitative tendencies of these middlemen. This practice also undermines the separation of implementing agencies from payment agencies. There were also cases where workers went to the bank in groups, possibly because they are

[8] In Angara block, the post office was taking Rs 70 from workers, out of which Rs 50 was reflected as the opening balance in their passbooks and Rs 20 was taken as an 'insurance premium'.

unfamiliar with the banking procedures and find security in numbers. But the general pattern, when workers were accompanied, was one of continued dependence on middlemen to collect their wages.

Table 6.2 Medium of Withdrawal

Reference group	Proportion (%) of respondents who:*			
	Withdrew in person	Went in person but someone 'helped'	Someone else withdrew	Did not withdraw
Block				
Angara	69	19	0	12
Mander	28	57	5	9
Karchana	56	44	0	0
Shankargarh	22	74	0	5
Gender				
Women	30	56	2	13
Men	45	48	2	5
Education				
Illiterate	27	67	2	5
Literate	53	36	2	9
Age of account				
Less than 6 months	35	60	1	4
More than 6 months	50	36	3	11
All respondents	41	50	2	7

Source: NREGA Field Survey, December 2008.
Note: * Each row gives the percentage distribution of 'medium of withdrawal' within the relevant group (with row entries adding to 100).

Passbooks are essential for tracking payments and withdrawals made through the workers' accounts, and presenting them at the bank or post office at the time of transactions is usually mandatory. However, we found that the distribution of passbooks among account holders was incomplete.[9] Further, in many cases there was

[9] In Bhaderwa panchayat, Karchana block, Rs 20 was taken from workers for issuance of passbooks.

no regular updating of passbooks. A positive finding in this regard was that in Angara block, everyone got their passbooks updated at the time of withdrawal of wages. In the sample as a whole, among workers who went to withdraw money on their own, 77 per cent got their passbook updated. But when the labourers went to withdraw their wages accompanied by someone else, the passbooks were updated in only 44 per cent of the cases (see Table 6.3).

Table 6.3 Updating of Passbooks

	Proportion (%) of sample workers who had their passbook updated	
Block	Among those who withdrew wages on their own	Among those who withdrew with someone else's help
Angara	100	100
Mander	60	13
Karchana	58	44
Shankargarh	46	56
All blocks	77	44

Source: NREGA Field Survey, December 2008.

All our survey respondents had put a signature or a thumb impression on a withdrawal slip when they went to collect their wages. The fact that procedural safeguards such as updating of passbooks and signing of withdrawal slips were observed in a majority of cases was somewhat encouraging, at least in comparison with the Deogarh experience. There were also positive signs of growing understanding and practice of these safeguards in the sample blocks, especially, but not only, in Angara.

System of Transfer

The flow of NREGA funds in the two sample districts is similar. In Allahabad district, the sanctioned amount comes directly into the gram panchayat account from the district headquarters. In Ranchi, the funds travel from the district to the block and then to the gram panchayat accounts.[10] From these, the funds are then transferred to the workers' accounts (in both districts). This is done in one of three ways: payment order, account payee cheques, and bearer cheques.

Payment Order

This is the most common instrument of transfer. In this system, the Sarpanch (in Allahabad district) or Panchayat Secretary (in Ranchi district) sends a letter to the bank or post office manager giving details of workers' names, account numbers, and the amounts due to them. On receipt of this payment order, the bank transfers funds from the gram panchayat account to the accounts of the respective workers. This process takes only one or two days, provided that the workers' accounts are in the same bank as the gram panchayat account—a practice that should be encouraged. We found no evidence of major delays in the transfer of funds in our survey.

In Angara block, once the money comes into the account managed by the panchayat secretary, he transfers it into the account of the abhikarta, who then withdraws the same amount and deposits it in the bank or post office where the workers' accounts are held. This process can cause considerable delays in payment of wages, and is also a dilution of the principle of separating the payment agency from the implementing agency.

The format of the payment order leaves much to be desired. In both survey districts, the payment order did not contain the name of the worksite, and in Allahabad district, the days worked by the labourer were also missing. In some cases, the payment order was made for four to five worksites together, or clubbed for many weeks. In such cases it becomes very difficult to verify the wage payments.

Another oversight of this system is that there is no provision for an official intimation to the workers, informing them that wages

[10] Even though there are no gram panchayats in Jharkhand, there are gram panchayat accounts, managed by the Panchayat Secretary. Elsewhere, these accounts are jointly managed by the Panchayat Secretary and the Sarpanch.

have been credited to their accounts. It is left to them to learn about the payments from an informal intimation (for example, from the Sarpanch or Secretary), or just 'from the grapevine'.

Account Payee Cheques

Here, the Sarpanch or Secretary writes account payee cheques, drawn on the gram panchayat account and payable to the workers, and distributes the cheques to them. Each worker then goes to the bank and deposits the cheque in his or her account. One advantage of this process is that the worker gets intimation of the money being credited into his or her account. We only encountered one case of payment through account payee cheques, in Taktaiya panchayat of Karchana block, but the process was not functioning as per the norm. The account payee cheques were not distributed among workers but were given directly by the Sarpanch to the bank manager. Most workers had no idea that an account payee cheque was even drawn in their name. The Sarpanch informed them that the money had been deposited in their accounts and the workers withdrew after signing the withdrawal slip. In these circumstances, the system of account payee cheques boils down to a convoluted and unwieldy payment order.

Bearer's Cheques

In Amilo gram panchayat of Karchana block, payment of NREGA wages was made through bearer's cheques. Some workers were given the cheque in hand and went to the bank themselves to encash the money. Others received cash at home and were not aware that any bearer's cheque had been issued. There were still others in whose names bearer's cheques had been issued and encashed, but who had never worked under NREGA and were completely unaware of the transaction. Being easy prey to corruption, bearer's cheques should not be used to pay NREGA wages.

FATE OF TRANSPARENCY SAFEGUARDS

'*We cannot give you the account details without the presence of the account holder.*' This statement of the manager of the Jharkhand Grameen Bank in Angara block of Ranchi district illustrates how the switch to bank payments has, in some respects, undermined earlier transparency safeguards. This has happened in several ways.

Transparency of Records

In order to obtain the payment orders, gram panchayat account statements, and workers' accounts statements, the survey teams went through a process of 'record hunting' in the selected payment agencies on the first day of the survey. Teams in all four blocks reported resistance from banks and post offices when they were asked to share NREGA-related records. Although the NREGA Guidelines clearly state that all NREGA-related information is in the public domain, and call for proactive disclosure of this information at all levels, bank officials argue that they are governed by their own rules which compels them to treat the details of all account holders as private. It was only after much coaxing that the survey teams were able to get hold of some of the necessary documents. By this time it had become clear that the entry of banks into the system of wage payments had considerably complicated the social audit process. This raises some troubling questions. How can the tension between the bank rules and the transparency provisions under the NREGA be resolved? Will banks be willing to amend their norms in order to disclose the details of NREGA-related accounts for public scrutiny?

Accentuated Neglect of Muster Rolls

After securing these records, the scrutiny of these documents brought a new issue to light. The introduction of bank payments has rendered the already neglected provisions related to the muster rolls almost non-existent. The muster roll is critical to the social audit process because it contains the attendance details and corresponding wages due to each worker at a particular worksite. Muster rolls are supposed to be available at every worksite, and read out in public before signatures are taken against the relevant wage payments, so that workers have an opportunity to verify the muster roll entries. This public verification of the muster rolls curbs the possibility of entering fake names and inflated figures. However, with wages of workers being deposited directly in their accounts on the basis of a payment order, muster rolls are no longer signed at the time of payment, and their maintenance is even more casual than it used to be. Unannounced visits of the survey teams to 11 worksites revealed that muster rolls were never there. This amounts to the dismantling of one of the key transparency safeguards under NREGA. In fact, it appeared that in some areas, muster rolls were not maintained at all—payment orders were filled directly from informal attendance registers maintained by worksite supervisors. In Karchana block (Allahabad district), when the Sarpanch was asked for the muster roll, he explained that it had not been prepared because the Panchayat Secretary was on leave. However, the payment order was in the survey team's hands, and was supposed to be based on the muster roll.

Job Cards

There is also a growing complexity in the maintenance of records, which is making it difficult, for instance, to match work attendance details with wages paid and received. In addition to the muster rolls, job cards are meant to serve as a personal record for each worker in which her/his attendance and payment details are entered. The job card, if regularly and accurately filled, can be a powerful document in the hand of each worker, enabling her to monitor her wage payments herself. Before the introduction of bank payments, the practice of filling job cards at the time of payments was encouraged. Although, even prior to the introduction of bank payments, job cards were poorly maintained, this practice is in danger of being pushed further into oblivion because now wages are no longer distributed openly at a public place where job cards can be filled simultaneously. In fact, it is not clear how job cards are supposed to be filled under the new system.

PEOPLE'S PERCEPTIONS OF THE BANKING SYSTEM

Workers' Preferences

A large majority (77 per cent) of the sample workers preferred NREGA wages to be paid through banks or post offices rather than in cash. In Angara and Shankargarh blocks, 94 per cent of sample workers stated a preference for the bank system, whereas a more mixed view was found in Karchana (85 per cent) and Mander (49 per cent) blocks (see Table 6.4). We observed that workers who had older accounts were better accustomed to using the banking system and also recognized its benefits. However, the preference for bank payments was not restricted to them, and nor did it vary much depending, say, on the gender or level of education of the respondents—it was fairly high across the board.

In general, the banking process was viewed in a positive light. There was openness to learning the procedures of this new system even among those who were illiterate and for whom this could be another disempowering hurdle. When we asked a worker why the abhikarta accompanied him to the bank, he replied '*Abhi to seekh rahein hain, agli baar khud jayenge*' (for now I am learning, later I will go on my own). In Mander block, it was heartening to witness an old and illiterate woman finding her way through the bank and completing all the procedures on her own.

One issue that concerned the workers is the distance between banks and their place of residence. Among the sample workers, 59 per cent lived within 5 km of the bank or post office and 41 per cent had to travel over 5 km. In some villages of Mander and Shankargarh blocks, the nearest bank was more than 10–15 km away and the workers com-

Table 6.4 Workers' Preferences and Integrity of Records

	Proportion (%) of respondents who prefer bank/PO payments to cash payments	Proportion (%) of workers who confirmed that their bank/PO account records were correct*
By block		
Angara	94	87
Mander	49	78
Karchana	85	95
Shankargarh	94	86
By gender		
Women	77	89
Men	77	84
By education		
Illiterate	81	86
Literate	75	85
By distance from bank/PO		
Less than 5 km	85	84
More than 5 km	67	87
By age of account		
Less than 6 months	75	86
More than 6 months	80	85
All respondents	77	85

Source: NREGA Field Survey, December 2008.
Note: * Excluding 11 per cent of workers who were unable to verify their bank records. If those are included, the overall proportion of sample workers who confirmed that their account records were correct comes down from 85 per cent to 76 per cent.

plained of a day's earnings being lost in travelling to the bank each time they had to collect their wages. This is also one of the reasons why many workers prefer to go to the bank with the Sarpanch or contractor: they want to make sure that they are able to withdraw money the same day and hence avoid another long trip to the bank. Note that, in spite of the distance and associated problems, there was a greater preference for bank payments among those who lived further away from the nearest bank or post office (see Table 6.4).

In Allahabad district and Mander block of Ranchi district, the bank accounts were scarcely used for the purpose of savings—most workers withdrew their entire wages as soon as they learnt that their accounts had been credited. In Angara block, however, the concept of saving had taken root. Many people who preferred bank payments stated 'the possibility of saving' as one of their main reason. For instance, in some cases, workers who were paid Rs 1,080 withdrew the bulk but kept Rs 80 in the bank, creating a small saving for the future.

We also found that not all banks and post offices functioned in the same way. In Angara block, the only block where post office payments were sampled, it was found that the bank system was working better than post offices. The Jharkhand Grameen Bank had computerized records (much better maintained than the manual log journals in the post offices), adequate staff (as opposed to the single post master operating the branch post offices), and secure arrangements for keeping large sums of money (unlike the post master at the Jonha branch office, who was scared of keeping large sums of money). We also observed the better functioning of nationalized banks in both Allahabad and Ranchi districts compared with the cooperative bank in Deogarh, which was openly flouting rules and colluding with corrupt contractors. The nationalized banks seem to have stricter norms, better records, and more effective supervision. Overall we found that more than 89 per cent of the sample workers who went to withdraw their NREGA wages found the banking staff 'helpful', but 38 per cent of illiterate workers who went unaccompanied to the bank to withdraw wages complained of some harassment by bank officials. Nevertheless, we found no evidence of bank staff accepting bribes.

Verification of Bank Records

An important aim of the survey was to verify the bank records with NREGA workers. After the relevant payment order and account details were shown and explained to them, 76 per cent of the sample workers confirmed the accuracy of the bank records, while 13 per cent found discrepancies (the remainder, 11 per cent, were unable to verify their bank records); see Table 6.4. This stands in stark contrast with the findings of the earlier social audit in Deogarh, where workers' accounts had been grossly manipulated. The Deogarh experience showed that, in a feudal and exploitative social setting, middlemen are able to 'outsmart' the banking system, and incorporate it in the system of corruption. The larger survey in Allahabad and Ranchi districts presents a more positive and hopeful picture of the system of bank payments. Banking norms such as issuing and updating of passbooks, use of signed withdrawal slips, presence of the account holder at the time of withdrawal, and cooperative staff attitudes were better observed than in Deogarh. In this more favourable environment, the transition to bank payments seems to have many positive aspects. In particular, it does help to reduce the extent of corruption—without eliminating it completely, as discussed later.

In connection with these positive findings, our experience in Angara block deserves special mention. The high levels of awareness compared to the other blocks, better maintenance of bank records, familiarity with banking procedures, and an understanding of the benefits of saving through banks are significant achievements in Angara. The field investigators felt that the Maoist influence in some gram panchayats, the commitment of the Block Development Officer (a local Adivasi woman), the leadership role played by a school teacher in one of the sample gram panchayats, and repeated visits by different survey and social audit teams (partly due to Angara's accessibility from Ranchi) were among the possible reasons why NREGA, in general, and the bank payments system, in particular, are doing relatively well there. While the reasons for effective functioning of the bank payment system in Angara need to be investigated further, this is an experience we can draw some lessons from.

METHOD AND EXTENT OF CORRUPTION

In the earlier system of cash payments, it was relatively easy for the implementing agencies to embezzle wage funds, by entering inflated figures (bloated attendance or fake names) in the muster rolls and pocketing the difference. Under the new system of bank payments, fudging the muster rolls is not enough, since the inflated payments are directed to workers' accounts rather than to the pockets of the implementing agency. Thus, siphoning off the wage funds requires some means of retrieving the inflated payments from the workers. This can be done in at least three ways: deception, collusion, and plain exploitation. Our survey uncovered cases of each of these three methods of embezzlement.

Deception

In Chatra gram panchayat, Angara block, we found a case of rank deception, similar to Deogarh. Money was being embezzled by the abhikarta (Sandip Kachhyap), in collusion with the local post master, from the accounts of NREGA labourers without their knowledge, after inflating figures in the muster roll.

In Mander gram panchayat of Ranchi district, workers were made to sign on the withdrawal slip in the premises of the Ranchi-Khunti Central Cooperative Bank and were then sent home. The abhikarta then withdrew their wages and paid them in cash at their homes. Most of the sample workers there claimed that they did receive the wages recorded against their name on the payment order. However, the fact remains that the withdrawal of wages without the account holder's presence is a dangerous and unlawful process, and can easily lead to embezzlement of funds.

Collusion

In four gram panchayats out of nineteen, the survey teams found evidence of fraud associated with fake names in the payment order.

In Banjhila panchayat of Mander block, most of the workers listed on the payment order belonged to the abhikarta's family. Here there is ample scope for inflating the muster roll since wages will be deposited in the accounts of family members. We have encountered this pattern in previous surveys in Jharkhand as well, where members of the abhikarta's family, although listed on the muster roll, did not work for a single day and the actual work was done by workers from other panchayats for meagre amounts. In cases like these, where workers (fake or genuine) collude with the implementing agency, the system of bank payments is not much of a protection against fraud.

In Kakram gram panchayat of Allahabad district, names of many upper caste men were included in the payment order even though the villagers said that these men had never worked on NREGA worksites. In Akauria panchayat of the same district, almost half of the names on the payment order were fake. In Chatra panchayat in Angara block, up to 10 fake names were found on the payment order.

Exploitation

Even when genuine workers are listed on the muster rolls and are paid through banks, it does not guarantee that there will be no fraud. Almost every third worker in Allahabad district said that after withdrawing the wages (alone or accompanied by someone), he or she gave a share to the Sarpanch—possibly, but not necessarily, to return 'advance wages' paid earlier by the Sarpanch. The ground reality is that, before the work begins, some workers make a 'deal' with the Sarpanch (or contractor), whereby they get work in return for agreeing to work for less than the minimum wage. The Sarpanch or contractor shows full payment of minimum wages on the muster rolls, and retrieves the difference from the workers after the money is credited to their accounts.

In Saidabad block of Allahabad district, we observed during field testing that inflated entries were made in the muster rolls with the knowledge of the labourers. After withdrawing their wages from the bank, the labourers gave the excess amount to the Sarpanch. The workers complained that they had no choice but to comply, as work was scarce and they would not be employed the next time if they resisted. In Mander block of Ranchi district, half of the workers who were accompanied by the contractor at the time of withdrawal gave him part of their earnings outside the bank.

As these examples illustrate, the social context has an important bearing on the functioning of the system of bank payments. Once a labourer's wages are withdrawn from the bank account, it is her relationship with (say) the Sarpanch or contractor that determines her share. In the feudal set up of some of the areas we surveyed, the workers have no choice but to agree to the work and payment conditions set by the Sarpanch or contractor. These conditions are sometimes downright exploitative, as we saw in Ganjebari gram panchayat in Deogarh where NREGA work was being carried out at an 'agreed' rate of Rs 60 per day, whereas the minimum wage for Jharkhand is Rs 92 per day. The workers were resigned to get paid less than their due. As one of them replied when asked why he accepted unfair payment, '*Kaun sahi daam deta hai*?' (Who will ever pay the full wage?)

RECOMMENDATIONS

We began by presenting the rationale behind the introduction of bank payments, widely publicized by the Central Government. Earlier investigations in Deogarh district of Jharkhand (and, before that, in Orissa) raised serious concerns about the role and potential of the banking system in streamlining NREGA wage payments and reducing corruption. Our survey then sought to probe these issues further. As compared to Deogarh, our findings not only revealed a more encouraging picture of the bank payments system, but also its limitations in fighting corruption. Before concluding, we present some recommendations borne out of our survey experience.

First, to facilitate efficiency in wage payments and monitoring, preference should be given to centralized banks and financial institutions with computerized records. Further, a list of all the payment agencies involved in NREGA wage payments should be made available at the block office and to the Ministry of Rural Development.

Second, to ensure accountability within this new system, banks must be brought under the ambit of the Act's transparency provisions. The Reserve Bank of India should direct banks to follow certain minimum safeguards, such as:

- money should be withdrawn only in the presence of NREGA workers;
- passbooks should be issued to all account holders;
- passbooks should be updated when money is withdrawn;
- all NREGA-related documents (including details of bank accounts of NREGA workers) maintained by the banks should be open to public scrutiny; and
- bank statements of gram panchayat accounts should be proactively disclosed at the end of each financial year.

Third, to restore public scrutiny of wage payments, and reinstate the public reading of muster rolls and filling of job cards, two methods of wage disbursal can be adopted. One, account payee cheques can be handed directly to all workers in a public place. Two, direct payments to the workers' accounts (based on payment orders) can be combined with the public distribution of 'wage slips' to all workers, informing them that their account has been credited and giving them the requisite details.[11]

Fourth, social audits of NREGA works should now include verification of bank records, including payment orders. Also, a model payment order should be designed and adopted by all state governments, to promote transparency and facilitate verification.

[11] The second approach (wage slips) is incorporated in the latest version of the NREGA Guidelines (available at www.nrega.nic.in).

CONCLUDING REMARKS

The survey findings are, in some ways, encouraging. We found that the direct transfer of wages into workers' bank accounts is a substantial protection against embezzlement, provided that banking norms are adhered to and that workers are able to manage their own accounts. Respondents had a fairly positive attitude towards bank payments, and an interest in learning how to use the banking system. While the rushed transition to bank payments (in 2008) created much confusion and chaos, the prospects of effective use of banks as a payment agency for NREGA seem reasonably good.

However, the survey points to some serious issues related to the use of post offices as a payment agency, including poor record-keeping and their inability to cope with mass payments of NREGA wages (these issues require further probing, given that there were few post offices in our sample). In remote areas, large distances to the nearest bank or post office also cause much hardship to NREGA workers.

Further, it is important to realize that that this new system of wage payments is far from foolproof. As workers familiarize themselves with the banking process, cases of embezzlement through 'deception' and 'exploitation' will reduce (in fact, they have already declined substantially), but the possibility of embezzlement through 'collusion' remains. The risk of manipulation is particularly high in areas with a feudal and exploitative social structure, where NREGA workers are easily manipulated. This is, perhaps, the main message of the Deogarh scam, where the banking system was swiftly integrated into a powerful nexus of corrupt contractors, politicians, and bureaucrats. Even in Allahabad and Ranchi districts, a similar situation emerged in specific gram panchayats.

This continued vulnerability points to the need to revive, adapt, and strengthen the earlier transparency safeguards related to wage payments. Possible steps in this direction (aside from strict enforcement of the more traditional safeguards) include bringing the bank's NREGA-related documents in the public domain, proactive disclosure of the gram panchayat bank account details, and distribution of cheques or wage slips in a public place along with reading aloud of muster rolls and maintenance of job cards.

Ultimately, the best protection against embezzlement is the empowerment of NREGA workers. As they learn to defend their rights under NREGA, manage their own bank accounts, and even build collective organizations, the crooks are likely to find it much harder to manipulate the system.

7

Employment Guarantee and Child Care*

Sudha Narayanan#

Recent social audits of the National Rural Employment Guarantee Act (NREGA) indicate that the programme can have a positive impact on the social and economic well-being of rural labourers and their families. In particular, it holds the powerful prospect of bringing major changes in the lives of women (see Chapter 4). This is especially true in a state like Tamil Nadu, where women constitute an overwhelming proportion (more than 80 per cent) of NREGA workers.

At the same time, however, some significant challenges frustrate this transformative promise of the NREGA. One of them is the issue of child care, which is easily overlooked. To examine this aspect, a survey of crèche facilities and child care practices of working women was conducted in Viluppuram district (Tamil Nadu) in July 2007, on the sidelines of a social audit of the NREGA.[1] The findings indicate that child care is a significant problem for many of them. This is particularly true for mothers of children below the age

* Originally published as 'Employment Guarantee, Women's Work and Child Care', *Economic and Political Weekly*, 43 (9): 10–13, 1 March 2009.

Thanks are due to the post-graduate students and faculty of the Department of Economics, Stella Maris College (Aut.), Chennai, for helping to conduct the survey which is the basis for this essay. I also thank—without implicating—Kiran Bhatty, Jean Drèze, Reetika Khera, and Vivek Srinivasan for their valuable comments and suggestions.

[1] Details of the social audit itself are available in NREGA Watch Tamil Nadu (2007).

of three years. This essay elaborates on the difficult predicament of young mothers in Viluppuram district who work under the NREGA, even as it plays a positive role in their lives.

WOMEN'S PARTICIPATION IN NREGA

The survey, conducted during 29–31 July 2007, covered 11 villages[2] and 15 NREGA worksites located in two blocks of Viluppuram district (Tirukoviloor and Tiruvennainallur). Of these works, two had been completed at the time of the survey, while the others were ongoing.[3] A total of 104 women workers with at least one child below the age of six years were interviewed. The questions relating to child care focused on the *youngest* child of the respondent.

The average age of the women was 27 years, ranging from just 19 years to 40 years (Table 7.1). The mother of the youngest child in the sample was already at the worksite despite having given birth just 17 days prior to the survey. At the NREGA sites, all these women were involved in *mannuvelai* or earthwork—mainly carrying mud from the site to its peripheries using minor implements.

Table 7.1 Socio-economic Background of Women NREGA Workers

Average age	27 years
Average household size	4.5
Proportion (%) who are illiterate	49
Proportion (%) who have completed middle school	5
Proportion (%) who belong to landless households	60
Proportion (%) who belong to SC, BC, or MBC communities	87
Proportion (%) who belong to agricultural labour households	39

Source: Survey of 104 women with at least one child below the age of 6 years, who are working at NREGA worksites in Viluppuram district; the survey was conducted during 29–31 July 2007.

[2] The villages surveyed included Eravalam, Konakkalavadi, Katchikuppam, Kolaparai, Nedumudaiyan, Panapadi, Poyyarasur, Sholavandipuram, T. Edapalayan, Thathanur, and Vengur.

[3] Wherever possible, the respondents were selected from the muster rolls and the interviews were conducted at the worksite.

Most of the women interviewed belonged to the Scheduled Castes, 'Backward Classes', or 'Most Backward Classes'.[4] In a state where the literacy rate for women is 65 per cent (in 2001), close to half the respondents (49 per cent) were illiterate. A mere 6 of the 104 respondents had studied beyond primary school, although one was a graduate (Table 7.1). Only around a third of the respondents reported that their household owned any land, and the average land ownership (among those who did own land) was only around one acre. The main occupation of a majority of these women was working on others' fields as agricultural labourers. Even among those who owned land, many nevertheless eked out a living working on others' lands. The respondents were clearly from marginalized and disadvantaged communities.

It is not surprising, therefore, that for some of these women, the NREGA was indispensable—a lifeline, they said. Some of them even said that they would 'starve' without the NREGA. As many as 41 per cent declared that the NREGA had been the only source of income for the household in the past few months (Table 7.2). At that time of the year (in late July), no agricultural work was available in the area. Some respondents claimed that their land was 'uncultivable' anyway, so they had to abandon cultivation leaving the land fallow; in the absence of alternate livelihoods, the NREGA was the only option.

Table 7.2 NREGA as an Employment Opportunity for Women

Proportion (%) of respondents who:	
Said their household had no other source of income in the past few months	41
Stated that it was their own decision to work on NREGA	95
Prefer wages in cash (rather than in kind, or as combination of cash and kind)	84
Keep all or part of the wages they earn on NREGA	70
Felt that NREGA is 'very important' for the economic well-being of their household	73

Source: Survey of 104 women with at least one child below the age of 6 years, who are working at NREGA worksites in Viluppuram district; the survey was conducted during 29–31 July 2007.

[4] In Tamil Nadu, Backward Classes (BCs) and Most Backward Classes (MBCs) are together equivalent to the Other Backward Classes (OBCs), used commonly elsewhere in India (see www.tn.gov.in/department.\bcmbc.htm).

In general, even women who were not so utterly dependent on the NREGA perceived it as giving them a sense of independence and security. It also offered the possibility of staying on in their village.

The wages they earned as NREGA workers enabled them to accomplish a number of things—ranging from paying their debts or retrieving pawned gold to spending on children's health and education or saving in chit funds, apart from meeting day to day household expenses. One woman used her wages to work her fallow land, and another bought insurance for her children! The fact that most of the women interviewed either kept the wages they earned (51 per cent) or shared them with their husbands (19 per cent) indicates, possibly, one kind of independence (Table 7.2). An overwhelming proportion of the respondents preferred to receive cash for their work (rather than grain, or a combination of cash and grain). Some commented that they knew 'better than the government how to spend the money' (Table 7.2). Others pointed out that since subsidized grain was available from the Public Distribution System, they were happy with cash wages.

The NREGA offered security too, as agricultural work was only intermittently available. Now, said a woman, 'we no longer have to go place to place looking for work. It is available right here at our village'. They explained that without the NREGA, they would migrate to Bangalore or Chennai, even Andhra Pradesh and Kerala, to work on construction sites under difficult conditions.

One woman's husband was a 'drunkard' and she felt the NREGA was something she could fall back on. The NREGA offered, in their words, a 'more comfortable life' and 'a little happiness'. One of them said simply that she was 'happy to work with others'.

As the survey found out, however, the NREGA can be transformative in less obvious ways. For instance, in Vengur village, earlier (before the NREGA works commenced) there was a severe problem with water scarcity. Now, we were told, the problem had been largely resolved, as water was available from a pond constructed under NREGA when it was not in the pipe. This had made things easier and life was 'more comfortable'. Another woman pointed out that NREGA had enabled her to purchase insurance for her children, as she is now recognized, for the first time, as 'working'.

The NREGA can sometimes empower whole communities as well. In Thathanur village, residents were all dependent on one single family that owned all the land surrounding their hamlet. Over the years, a woman explained, these zamindars had expanded their sugarcane fields and steadily encroached on their hamlet. Yet, they could not protest, since they were at the zamindars' mercy. Now with the NREGA providing an alternative, they did not feel this dependence anymore.

THE NREGA AND CHILD CARE

Despite the obviously beneficial role of the NREGA, these young mothers face some difficulties on a daily basis. Chief among them, it seems, is the issue of child care.[5]

The NREGA clearly states that in the event where there are at least five children under the age of six years at the worksite, one of the female workers should be deputed to look after them and she should be paid the same wage as other NREGA workers.[6] Yet, around 70 per cent of the women interviewed said that there were no child care facilities at the worksite. Of the remaining 30 per cent, many were unsure if the 'shed' at the worksite was really meant to be a crèche. Only a few worksites seemed to have some arrangement for child care, with one or two elderly women taking care of the children brought to the worksite. Disturbingly, close to 65 per cent of the respondents were unaware of this basic entitlement.

[5] Another major problem relates to morbidity levels. Three-fourths of the women reported having some health problem, such as body ache, dizziness, fatigue, or ulcers.

[6] 'In case the number of children below the age of six years accompanying the women at any site are five or more, provisions shall be made to depute one of such women to look after such children' (NREGA 2005, Schedule II, Section 28).

WHEREABOUTS OF THE CHILDREN

Where then were the children while their mothers worked on the NREGA? Of the 104 women, almost 50 per cent left their children at home, while 19 per cent brought their children to the worksite. About 12 per cent of the respondents reported leaving their children at the *balwadi* or *anganwadi* and around 11 per cent at schools (Table 7.3).

Table 7.3 Whereabouts of NREGA Children (Age 0–6 years)

Age group	Number of children in the sample	Where was the child while the mother was working on NREGA? (Percentage distribution)					
		Home	Worksite	Anganwadi or balwadi	School	Worksite crèche	Total
Below 1 year	21	76	14	5	0	5	100
1–3 years	44	52	25	5	5	13	100
3–5 years	25	44	16	32	0	8	100
5–6 years	14	7	14	14	65	0	100
Total	104	49	19	12	11	9	100

Source: Survey of 104 women with at least one child below the age of 6 years, who are working at NREGA worksites in Viluppuram district; the survey was conducted during 29–31 July 2007.

Most of the children who accompanied their mothers to the worksite were either left in the shade nearby or kept near the spot where the mother was working. One mother worried that the child 'kept following her around the worksite'. While keeping a child at the worksite is difficult enough on 'normal' days, it becomes even more problematic in harsh weather or when the child is sick, if there is no child care facility. At the worksite, children who were not breastfed ate what their mothers brought for themselves. For most, this is simply rice, sometimes cooked the previous day. For others, it is rice with vegetables or *sambar*, and still others it is *koozhu* (a kind of porridge).[7]

[7] In a village in Tirukoviloor, women claimed that they had not eaten vegetables for months, save for potato that was purchased occasionally from Tirukoviloor town 45 minutes away.

In general, it seemed that women were being dissuaded from bringing their children to the NREGA worksite. Some were apparently turned away from the worksite if their child accompanied them. Others were told: 'If you want to feed your child, don't come here, go home.' A few women reported that whenever they brought their children to the worksite, their wages were cut. Those who brought their children regardless were often 'harassed' by the supervisor or by their co-workers. For instance, one was told 'If you keep breast-feeding your child, who will do your work?' In fact, of those who reported some form of harassment at the workplace from supervisors and colleagues, close to half stated that such harassment was related to child care.

Consequently, even women who preferred to have their children in their own care often had no choice but to leave them at home. In most cases, these children were looked after either by their siblings or by older relatives. Other children were left to their own devices—sometimes roaming around the streets, with their mothers relying on the neighbours' goodwill to keep an eye on them. One child was tied to a table at home, with food left on a plate beside it. There were even cases where babies as young as 5 to 10 months old were left at home, unattended. As one might expect, mothers were anxious about the welfare of their children. One NREGA mother worried all the time about her child—constantly carrying the image of the open water tank near the house where her toddler would be playing.

Women with older children (within the reference age group of 0–6 years) did not seem to face such difficulties. A large proportion of mothers of children over the age of 3 years reported sending their children either to the anganwadi or to schools. For instance, one-third of the children in the age group 3–5 years were sent to the anganwadi (Table 7.3). Among those aged 6 years, four-fifths went to either the school or the anganwadi.

It has been argued that child care facilities at NREGA worksites are not required in Tamil Nadu, as there are anganwadis and balwadis in every village.[8] It is certainly true that Tamil Nadu has an impressive network of balwadis and anganwadis. In this respect, Tamil Nadu is far ahead of most other Indian states.[9] Where these facilities work well, the mothers seemed quite content to leave their older children there. Some of them, in fact, felt that the worksite was 'no place for children'. In the better cases, the anganwadi was open regularly, the helper fetched and dropped the children, and nutritious food (including eggs) was being provided.

However, as the survey reveals, this does not obviate the need for crèches at the NREGA worksites. In some villages, the anganwadis were in poor shape. One mother complained that the anganwadi provided only food and little else. Some complained that the anganwadi did not provide children 'proper food'. In a couple of villages, the survey team was informed that the 'teacher' rarely attends the anganwadi. Under these circumstances, the mothers preferred to leave their children under the care of relatives and neighbours.

Further, many families are still deprived of convenient access to an anganwadi. The opening hours of anganwadis are different from those of NREGA worksites, and often shorter. In Tirukoviloor block, for instance, women in many villages complained that the anganwadi was open only from 8 AM to 12 PM. Once food was distributed, it was 'locked up' and children were sent away. What would their children do until the women returned? One mother felt that the anganwadi was too far—in another hamlet, a mile away. She told us, 'walking to it is dangerous, so my children have never been there'.

[8] A public statement to this effect was made by M.K. Stalin (Local Administration Minister, Government of Tamil Nadu) at the time of the social audit of NREGA in Viluppuram: 'Admitting there was room for improvement, he said some of the negative findings could not be acted upon... since Tamil Nadu had multiple anganwadis or balwadis in each village, the suggestion that a crèche was needed would not be acted upon' (quoted in Radhakrishnan 2007).

[9] See Citizens Initiative for the Rights of Children under Six (2006) and Swaminathan (1991).

Even when the anganwadi or school seems to work for older children, it is not a satisfying option for the younger ones. Indeed, it is often better for small children to stay close to their mothers unless the anganwadis are of exceptional quality, which is rarely the case. Only 5 per cent of the infants were left at the balwadi or anganwadi. Three-fourths of the mothers of infants left their babies at home, while only around a fifth brought them to the worksite. One mother sent the older siblings to the anganwadi, but preferred to leave her 6-month-old at home with an aged relative. Another reported that she would be very happy to bring her infant to the worksite crèche should one be available. She explained that she used to breastfeed her child 10–12 times a day, but because she had been forbidden to bring her infant to the worksite she was now able to feed the child only 5–6 times.

THE NEED FOR CRÈCHES

Under these difficult circumstances, an overwhelming proportion (almost 85 per cent) of the mothers who left their children at home said that if a crèche was provided at the worksite, they would certainly bring their children, particularly the young ones. Most felt that a crèche at the worksite would enable them to keep an eye on the children without being distracted from work. Clearly, the survey provides ample evidence of the urgent need for crèche facilities at the worksite.

Further, some women mentioned that because of the problem of child care, they were often unable to join the NREGA worksites at all, critical as this was for the economic well-being of the family, especially for those who are landless and illiterate. Lack of child care facilities prevented many of these women from claiming their entitlement under the Act. As one mother put it: 'If there were someone to take care of my child, why would I not go to work? Is it (the NREGA) not important for my very survival?'

Simple child care facilities at NREGA worksites could go a long way in addressing these concerns. In any case, these facilities are mandatory under the law. What is lacking in the law, as well as in the Operational Guidelines of NREGA (Government of India 2006), is a blueprint for effective child care facilities at the worksite. The Act states that a woman worker should be deputed to look after young children, in the event where at least five children below the age of six years are present at the worksite. This is a step forward, but Guidelines are also needed to ensure that shade, food, and other basic amenities are available for these young children at the worksite. Cost norms are also required, along with specific instructions as to how the costs are to be incorporated in the financial estimates (for example, under the 'materials' component of the programme).

Another important issue needs to be addressed in this context. As things stand, women workers are not entitled to child care facilities at the worksite unless five children at least are present. However, as this survey makes clear, many women are unlikely to bring their children to the worksite unless child care is available there in the first place. Thus, the real extent of the demand for child care facilities at the worksite is 'hidden' because women leave their children at home, even though they would bring them to the worksite if child care facilities were available. One way of addressing this problem would be to prescribe that a crèche has to be provided if at least five children are present at the worksite *or* if at least five workers (male or female) demand child care facilities.

To conclude, the provision of effective child care facilities at NREGA worksites is an important issue that calls for creative thinking and action. Tamil Nadu is well placed to take the lead in this field, given its earlier achievements in the domain of child care. This would not only be a step forward for Tamil Nadu but also an example for the country as a whole.

8

The Group Measurement Experiment in Jalore*

Reetika Khera#

INTRODUCTION

Rajasthan is seen as the forerunner with respect to the implementation of the National Rural Employment Guarantee Act (NREGA), both in terms of scale of works and transparency safeguards. This combination has meant that large numbers of people have benefited from the NREGA in the state. The scale of NREGA works in Rajasthan is impressive: according to official statistics, in 2006–7 and 2007–8, Rajasthan generated 77 days and 68 days, respectively, of employment per rural household (in the districts where NREGA was in force), the highest in the country (see Chapter 2).

More recently, there have been positive reports of Rajasthan's efforts to improve worksite management.[1] Proper worksite management is essential for at least three purposes: ensuring good working conditions

* Originally published as 'Group Measurement of NREGA Work: The Jalore Experiment', Working Paper No. 180, Centre for Development Economics, July 2009.

The fieldwork for this essay was done in collaboration with Shiva Dhakal and Vivek S. Thanks are also due to Nikhil Dey for advice and suggestions, and to Rohit Kumar (District Collector, Jalore) for helpful information about the Jalore experiment. Thanks to Jean Drèze for helping me think through the issues raised here.

[1] See Iyer (2007) and Kumar (2007); also Ridge (2008).

and the provision of essential worksite facilities;[2] implementing the transparency safeguards; and providing technical supervision to ensure satisfactory labour productivity and asset creation.

Related to effective worksite management, an important issue that has not been resolved yet is that often NREGA labourers in Rajasthan are not paid the statutory minimum wage. Low wages are commonly attributed to low productivity on worksites. This means that labourers do not (or are unable to) perform the 'task' required to earn the minimum wage. There could be several reasons for this: excessive productivity norms, confusion or lack of awareness regarding the task that must be performed to earn the minimum wage, poor worksite supervision arrangements, and poor work incentives related to the system of wage calculation.[3]

This brief note takes a closer look at an experiment of training mates (worksite supervisors) in Rajasthan to improve worksite management.[4] It is based on a four-day field visit (11–14 February 2008) to Jalore district where this experiment is said to have been a success. A team of three researchers visited nine ongoing worksites from two blocks of Jalore (Raniwara and Jalore) and two completed worksites.[5]

The gram panchayats visited include Bakra Road (one worksite), Leta (two worksites), Oon (one worksite), and Sankarna (three worksites) in Jalore block. For this block we got a list of gram panchayats

[2] The following worksite facilities are mandatory under the Act: shade for periods of rest; drinking water; first aid. If more than five children under the age of six years are present at the worksite, one female worker should be deputed to look after them and paid the minimum wage.

[3] Discussions with labourers suggest that poor, faulty, or non-existent measurement by Junior Engineers could also have a bearing on the low wage rates. There were frequent complaints regarding the wage not being commensurate to the output and of the 'lead and lift' not being taken into account. While it is true that Junior Engineers are overworked, there is no reason why poor labourers should pay the price for this.

[4] See Iyer (2007) and Kumar (2007) for more details on this experiment.

[5] Preliminary observations from a more detailed survey conducted in Dungarpur and Sirohi districts in May–June 2008 are also reported in the concluding section.

with ongoing works. From this list, we selected Bakra Road and Sankarna because they were served by buses and Leta and Oon because these were accessible by bicycle. The closest gram panchayat was Leta (6 km from Jalore district headquarters) and the furthest was Bakra Road (about 25 km away). We also visited two gram panchayats in Raniwara block on the recommendation of the District Collector and Block Development Officer.

THE WAGE PAYMENT SYSTEM

The NREGA permits wage payments on daily rate as well as on piece rate. Rajasthan has followed the piece rate system, whereby wages are paid according to the work performed, and a prescribed 'task' must be completed in order to earn the minimum wage. For instance, for digging, the prescribed task consists of a given number of cubic feet, which varies by soil type and also takes into account lead (the distance the earth is carried) and lift (the gradient). The details of these productivity norms are listed in the 'Schedule of Rates'. Under the Act, the Schedule of Rates has to be such that 'a person working for seven hours would normally earn a wage equal to the [minimum] wage rate'.[6]

Further, following the earlier tradition of public works in Rajasthan, wage payments on NREGA works are based on 'collective measurement'. The total output (for example, cubic feet of earth dug) of all the workers employed at a particular worksite is measured once, collectively, at the end of a fortnight. The total output is divided by the total task (required to earn the minimum wage). Thus, if total task equals total output, then all labourers earn the minimum wage. If the total output is less than the total task, labourers earn proportionately lower wages.[7]

[6] A circular issued by the Ministry of Rural Development on 14 January 2008 extended the length of the working day from seven hours to nine hours; a follow-up circular, dated 28 May 2008, clarified that this would include a one-hour break (for further details see www.nrega.nic.in).

[7] Under this system, the minimum wage is, effectively, the maximum that a labourer can earn.

Under the collective measurement system, all labourers earn the same wage, based on their joint effort. In this system, in order to earn the minimum wage, labourers would have to cooperate with each other and work towards producing an output that equals the prescribed total task. If some labourers do not cooperate, it is likely to affect the work incentive for the others also, driving the wage rate down for all workers.[8]

The poor work incentives associated with the collective measurement system appear to be the main reason why Rajasthan has witnessed some of the lowest NREGA wages. The average wage earned in Rajasthan in 2006–7 was Rs 51 per day, much lower than the statutory minimum of Rs 73 per day, and less than the average wage in any other state (see Chapter 2).[9] In February 2008, we came across similarly low wages (starting from Rs 30 per day) in Jhalawar, Jalore, and Barmer districts.

To address this problem, the Government of Rajasthan recently began an experiment of group measurement (as opposed to collective measurement), in collaboration with Rozgar Evam Suchna ka Adhikar Abhiyan.[10] Briefly, this experiment entailed the formation of groups of five workers at a worksite (typically more than 40 labourers work at any given worksite). This experiment required that there be trained 'mates' (worksite supervisors), who would not only mark attendance but also assign each group its 'task' and measure the 'output' of the group. Both assigning and measuring are to be done on a daily basis. Workers are then paid based on the output of the group, rather than of the worksite as a whole. This was expected to lead to higher work incentives, labour productivity, and wages. Aside from this, the posting of trained mates at NREGA worksites was expected to further the general objectives of improved worksite management, mentioned earlier.

[8] This phenomenon has been referred to as an 'inefficient work culture' by some (see, for instance, Kumar 2007).

[9] See also Drèze and Lal (2007). From 1 April 2008, the minimum wage in Rajasthan was increased to Rs 100 per day (from Rs 73).

[10] This experiment was later extended to Rajasthan as a whole (also discussed later).

GROUP MEASUREMENT IN PRACTICE

Mate Training

Of the nine worksites that we investigated, two did not have any mates. We met trained (including semi-trained) mates at seven out of nine worksites.[11] Four sites had *mahila* (female) mates; three mates were men. The mates we met said that the training covered the following matters:

1. Maintenance of muster rolls
2. Basics of work measurement
3. Maintenance of the measurement sheet or '*mate maap pustika*' (MMP)
4. Provision of worksite facilities (for example, medicine kits)

Apart from this, it is not clear how much they were told about the Act. One mate we met did not know the minimum wage whereas another did not know about the work application procedures or the unemployment allowance.[12]

In Jalore, mahila mates have been trained in large numbers. The experiment of training of mahila mates was quite impressive. When I met one woman from Raniwara gram panchayat, and asked her why she was not working on the NREGA sites even though she had not exhausted her 100 day entitlement, she said, '*ab to mate ka hi kaam karna hai*' (now I only want to work as a mate). Allowing women who have studied up to class 5 or 8 to train as mates has enabled the creation of a large pool of mahila mates—as many as five or six in each revenue village, according to the District Collector.

The mates had formed groups at many worksites and most knew about the task required to earn the minimum wage. Generally, they also

[11] The reason why there were untrained mates at the other worksites is that in those villages, the trained mates had exhausted their quota of 100 days of work.

[12] See Kumar (2007: 3–6) for a detailed discussion of what the training is supposed to cover. It is possible that the mates we met retained only part of what was discussed at the training.

had the mate's kit consisting of the MMP, a calculator, and a measuring tape. At some worksites, we even came across some child care facilities and provision of a tent to provide shade for period of rest.

Group Formation

In order for group measurement to happen, the formation of groups (at the beginning of the fortnight, when new muster rolls are issued) is essential. At some worksites, however, groups had not been formed. Where groups had been formed, the names of labourers had been recorded group-wise on the MMP. The groups were self-selected, that is, labourers had decided on their own who would be part of their group (this is how it is meant to happen).

Group Measurement

Group measurement was not happening at any of the worksites that we visited. The practice seems to be that the mate marks out the task at the beginning of the day. Whether they measure accurately, or at all, at the end of the day was not clear.[13] The common practice seemed to be to credit each group with the full task in the MMP. In the absence of group measurement, different groups were *not* getting different wages.

We were told that there were a few instances of group-wise measurement in the past but that these had stopped. In one gram panchayat in Raniwara, measurements were made separately for each mate's groups (that is, separate measurement for each of the mates so that all the groups supervised by him/her got the same rate). This—different rates for workers supervised by different mates (rather than for different groups) on the same worksite—led to a fight. The labourers said '*aap log hamare mein phoot daal rahe hain*' (you are creating divisions amongst us labourers). This was resolved by agreeing that all workers would get the same rate.

[13] At one of the worksites, where we were present at 5 PM, no measurement was done and the labourers left with us. This is also the only worksite where every single labourer was sitting idle when we arrived.

REASONS FOR IMPROVED PRODUCTIVITY WITH GROUP MEASUREMENT

Group formation (GF) and group measurement (GM) can increase labour productivity for three distinct reasons:

1. Improved work incentives
2. Better monitoring
3. Greater clarity regarding the task

Improved Work Incentives

Under the collective measurement (CM) system, the wage earned by each labourer is not directly related to his or her effort. It depends on the effort of all those who are working at the same worksite. Under GM, labourers earn according to their group's output, linking productivity more directly with the rewards. To that extent, GM leads to better work incentives. However, for productivity to improve in this manner, both GF and GM are required. GF alone will not enhance work incentives.

In Jalore, the District Collector, block officials, and the Junior Engineer claimed that both GF and GM were in place. As mentioned before, this was not borne out at the worksites that we visited—only GF was being practised.

Officials also claim that now everyone does the full task. Many labourers, mates, and most officials claimed that the task done had increased as a result of the formation of work groups. To substantiate this claim, they point to the rising wage rate: the wage rate in Jalore district has shown a steady upward trend since the introduction of GF and GM: starting at Rs 45–48 per day in May 2007, it was nearly touching Rs 70 in November–December 2007.[14]

This rise in wages could be due to an actual increase in output, or, simply, to the fact that *recorded* output has increased (without an increase in productivity). As discussed later, it is quite possible that productivity did increase, in spite of the absence of actual group

[14] See Kumar (2007: 7).

measurement. But mates generally have no incentive to actually measure the output every day or to record the actual output as measured by them (if they do measure).

I also noticed a tendency to 'over-measure', in the sense that the mate, irrespective of the output, records in the MMP that each group has completed the prescribed task. It seems that mates just *record* that the full task has been done. At least at one worksite, the mate was filling in the measurement for all days of the fortnight, in front of us. At yet another worksite, the mate was filling in the measurement for that particular day, even though he had not measured and nor was the day over yet. The way the MMP had been filled indicated that they had just put the same numbers down for each team. I suspect similar practices are common at other worksites as well, because of the 'look' of the MMP (with uniform entries for all groups).

It is not clear what incentive the mates have to measure output honestly (or at all). In principle, if a mate over-measures, he or she will be 'caught' when the Junior Engineer does the collective measurement at the end of the fortnight. From this brief survey, it was not very clear how often discrepancies arose between the mates' MMPs and the Junior Engineer's measurements, and how these discrepancies were resolved. It seemed that in some cases, the Junior Engineer's measurements 'overrode' the MMPs as far as wage payments are concerned; this would amount to falling back on collective measurement. In other cases, the Junior Engineer probably accommodated the MMP by adjusting his own estimates. This undermines the verification role of the Junior Engineer's measurements and opens the door to over-measurements by the mates.

Thus, the rising trend in wages could reflect 'over-measurement' on the part of the mates as much as actual improvements in productivity at NREGA worksites.[15]

[15] It is also worth noting that there have been periodic revisions of the Schedule of Rates in Rajasthan during the last few years, with the standard 'task' being relaxed each time. This, in itself, would contribute to higher wages, even in the absence of any change in productivity.

Better Monitoring

Peer Monitoring

When labourers are working in groups of five, it is easier for them to monitor each other and to pull up any 'shirkers' amongst them, than when they work in groups of 40 or more (which is generally the case under collective measurement). Shirking becomes more difficult under these circumstances.[16]

At one of the worksites that we visited in Sankarna panchayat, women said that working in groups was better because earlier the better-off labourers, to whom the wage rate did not matter much, would sit around; this harmed those of them who needed the money and wanted a better wage rate. With smaller groups, it was easier for them to monitor each other. Besides this, women at other worksites also said that working in smaller groups allowed them to divide tasks (for example, digging, loading, carrying) amongst themselves in a more efficient manner.

Mate Monitoring

The formation of groups also enables better worksite supervision by the mate. It becomes easier for the mate to spot which group(s) are lagging behind in the completion of their task. This also puts pressure on the labourers to work because closer monitoring by the mate is possible.

In larger groups, NREGA labourers said that each one thinks that the other will work, or that it was not clear how much they were supposed to do, and the mate could not single out one set of people to pull up for poor productivity until it was too late.

The bottom line is that working in groups facilitates work monitoring—both peer monitoring and supervision—on the part of the mates.

[16] There is anecdotal evidence that, in Rajasthan, there is a tendency for some people to join the worksites without intending to do much work. However, it is not clear how serious or widespread the problem is. We have not heard of this being a serious problem in other states.

Greater Clarity regarding Task

With collective measurement, when labourers work in batches of 40 or more, it is difficult for them to understand the task required to earn the minimum wage. In smaller groups, the task can be marked out more easily. Discussions with labourers indicated that improved clarity regarding what is required of them is an important factor in raising productivity.

For instance, labourers working in groups of 40 or more may not understand how much earth exactly they need to dig in order to earn Rs 73 per day (the minimum wage at the time of this investigation). When groups are formed, the task for each group of five is marked out for them and makes the job of completing it easier. Thus, even if each group's output is not measured separately at the end of the fortnight, the labourers may have achieved more output than before just on account of having better understood what is required of them.

We also tried to understand the labourers' perspective on GM versus CM. It was not clear whether labourers prefer GM or CM. Some said that they preferred not to work in groups because the aged and other physically weak persons would be the losers in a group measurement system. Able-bodied persons may not be willing to allow older persons in their group, for fear of a reduction in their own wage rate. On the other hand, if the older persons are from their own family or caste, or if there are other forms of solidarity amongst the labourers, then older persons may be grouped with the able-bodied. For instance, in other places labourers said that if old people do show up for work, then they spread them across different groups, so that their 'burden' can be shared by everyone. Similarly, we met a disabled man who had worked as a mate but who felt that the GM system was not good for the disabled because nobody wanted them in their group.

Sometimes women said that they preferred working in groups because they can finish their task early, and work at their own pace. But follow-up questions revealed that they can rarely finish the task early, and even if they are able to do so, they have to stay at the worksite until 5 PM because they worry about 'checking' (they will be marked absent if they are not around). If labourers are allowed to pace themselves and leave early when they complete their day's task it would greatly strengthen the argument in favour of GM. This is especially true of women who often combine NREGA work with household chores and other responsibilities.

WORKSITE MANAGEMENT IN RAJASTHAN: POSTSCRIPT

As part of the NREGA Survey 2008, the survey teams in Rajasthan covered 10 worksites each in Dungarpur and Sirohi districts and interviewed 200 workers employed at these worksites. The findings of this survey confirm that worksite management is much better in Rajasthan than in most other states. Close to 80 per cent of the worksites visited had trained mates. This has enabled the implementation of transparency safeguards in the state: muster rolls were available at 86 per cent of the worksites, labourers at all worksites said that they signed the muster roll at the time of payment of wages, and corresponding entries were simultaneously made in their job cards. In the other survey states, investigators were able to find muster rolls at only one out of every 10 worksites visited (see Chapter 3 for more details).

Further, the presence of trained mates has also meant that basic worksite facilities are more likely to be found in Rajasthan than in any of the other survey states. For instance, most of the worksites in Rajasthan had drinking water, compared with just half of the worksites in the other states.

Where trained mates had been posted, they had been told about the formation of groups and in many cases they had also been provided with an MMP to record group-wise measurements.

However, as with our own investigation in Jalore, the investigators found that in almost all cases, wages were still being calculated on the basis of collective measurements made by the Junior Engineer. Labourers at all worksites reported getting less than the minimum wage. The average wage earned was Rs 71 per day, as against the statutory minimum of Rs 100 per day in Rajasthan at that time.

CONCLUSION

The main purpose of the mate training experiment in Rajasthan was to improve labour productivity. I find that its impact on raising labour productivity is unclear. The experiment, however, has much to contribute to better worksite management.

While groups had been formed at most of the worksites we visited, not a single worksite was practising group measurement. It is, therefore, difficult to attribute the rising wage in Jalore to the driving out of shirkers through GM, as has been claimed.

The main impact of this experiment on labour productivity seems to operate through the formation of groups. If the wage rate has been increasing on account of improved productivity (rather than due to inflated measurement), it is probably because GF facilitates better worksite supervision and peer monitoring, rather than on account of greater work incentives. Further, GF can have an impact on productivity because of the greater clarity amongst labourers regarding the prescribed task. Group formation alone seems to affect productivity, independently of group measurement. Even that is a significant achievement given that low productivity is a genuine problem on NREGA works in Rajasthan.[17]

The uncertain impact of trained mates on labour productivity does not detract from the value of this initiative as a step towards better worksite management. Trained mates are definitely required at NREGA

[17] I witnessed an extreme example of low productivity in Chohtan block of Barmer district, at a worksite where approximately 250 workers were employed, but very few were actually working at the time of my visit. This worksite was like a large picnic, with groups of labourers sheltering themselves under trees, cooking, and resting, until our arrival. This is not a general pattern (it is the worst I have seen, as far as labour productivity is concerned), but it does illustrate the vulnerabilities of the collective measurement system.

worksites, and have much to contribute (for example, in terms of better provision of worksite facilities, improved record-keeping, and implementation of the transparency safeguards), whether or not GM is practised.

The training of mates has certainly helped to protect the entitlements of labourers—in the sense of provision of mandatory worksite facilities, as well as protecting them from corrupt practices. Rajasthan is still among the few states that have taken the transparency safeguards, prescribed in the NREGA Operational Guidelines and in the Act itself, seriously.

9

Empowerment Guarantee Act?*

Reetika Khera#

INTRODUCTION

As many observers have noted, the National Rural Employment Guarantee Act (NREGA) is a unique opportunity for rural labourers to organize. Conversely, building strong workers' organizations is an essential condition for the success of NREGA. The recent history of Jagrut Adivasi Dalit Sangathan (JADS) in Badwani district (Madhya Pradesh) is one interesting example of this complementarity.

I spent four days in Pati block (Badwani district) in June 2006 and again in May 2008, as part of a survey team looking at the implementation of NREGA in this area. The 2006 survey involved worksite visits. The NREGA Survey 2008 (discussed in Chapter 3) covered two districts of Madhya Pradesh (Badwani and Sidhi), and two blocks in each district. Along with worksite visits, it included interviews with 50 randomly-selected NREGA labourers in each block (10 from each of the five sample worksites in the relevant block). The sample blocks in Badwani district were Pati and Rajpur.

* Originally published as 'Empowerment Guarantee Act?', *Economic and Political Weekly*, 43 (35): 8–10, 30 August–5 September 2008.

I am grateful to the field investigators who conducted the fieldwork in Badwani. The fieldwork would not have been possible without help from the Jagrut Adivasi Dalit Sangathan. I would like to thank the members of the Sangathan, especially, for hosting the survey team and for giving us their time. Special thanks are due to Madhuri Krishnaswamy for her support in Badwani and for comments on this essay. I would also like to thank Jean Drèze and Nandini Nayak for helpful comments and suggestions.

Pati, once covered with lush teak forests, now has a depressing lunar landscape of denuded hills, where only subsistence agriculture is possible. As a result, many households survive on wage labour and seasonal migration. The JADS, a labour union, has worked there for many years on issues of tribal land rights. Since the NREGA was launched on 2 Februrary 2006, JADS has also struggled for workers' entitlements under NREGA: employment on demand, minimum wages, timely wage payments, and the unemployment allowance, among others.

Madhuri Krishnaswamy has been working in Badwani since 1993 and has been part of the Sangathan since its inception. Her involvement and vision have been crucial in inspiring and guiding the work of Jagrut Adivasi Dalit Sangathan. Speaking to her about the NREGA, one realizes that for JADS the teething phase in the implementation of this Act is over, and it is now dealing with 'second generation' issues, such as increasing the levels of people's participation in the planning process. This essay documents some aspects of that initial phase of struggle, the results of that struggle, and also some of the second generation issues that face the Sangathan now.

EDUCATE, ORGANIZE...

The JADS is an unregistered organization with a membership of 3,500 families in 2007 and is active in three blocks of Badwani district. All the organizational work is managed by members, all of whom are local residents, who volunteer their time for the Sangathan's work. There are no paid employees. It has an informal organizational structure, where the district committee members and area committee members share work responsibilities. The Sangathan has been working on a range of issues related to workers' rights (including control over local resources—land, water, and forests among others), and also took up NREGA-related issues as soon as the Act came into force in February 2006.

This organizational work has achieved important results. To start with, most labourers are aware of their rights under the NREGA—in the 2008 survey, we found that 88 per cent of the sample workers in Pati knew that they are entitled to 100 days of work, 74 per cent were aware of the minimum wage, and 76 per cent knew that wages were supposed to be paid within 15 days (see Table 9.1). Another striking example of the high level of engagement and awareness is that many Sangathan members in Pati were aware of the increase in the statutory minimum wage in Madhya Pradesh to Rs 85 per day (from Rs 69), even though the increase had come into force just a few days before the survey began. We were also amazed when we found that many women in this area were aware of their right to have child care facilities at the worksite.

Table 9.1 Status of NREGA in Pati vs Other Survey Areas

	Badwani district		Other districts
	Pati	Rajpur	
Proportion (%) who are aware of their entitlement to			
100 days of work each year	88	37	51
the minimum wage	74	58	62
timely wage payments	76	41	56
Proportion who had got work in response to a written application	92	17	19
Number of days of work obtained in the past 12 months	85	23	41

Source: NREGA Survey 2008 (see Chapter 3 for details).

What is perhaps more significant is that apart from awareness of their entitlements, Sangathan members are aware of the process through which these can be claimed. To illustrate, even at the time of my first visit in June 2006, most of the workers had gone through the formal process of applyling for work. In May 2008, 92 per cent of the respondents from Pati block had obtained work in response to a written application.

The high levels of awareness, and also the fact that demand-driven employment has taken root in Pati, are significant achievements. This is clear when we contrast awareness levels in Pati with those in Rajpur block (where this kind of organizational work is yet to happen) and in other survey districts (see Table 9.1). For instance, in Rajpur and other survey districts less than one-fifth (17 and 19 per cent, respectively) of the sample workers had applied for work in writing. In fact, in most of the sample districts, the work application process was simply not in place, defeating the whole principle of demand-driven employment (most job-card holders were just waiting for NREGA works to open). The activation of this process in Pati is a major step forward.

Many other examples can be given of the effectiveness of the Sangathan's work of educating and organizing. These include payment of statutory minimum wages and high levels of employment under NREGA. In Pati, the payment of minimum wage is a matter of routine now. This has been achieved after a period of struggle which included refusal to accept anything below the minimum wage. Besides this, in 2007–8, many Sangathan members were able to work for a full 100 days on NREGA (the upper limit under the Act). Among the workers interviewed in Pati, the average number of days of employment during the 12 months preceding the survey was as high as 85 days, compared with just 23 days in Rajpur block. Very few districts in the country, except in Rajasthan, can boast of similar levels of employment. The corresponding average for the two districts surveyed in Rajasthan (Dungarpur and Sirohi) is 71 days. However, Pati's record is mainly an achievement of the people, unlike in Rajasthan, where the high level of employment generation is primarily the result of proactive efforts of the district administration.

Indeed, the most heartening aspect of the Sangathan's work in Pati is the sense of empowerment that one gets from its members. Two snippets of conversations are illustrative of this. The first pertains to a fine levied by Sangathan members (at the rate of Re 1 per day of delay) on the panchayat secretary for delayed wage payments. Under the Act, wages are supposed to be paid within 15 days, but this time limit is routinely violated without any sanction being imposed. While a fine of one rupee per day of delay may seem trivial, the stigma associated with being fined is likely to have a deterrent effect (the concerned secretary was certainly anxious to avoid any such delays). This fine is an interesting example of the determination of the Sangathan members to assert their rights.

The other example is related to the introduction of bank payments of NREGA wages. When asked what he thought about the introduction of bank payments, Malubhai said he was not sure: it would involve the cost of getting to the bank, which was in the neighbouring village, but would reduce the risk of being cheated. Since there was an order from the district administration, he said that they were willing to try it out. If they were not happy, all they needed to do was launch an agitation to revert to the old system of payments. This confidence of Sangathan members in their ability to change the way things work contrasts sharply with the general resignation and fatalism we have observed among NREGA workers elsewhere, even in the face of gross exploitation.

What has empowered the Sangathan members so? I believe that the June–October 2006 struggle for unemployment allowance has much to do with this. In June 2006, five months after NREGA came into force, the Sangathan launched a five-month struggle for the payment of unemployment allowance. The fruits of that struggle were easy to see two years later.

...AGITATE: THE UNEMPLOYMENT ALLOWANCE

As mentioned earlier, JADS has focused on creating wide awareness of NREGA entitlements and the *process* whereby people can claim these entitlements. In 2006, when they were offered work without applying, they insisted on applying. They had also understood the importance of demanding a receipt when applications for work are submitted. Many Sangathan members had gone through the entire process of applying for job cards, then for work, and, finally, for the unemployment allowance (in cases where work was not provided). On 7 June 2006, the unemployment allowance became due to more than 2,000 labourers of Pati. This opened a new chapter in the Sangathan's eventful history.

The NREGA states that if work is not provided within 15 days of an application being made, the applicants are entitled to an unemployment allowance at the rate of one-fourth of the minimum wage for the first 30 days, and one half thereafter. While the bulk (about 90 per cent) of employment costs is borne by the Central Government, the unemployment allowance is to be paid by the state governments. Thus, one role of the unemployment allowance is to act as a 'fine' on the state government if it fails to implement the guarantee. Seen in this light, the payment of the unemployment allowance plays a key role in the realization of the work guarantee. If the unemployment allowance is not paid, the work guarantee itself becomes very weak.

However, the Madhya Pradesh government (as well as other state governments) has found various means to evade the payment of unemployment allowances. One escape route is to provide work within 15 days of an application being made, but only for a few days.[1] In Pati, in 2006, we came across applications for 30 days of employment, but labourers barely got 10 days of employment. This tactic, effectively, defuses the demand for unemployment allowance, even though labourers remain, strictly speaking, legally entitled to it as long as the number of days of employment falls short of what they have demanded.

Another escape route was to entangle villagers in a web of paperwork. When villagers submitted applications for the unemployment allowance, the administration surpassed itself in finding flaws in their applications. For instance, applicants were told that they had not used the correct form (Form 14), or that they had not

[1] In 2005, while conducting a field survey in Dahanu (Maharashtra) I learnt that this tactic was also being used there: there had been cases of work being provided for as little as two days in order to evade the unemployment allowance.

attached a copy of their work application along with the application for the unemployment allowance. The spurious nature of these objections is evident from the fact that, say, requests for Form 14 were met with a blank look from the block officials, who had never heard of it.

The Sangathan did not give up. In the face of threats of violence and fake cases against their members, they continued to put pressure on the administration to pay the unemployment allowance. Finally, in October 2006, unemployment allowance was paid to 1,574 labourers of 8 gram panchayats of Pati block, making this the first instance of payment of unemployment allowance in the country.

This victory seems to have turned the channel of accountability on its head. In most places that I have visited, the Panchayat Secretaries (also known as the *Sevaks*) feel that they are accountable only to block level officials. In Pati block, for the first time, it seemed that the Panchayat Sevak was actually a 'sevak' of the villagers. A conversation with Virendra Patel, the Panchayat Sevak of Ubdagarh panchayat (one of the gram panchayats where unemployment allowance had been paid in October 2006) illustrates this point.

On 8 April 2008, more than 1,000 workers in Ubdagarh village put in a group application for work under the NREGA. They were demanding 30 days of work on Cattle Prevention Trenches (CPT) work in their village. It is heartening to note that the concerned authorities provided them work within 15 days (as stipulated under the NREGA). Further, the Secretary informed us that another 600 residents of the village had caught on to the 'demand-driven employment' principle of the NREGA (learning from the JADS members) and put in a separate work application. Patel has managed to ensure employment for these workers as well. It is noteworthy that when Patel talked about this episode, he seemed to suggest that he did not have an alternative—if he had not provided work, he would have had to pay them the unemployment allowance.

LOOKING AHEAD: PARTICIPATORY PLANNING AND TRANSPARENCY

Probing further, I found that the residents of Ubdagarh were happy about being given work but were agitated that the work opened was not what they had demanded. The Sangathan members had demanded contour trenches (also called CPT by the local residents) in their collective work application and also in the gram sabha. On verifying the gram sabha minutes for 2 February 2008, we found that the first resolution pertained to NREGA works; it included a list of 22 works, of which the first two were contour trenching works. Instead the applicants have been given employment on a road work (listed third on this list).

This is not the first instance of a mismatch between what was demanded and has been provided: earlier, when they had demanded a *medh bandhi* (land improvement work on private lands), contour trenching work was opened. The Sangathan members are very keen on medh bandhi and CPT works because of the benefits to their lands (and the forest) from such soil regeneration and water conservation works. As Shivjia Barela of Ubdagard says, '*CPT mein bahut fayda hai—chara hoga, pani rukega, aur mitti bachti hai*' (CPT is very useful—we can grow fodder, prevent water from running off, and also conserve top soil on our lands).

Overriding the decisions of the gram sabha, in the matter of selection of NREGA works, is not confined to Ubdagarh. Similar complaints have come to light from other gram panchayats in the area.

In this remote village of Pati block, the villagers are emphatic about NREGA funds being put to good use, rather than being spent with the sole purpose of providing them employment only. While they are keen that employment must be provided, they are equally concerned about the creation of useful assets. The Sangathan is now dealing with what might be called second generation issues (compared to the issues that are being dealt with in other states). They are demanding to know why a proposal passed in the gram sabha has been overturned.

The attempt at participatory planning has also brought the issue of transparency to the fore. The Sangathan is demanding transparency in the decision-making process and that transparency safeguards prescribed in the Operational Guidelines be taken seriously. For instance, JADS has been able to ensure that wages are not embezzled by activating the 'monitoring and vigilance committees', which in most other places exist—at best—on paper.[2] Apart from participating in these committees, Sangathan members visit worksites regularly and maintain their own attendance records as a means of crosschecking the official 'muster rolls'. In 2006, in Bamnali, for instance, the Sangathan's records indicated that 510 persons were employed, but 535 names had been entered in the muster rolls.

The effective implementation of NREGA in Pati block goes beyond the ability of its residents to claim their rights. This is brought out by the high levels of engagement with the programme in terms of planning, implementation, and monitoring. As Madhuri Krishnaswamy put it, 'The struggle for the enactment of the NREGA was associated with a larger vision.' Apart from its immediate aim of being a form of social security for the rural poor by providing them local employment, it was expected that NREGA would contribute to activating gram sabhas, to empowering women, and to the development of rural areas. In this sense, JADS has fully imbibed the spirit of NREGA, looked upon as an opportunity to promote the overall development of the village as well as to alter the balance of power in the village society. Aside from showing that it is possible to make NREGA work, the Sangathan's experience also provides important insights into the transformation that is possible if the Act is effectively implemented.

[2] The Panchayat Sevak said that the first day at a new worksite was hectic because, apart from handing over the muster rolls to the mates and arranging worksite facilities, he also had to institute the Vigilance Committee for the worksite. While some of this needs to be taken with a pinch of salt (for example, we did not find crèches at any of the worksites), Vigilance Committees are active in Sangathan areas.

PART III

CONTRASTING EXPERIENCES

10

Orissa

Ten Loopholes and the Silver Lining

Jean Drèze, Reetika Khera, and Siddhartha#

INTRODUCTION

This part of the book presents a few short 'case studies' of the National Rural Employment Guarantee Act (NREGA) in different states. The intention is, partly, to shed further light on the ground realities, and, partly, to give a sense of the contrasts between different states as well as of the evolution of NREGA over time. These case studies are part of a series of field investigations that were conducted between 2007 and 2009, using much the same methods as with the 'NREGA Survey 2008' discussed in Chapter 3. Many student volunteers (from University of Delhi and elsewhere) participated in these field surveys, and we take this opportunity to thank them all, as well as the local volunteers who made invaluable contributions to this endeavour. The first survey took place in three districts of Orissa (Balangir, Boudh, and Kalahandi) during 3–12 October 2007, in response to reports of widespread embezzlement of NREGA funds in that area. In each of the three districts, two blocks were selected at random, and within each block, five randomly-selected gram panchayats were studied. The survey included careful verification of muster rolls for one randomly-selected NREGA work in each of the 30 sample gram panchayats.

We are grateful to Rajkishor Mishra and Umashankar Behera for helping to coordinate this survey and train local volunteers.

The verification of muster rolls for the 30 sample worksites shows that only 60 per cent of the days of employment recorded in the muster rolls were confirmed by the concerned labourers (see Table 10.1). The corresponding discrepancies in wage payments may be even larger. However, this is hard to ascertain as the verification of wage payments poses considerable difficulties, for instance, due to the 'clubbing' of payments for several labourers in the muster rolls. In fact, one of the main conclusions of the muster verification exercise is that, for reasons discussed later, the NREGA records in Orissa are virtually unverifiable.

Table 10.1 Findings of Muster Roll Verification

District	Block	Number of sample labourers*	Total days of work according to labourers	Total days of work according to muster rolls	Ratio (labourers/ muster roll) (%)
Kalahandi	Narala	87	1,158	2,141	54
	Lanjigarh	96	1,653	2,740	60
Bolangir	Belpada	88	1,036	1,769	59
	Tureikela	107	910	1,742	52
Boudh	Boudh	115	1,691	2,217	76
	Kantamal	99	1,178	2,085	56
All sample blocks		**592**	**7,626**	**12,694**	**60**

Source: NREGA Survey conducted in six randomly-selected blocks of Balangir, Boudh, and Kalahandi districts during 3–12 October 2007. In each block, five gram panchayats were selected at random, and in each gram panchayat, muster roll verification (covering 30 labourers selected at random from the muster rolls) was done for one worksite. The results show that the number of days worked according to the labourers was only 60 per cent of the total employment days recorded against their names in the muster rolls.

Note: * Excluding those who were unable to remember their employment details.

This note presents a few general observations about the reasons why NREGA in Orissa appears to be particularly vulnerable to corruption. This is, indeed, an issue of overwhelming importance at this time: NREGA has tremendous potential in Orissa (especially, in deprived areas such as the sample districts), but corruption threatens to derail the entire programme.

TEN LOOPHOLES

The survey findings suggest that Orissa's Employment Guarantee Scheme is highly vulnerable to corruption. Ten specific sources of vulnerability are identified in this section. The main focus is on works implemented by the gram panchayats.

The term 'loopholes', used in the title of this section, should not obscure the possibly intentional character of some of these vulnerabilities. At least some of them reflect a deliberate sabotage of the transparency safeguards, aimed at perpetuating the traditional system of extortion in rural employment programmes. We shall return to this.

Faulty Design of Job Cards

The main purpose of the job card is to enable NREGA labourers to 'verify' their own employment and wage details. In Orissa, this purpose has been defeated from the start due to the faulty design of the job card. In particular, there is no column for 'wages paid' in the job card, making it impossible for workers to verify their wage payments. Even the number of days worked is hard to verify, as the names of the labourer and the worksite have been replaced by 'codes'. To decipher a labourer's code, one has to refer to page one of the job card, which is often in English! The worksite code, for its part, is plain Greek for the card holder. As for employment dates, they are supposed to be written in a rectangle divided into four boxes, but these are filled in different ways by different functionaries, further confusing the reader. In this and other ways, the job card is virtually unreadable, even for trained investigators—let alone semi-literate labourers.

Erratic Maintenance of Job Cards

The problem of the faulty design of job cards is compounded by irregular maintenance. In most of the sample villages, job card entries were incomplete or even blank. Even when entries were made, they were often illegible, or hard to read for one reason or another. Perhaps, it is not surprising that little attention is paid to the maintenance of job cards, since the cards (as presently designed) are little more than symbolic documents. Further, there is some lack of clarity as to who is to be held accountable in the event where job cards are not adequately maintained.

Incomplete Distribution of Job Cards

In many of the sample villages, the distribution of job cards was incomplete. Cases were even found of entire hamlets where just a few households had a job card (in spite of an evident demand for job cards from others also). Even among those who were given a dated receipt after applying for registration, some did not have a job card. Aside from depriving many rural households of their entitlements under the Act, the incomplete distribution of job cards has led to problematic 'adjustments' in the records to accommodate workers without job cards at the worksites (discussed later). These adjustments open the door to further adjustments that serve different purposes.

'Adjustments' in the Muster Rolls and Job Cards

In many of the sample gram panchayats, it was observed that various adjustments in the muster rolls and/or job cards had become routine practice. For instance, a worker without a job card is often accommodated by clubbing his/her wages with those of someone who has a job card, under the latter's name. Similarly, team work performed under the piece-rate system is often recorded under the name of the team leader alone. Sometimes, adjustments are also made to meet the requirements of the on-line Monitoring and Information System

(MIS). These and related practices, well-intentioned as they might be in some cases, send a dangerous signal that records can be 'adjusted', and open the door to further, arbitrary adjustments. In fact, the pressure to make adjustments in some circumstances (for example, meeting the requirements of the MIS) seems to have become a convenient excuse for fraudulent practices.

Lack of Transparency in Muster Rolls

Lack of transparency in muster rolls had several aspects in the sample gram panchayats. First, there are 'dual' records: for instance, authentic attendance details are taken in informal notebooks (*kaccha* muster rolls) at the worksite, while official (*pacca*) muster rolls are filled—and often fudged—elsewhere. Second, muster rolls are rarely accessible for public scrutiny. 'Live' muster rolls were not kept at the worksite (as per NREGA Guidelines) in any of the sample gram panchayats, and 'completed' muster rolls were typically kept at someone's home rather than at the Panchayat Bhawan. Third, like the job cards, muster rolls are difficult to verify. Indeed, the earlier discussed 'adjustments' make it possible to justify almost any discrepancy between the muster rolls and the workers' testimonies. The lack of transparency in work measurement (see later) further exacerbates this problem.

Rigid MIS

The Government of Orissa has taken a pioneering initiative in operationalizing the centrally-designed MIS. This MIS can be of great help in achieving some discipline and consistency in record-keeping. However, in this initial phase, the rigidities of the MIS have played a role in promoting adjustments in the written records.

For instance, a muster roll can accommodate a worker without a job card, but the MIS cannot. Similarly, the MIS does not allow employment to be given to a household that has already secured

100 days of NREGA employment in the current financial year. These hurdles are typically overcome by making adjustments, either in the written records or at the data entry stage (for example, clubbing two workers' wages in the same muster roll entry). Thus, instead of alerting users to possible inconsistencies and irregularities in record-keeping, the MIS often covers them up.

Continued Hold of Contractors

Private contractors are banned under NREGA. However, in a majority of the sample gram panchayats, the investigators found evidence of continued involvement of contractors, either directly, or indirectly (for instance, through dummy 'Village Labour Leaders').[1] The contractors, in turn, are often under the control of local political leaders. They milk the system by exploiting labourers, fudging muster rolls, and cheating on the material component. A major part of the loot is recycled through the so-called 'PC' (percentage) system, whereby various functionaries receive fixed percentages of NREGA funds. According to fairly reliable testimonies from contractors and others, the PC system—where it applies—absorbs about 20 per cent of NREGA funds in the sample blocks of Balangir and Kalahandi districts.

Vulnerability to Local Collusion

In Orissa, NREGA funds are transferred directly from the district to gram panchayat accounts after a project is sanctioned. Thereafter, gram panchayat functionaries (the *Sarpanch*, the Secretary, the Executive Officer, and the VLL) are in control of almost everything: funds, accounts, payments, muster rolls, job cards, and even work measurements. The Junior Engineer's work measurements are supposed to act as a 'check'

[1] The Village Labour Leader (VLL) is supposed to be selected by the gram sabha for the purpose of 'supervising' a specific worksite. The VLL is supposed to be a mere worksite supervisor, who earns wages at the same rate as other labourers (see Chapter 14 for more details).

against inflated muster rolls, but, in practice, the measurements are often done by gram panchayat functionaries and copied or endorsed by the Junior Engineer in the 'measurement book'. In any case, suitable inducements can often secure the cooperation of the junior engineer. Thus, in the event of collusion among gram panchayat functionaries, very little is left by way of checks and balances.

Cryptic Work Measurement

In Orissa, Junior Engineers are supposed to carry out regular (for instance, weekly) measurements of the *individual output* of each NREGA worker, and to note the individual measurements in their measurements books. In practice, this is rarely done, and indeed it would involve an unmanageable work burden for the Junior Engineers, at current staffing levels. What seems to happen, instead, is that gram panchayat functionaries (usually the Executive Officer and/ or VLL) do most of the measurements, and the Junior Engineers just check them, for example, by measuring the collective output at the end of the week. Since the initial measurements are 'unofficial', there is no authorized record of them. Further, 'team measurement' is often practised instead of individual measurement, to keep things manageable. While muster rolls include a column for 'wages as per measurement', it is impossible to verify wage calculations without having access to the measurement book *or* the unofficial notebook, both of which are zealously sheltered from public scrutiny. This expands the scope for making creative entries in the muster rolls, and makes it all the more difficult to verify them.

Other Vulnerabilities

So far, we have focused on vulnerabilities that are *specific* to Orissa's Employment Guarantee Scheme (as it functions on the ground). To these must be added some *general* vulnerabilities of NREGA, not confined to Orissa. These include:

Staff Shortages

In Orissa, as in many other states, there is a severe shortage of NREGA staff, from top to bottom. For instance, the responsibility for implementing NREGA is typically imposed as an 'additional charge' on overworked Block Development Officers (at the block level) and Executive Officers (at the gram panchayat level). Gram Rozgar Sevaks are yet to be appointed in most gram panchayats, and the system is also short of technical staff, such as Junior Engineers. All this makes it harder, in many ways, to ensure effective monitoring of NREGA, and also creates a temptation to rely on contractors to fill the gap.

Dormant Gram Sabhas

There was little evidence of active involvement of the gram sabhas with NREGA in the sample gram panchayats. Typically, gram sabhas are poorly attended and controlled by the local elite. Resolutions are easily 'passed' by vested interests in the name of the whole village community. This makes it possible, for instance, for influential contractors to instal themselves (or their cronies) as the VLL with the sanction of the gram sabha or palli sabha.

Ritualistic Vigilance Procedures

In the sample gram panchayats, Vigilance Committees were inactive, when they existed at all. Similarly, social audits (where they had taken place) were still at a largely ritualistic stage, where government officials hastily read out various NREGA records (often in 'summary' form) to bemused villagers.

Lack of Grievance Redressal

Last but not least, one of the major flaws of NREGA in Orissa, as elsewhere, is the lack of grievance redressal procedures. The grievance redressal authorities (for example, Programme Officer and District

Programme Coordinator) are, essentially, the same as the implementing authorities, making it difficult to hold anyone accountable. And, while Section 25 of NREGA provides for penalties against anyone who 'contravenes the provisions' of the Act, there is no clarity as to when or how or by whom the penalties are to be imposed.

ASSESSMENT: NREGA AND THE TRADITIONAL EXTORTION SYSTEM

To sum up, most of the transparency safeguards under NREGA have broken down in Orissa. The records are virtually unverifiable, and the accountability mechanisms are also very weak. The main protection against corruption seems to be the complexity of the system: embezzlement of funds requires a certain amount of collusion, and manipulating a wide range of records. The MIS is also a protection of sorts, in so far as it does put muster rolls and other key documents in the public domain, and inspires fear among corrupt elements (especially those not familiar with information technology). But this leaves plenty of room for fraud, as the findings of our muster roll verification exercises illustrate.

In this vulnerable environment, Orissa is witnessing an attempted survival of the 'traditional' methods of misappropriation, involving dual records (kaccha and pacca), private contractors, and the PC system. The continuation of traditional arrangements for the siphoning off of employment funds has been helped in no small measure by the tolerance of contractors or quasi-contractors, and of arbitrary 'adjustments' in the records. Even when no embezzlement is involved, these adjustments constitute a fraud of sorts, since any tampering with the records is a form of corruption, and also because these adjustments lay the foundation for an entire system of misappropriation.

The silver lining is that the traditional system of extortion seems to be finding it harder and harder to survive. Contractors, for instance, do not seem to be particularly happy with NREGA; vulnerable as it may be, the system has become harder for them to control. They are apprehensive of a possible tightening of the checks and balances, and have started fading away in many places. In some of the sample gram panchayats (notably, in Boudh district), corruption levels in NREGA are already much lower, by all accounts, than in earlier employment programmes such as the Sampoorna Grameen Rozgar Yojana (SGRY) and the National Food for Work Programme (NFFWP). The main challenge is to accelerate this process of 'phasing out' of the traditional system of corruption, and the transition towards a transparent and accountable system.

PRELIMINARY RECOMMENDATIONS[2]

From the preceding section, it should be clear that most of the vulnerabilities of the Employment Guarantee Scheme in Orissa relate to *violations of the NREGA Guidelines.*

These include, for instance, poor job card maintenance, lack of transparency in muster rolls, and the continued involvement of contractors. Thus, the first priority is stricter enforcement of the Guidelines, and of the provisions of the Act, especially, the transparency safeguards.

Four measures would be particularly useful in achieving stricter enforcement of the Act and the Guidelines. First, whenever possible, *responsibility should be fixed* for specific aspects of the implementation of NREGA. For instance, the responsibility for the maintenance of job cards should be assigned to the Gram Rozgar Sevaks (and this should be clearly mentioned in their 'job charts'). This would make it easier to take action in the event where the provisions of the Act or the Guidelines are violated.

Second, credible grievance redressal procedures need to be put in place. In particular, Rules should be framed to activate Section 25 of

[2] We present here, without change, the recommendations that were made at that time. Many of them were later implemented, or at least taken up, by the Government of Orissa, with varying success.

NREGA, regarding penalties against contraventions of the Act. The Rules should list specific violations of the Act that would automatically attract penalties and clarify who is empowered to impose the fines.

Third, exemplary action needs to be taken in the event of confirmed violations of the Act, as happened in Boudh district on 12 October 2007 after the survey team uncovered a fake muster roll.[3] Localized as they may be, these instances of swift and firm action can have major 'demonstration effects', and send an important signal that corruption in NREGA will not be tolerated. Exemplary actions against contractors involved in NREGA could have a similar impact.

Fourth, there is need for wider awareness of the Act and Guidelines. During the survey, we often found that, say, gram panchayat functionaries (not to speak of labourers) had inadequate knowledge of the provisions of NREGA. Most of them are untrained and have no access to reader-friendly guidelines in the local language, such as 'primers' or introductory booklets. This kind of material needs to be developed and disseminated, along with a major expansion of training programmes.

Beyond this, specific steps are required to address the vulnerabilities discussed earlier. Some of these vulnerabilities (for example, faulty design of job cards) are relatively easy to remove, but others (for example, the continued involvement of contractors) call for sustained and wide-ranging action. Some preliminary recommendations are presented below, to initiate this process.

1. *Replacement of Job Cards*: Job Cards in Orissa should be re-designed and replaced by 1 April 2008 (the beginning of the next financial year). The new design should be reader-friendly and contain a column for 'wage payments' as well as a list of useful phone numbers including a Helpline number.

[3] The fake muster roll was shown to the District Collector, Shalini Pandit, who personally verified the facts on the spot, recovered the stolen money from the Panchayat Sevak, and took action against him.

2. *Maintenance of Job Cards*: Regular maintenance of job cards should be strictly enforced. In particular, responsibility should be clearly fixed for job card maintenance, for example, by assigning this task to the Gram Rozgar Sevaks specifically (as things stand, job card maintenance is not mentioned in their job chart). 'Collecting' people's job cards and keeping them in any place other than the Panchayat Bhawan should be considered as a contravention of the Act.
3. *Distribution of Job Cards*: A new registration drive should be conducted when the existing job cards are replaced. Adequate arrangements and instructions should be in place for issuing job cards on a continuous basis at the gram panchayat level, as and when someone applies.
4. *No Adjustments in the Records*: Adjustments in the records should not be allowed in any circumstances. Persons without a job card should be provided with one before they join a worksite. Each worker should be treated as an individual and no clubbing should be permitted.
5. *Transparency of Muster Rolls*: A uniform, single, numbered, well-designed muster roll should be used throughout the state. Accountability should be fixed for ensuring that live muster rolls are kept at the worksite, and that completed muster rolls are available for public scrutiny at the Panchayat Bhawan. Surprise checks should be conducted at worksites for on-the-spot verification of muster rolls. Consideration could also be given to the possibility of introducing the 'Tamil Nadu System', whereby, each labourer has to sign or thumbprint the muster roll every day by way of marking attendance.
6. *Trained Mates*: The VLL system should be phased out. Instead, worksites should be supervised by carefully selected and trained mates, as in Rajasthan. NREGA works implemented through gram panchayat should be executed by the Executive Officer with the assistance of the Gram Rozgar Sevak and trained mate.

7. *Transparent Measurement*: The current fictions of the work measurement system (for example, the myth of individual measurement by Junior Engineers) should be squarely faced. The present system cannot be implemented without a considerable expansion of technical staff. Alternatively, worksite supervisors (mates) could be trained to take measurements, and 'measurement sheets' could be developed for this purpose. Aside from other considerations, transparent measurement would help to prevent the embezzlement of wages in the name of piece-rate work.
8. *Staff Deployment*: Additional staff should be appointed as soon as possible, as per NREGA Guidelines, to facilitate the implementation of the Act, make collusion more difficult, and keep the contractors at bay. In particular, a Gram Rozgar Sevak should be posted in each gram panchayat. Also, the Programme Officer at the block level should be 'a full-time dedicated officer', not below the rank of the Block Development Officer (NREGA Operational Guidelines: 6).
9. *Separation of Payment Agencies from Implementing Agencies*: Wherever possible, payment agencies should be separated from implementing agencies. Many districts in Orissa are adopting bank payments as the separation device. This can go a long way in preventing the appropriation of wage funds and eliminating contractors. However, there are considerable difficulties with this approach, including the lack of preparedness of the banking system, the risk of further confusion in the record-keeping system, and lack of familiarity with banking procedures among NREGA workers. Alternative means of separating payment agencies from implementing agencies could also considered.[4]
10. *Awareness Drives*: Awareness drives urgently need to be conducted, as most labourers are still unaware of their entitlements under NREGA. A simple, reader-friendly primer on NREGA

[4] A useful precedent in this respect is the payment of wages through the Revenue Department in the context of drought relief works in Rajasthan.

should be made available to each gram panchayat. Related resources (booklets, pamphlets, videos, simplified guidelines, and so on) should also be prepared for training purposes. The practice of holding a weekly *Rozgar Divas* in each gram panchayat, as per NREGA Guidelines, should be vigorously activated.

11. *Helplines*: Each block and district should have a NREGA Helpline (for information as well as for complaints). Helpline numbers should be printed or stuck on each job card.
12. *Elimination of Contractors*: Last but not least, the ban on contractors should be strictly enforced. Exemplary action should be taken against contractors involved in NREGA as well as against functionaries who cooperate with them. The retrenchment of contractors should also be facilitated by expanding staff appointments, separating payment agencies from implementing agencies, and enforcing the transparency safeguards. Giving priority to labour-intensive projects (for example, 'earth works') would also help, as contractors tend to look for projects with a high material–labour ratio.

CONCLUDING REMARK

This essay would be incomplete without a mention of the tremendous potential of NREGA in the survey areas. Where work was available, it was generally found that workers earned close to (and sometimes more than) the statutory minimum wage of Rs 70 per day, and that wages were paid within 15 days or so. This is an unprecedented opportunity for the rural poor, and there was evident appreciation of it among casual labourers and other disadvantaged sections of the population. Some of them even hoped that NREGA would enable them to avoid long-distance seasonal migration, with all its hardships. Further, there is plenty of scope for productive NREGA works in these areas, whether it is in the field of water conservation, rural connectivity, regeneration of forest land, or improvement of private agricultural land. The challenges involved in 'making NREGA work' should always be seen in the light of these long-term possibilities, and their significance for the rural poor.

11

Himachal Pradesh

Assessment and Outlook

Siddhartha and Anish Vanaik[#]

This essay presents summary findings of an exploratory survey of the National Rural Employment Guarantee Act (NREGA) in Himachal Pradesh. This survey was conducted in Kangra and Sirmaur districts in December 2007. It was carried out with the help of students from Delhi University and Jawaharlal Nehru University, in collaboration with local volunteers. As with the preceding chapter, this account must be read bearing in mind that the survey took place at an early stage of the implementation of NREGA.

The NREGA was launched in Sirmaur district in February 2006, when the Act came into force, whereas Kangra district was one of the districts chosen for implementation in the second phase (beginning on 1 April 2007). In each district, two blocks were selected for the survey and within each block three gram panchayats were randomly selected. In each of the sample gram panchayats, the most recent completed NREGA work was selected for investigation, including a worksite questionnaire and verification of muster rolls.

The process of muster roll verification entailed recording labourers' testimonies about the wages they had received and comparing them with the corresponding muster roll entries. For this purpose,

We are thankful to the field investigators and local organizations for their valuable support.

muster rolls were collected a week in advance in eight out of the twelve sample gram panchayats. In the other four gram panchayats, muster rolls were sought by the field investigators, on arrival, from the gram panchayat office. Documents such as job cards, perspective plan, employment register, and job card register were also examined by the survey teams in all the sample gram panchayats.

NREGA IN HIMACHAL PRADESH

In some ways, the context of the NREGA in Himachal Pradesh (hereafter, Himachal, for short) is quite unique. The fact that Himachal has made rapid strides across a number of social indicators in the last few decades is just one aspect of this.[1] Another is that Panchayati Raj Institutions (PRIs) are fairly active and, compared to most other states, have a relatively good infrastructure. The Act also has some distinctive features in Himachal. In particular, the minimum wage paid to NREGA labourers (Rs 75 per day since April 2007) is significantly lower than market wages for comparable types of 'unskilled' work (above Rs 100 in both Kangra and Sirmaur). This contrasts with the situation in many other states, where NREGA wages are typically higher than local market wages. These distinctive features of NREGA, and its social context in Himachal, have an important bearing on the implementation of the programme, as discussed later.

The survey findings present a mixed picture of achievements and shortfalls (see Appendix 11.1). In some respects, relating for instance to the administrative culture, the participation of PRIs, and the creation of productive assets, NREGA seems to be doing quite well in Himachal. However, there are also serious inadequacies in many areas, such as awareness levels, job card design, application process, grievance redressal, and social audits. There is a definite sense that much more could have been achieved with the structures and capacities already in place in Himachal.

[1] For a detailed study of Himachal's social achievements, see Bhatty (2006b).

FINDINGS

Awareness Levels

Perhaps the most surprising finding of the survey was people's low level of awareness of their entitlements under NREGA, not to speak of the procedural aspects of the programme. While there was some general awareness of the promise of 100 days of employment under NREGA, few respondents were aware of the principle of demand-driven employment, the unemployment allowance, the transparency safeguards, mandatory worksite facilities, and related matters (see Appendix 11.2). This pattern was as visible in Kangra, where the Act had been in force for just under a year, as in Sirmaur, where NREGA was two years old at the time of the survey.

This is all the more striking as literacy rates are high in Himachal Pradesh, especially in the younger age groups. Indeed, most of the NREGA labourers we met were literate and the muster rolls generally bore signatures rather than thumb impressions. This situation is not merely indicative of the inadequate awareness generation efforts of the state government but also calls for devising newer methods of awareness generation.

Application Process

In Himachal, as in most other states, the work application process is yet to be put in place. Generally, work applications are a mere formality, followed (if at all) for the sake of nominal compliance with the guidelines. For instance, it seems to be a common practice for officials to collect advance signatures on the application forms, and to fill in the dates retrospectively as and when the work actually commences. Even though sheaves of completed or partially completed (dated and undated) work application forms can be found at the gram panchayat offices, very few labourers understood these applications as an expression of demand for work.

Wages and Payment

It was quite heartening to find that most workers were earning the statutory minimum wage of Rs 75 per day on NREGA works. Equally significant was the fact that at 10 of the 12 worksites surveyed, most of the labourers received wages within 15 days of the end of the week when work was done, in conformity with the Act. The one grey area was the worksite transparency safeguards. This is discussed in further detail later.

In Himachal, NREGA workers are paid according to the daily wage ('time rate') system. As noted earlier, the minimum wage (Rs 75 per day) is typically lower than the market wage, which ranged between Rs 90 and 125 per day in the sample gram panchayats (for casual agricultural labour). As a result, young men usually stay away from NREGA works. Even when they do come, there have been problems with achieving productivity norms, due to poor work incentives under the daily-wage system. On the positive side, assured wages and work close to home have encouraged many women to take up paid employment outside the household for the first time. The Act also appears to be very popular among the elderly, who have few other work opportunities. Nevertheless, the overall effect of NREGA wages being lower than the market rate has been to restrain the demand for work and to hold up the scale of NREGA employment.

Asset Creation

The variety of works that have been taken up under the NREGA in Himachal is particularly noteworthy. Apart from roads and ponds, which are routinely being taken up in NREGA works across the country, many other assets and structures have been built, repaired, or improved: gabion structures, traditional irrigation channels (*kul*s), step wells (*bavdi*s), burial grounds, playgrounds for children, boundary walls for schools, and so on.

This impressive diversity of works, which contrasts with the narrow range of NREGA works in many other states, is partly a reflection of the possibilities associated with the daily-wage system. This system dispenses (to a large extent) with the stringent requirements of work measurement that often restrict the range of possible works under a piece-rate system. However, the diversity of NREGA works in Himachal also testifies to the imagination that vibrant PRIs can bring to the process, when they are given adequate space and support.

Selection and Planning

One of the successes of the NREGA in Himachal is that PRIs have been active in the planning and selection of works. All, but one, of the sample gram panchayats had a 'shelf of projects', with a long list of potential NREGA works identified by the local community. Further, most of the worksites that were examined during the survey had been recommended by a gram sabha. These positive findings, in conjunction with what has already been said about the variety of works, indicate that NREGA in Himachal rests on relatively solid institutional foundations, on which much can be built.

State of Records

In all the sample gram panchayats, muster rolls were accessible and teams were provided with photocopies of them on demand. This included the four 'surprise' gram panchayats where survey activities were carried out without prior collection of muster rolls. It is important to mention here that the muster rolls were obtained without having to invoke the Right to Information Act or disclosure clauses under the NREGA. In many cases, even a letter of introduction was not required. This situation, which contrasts with the continued inaccessibility of muster rolls in many other states, reflects the general culture of administrative transparency in Himachal—another aspect of the solid foundations of NREGA in the state.

The basic NREGA records at the gram panchayat level (including job card register, employment register, applications register, asset register, and shelf of projects) were also made available to the teams by the Panchayat Secretaries at short notice. The registers were generally well maintained, as were the proceedings of the gram panchayat and gram sabha meetings. Discussions of NREGA-related matters often figured in these proceedings.

Here again, there was evidence of strong capacities at the gram panchayat level, especially in comparison with other north Indian states. The PRIs in Himachal are obviously capable of handling a complex programme such as NREGA, in a fairly transparent manner. One major qualification is the shortage of essential staff. For instance, in many gram panchayats the post of Secretary was vacant. In other cases, the Secretary was supposed to look after several gram panchayats. Even in cases where the gram panchayat had its own full-time Secretary, he or she was often overworked, with numerous schemes to implement aside from NREGA.

Productivity and Measurement

Low labour productivity under NREGA is a major concern in Himachal, especially among gram panchayat functionaries, programme administrators, and engineering staff. Measured work output (or 'progress', as it is called) often falls short of what is expected for a given number of person-days, based on the prescribed schedule of rates. Aside from being an issue in itself, low productivity often leads to a tussle between gram panchayats and the engineering staff, with the former having to pay NREGA workers on the basis of minimum wages, but the latter authorizing the release of funds based on 'measurement books' that may not tally with the amounts due as per muster rolls.

Various factors have contributed to low labour productivity under NREGA works in Himachal. First, workers are employed under the daily-wage system, which has no built-in work incentives, unlike the piece-rate system. Second, it is not possible to use the threat of dismissal to keep up productivity (as private contractors typically do when they hire labourers on daily wages), since employment is guaranteed. Third, worksite supervision is, in any case, quite informal. Typically, gram panchayat 'members' (ward *panchs*) step in as ad hoc supervisors of NREGA works in their wards, without any special training or authority.

Fourth, as mentioned earlier, the NREGA workforce in Himachal consists mainly of persons (including many elderly men and women) who are unable to get employment on the private labour market, possibly due to low productivity. Finally, even the relatively healthy and hardworking labourers may not be inclined to exert themselves when they work side by side with persons who work at a much slower pace. All this makes it quite difficult for the gram panchayats to ensure adequate 'progress'.

On the positive side, the daily-wage system allows a much greater variety of works to be taken up, as mentioned earlier. This offsets, to some extent at least, the losses involved due to low labour productivity on NREGA worksites.

Transparency Measures

Surprisingly, given the general culture of administrative transparency in Himachal, and the accessibility of NREGA records (discussed earlier), the survey points to a serious neglect of many transparency safeguards. For instance, at 10 out of 12 worksites, attendance was not recorded in muster rolls. Instead, the use of informal attendance book (*kaccha khata*) persists in most of the sample gram panchayats. Further, discrepancies were found (especially in Sirmaur) between the muster rolls and labourers' own statements about the number of days they had worked and the wages they had received.

Other measures intended to create transparency at the worksite were also neglected. Mandatory worksite boards (with details of amount sanctioned, implementing agency, wage rate, and related information) were found at only two out of the 12 sample worksites. Similarly, NREGA provides for the payment of wages in front of all the labourers in a public space. Payment details are supposed to be read out aloud, enabling labourers themselves to check the relevant information before signing the muster roll. At more than half of the sample worksites, however, this practice was not being followed. Instead, wage payments were made in an ad hoc fashion, sometimes at the residence of the labourers, at other times elsewhere. Due to the violation of many transparency safeguards, the system remained vulnerable to corruption. Indeed, a few clear instances of misappropriation came to light during the survey, notably in Minta gram panchayat (Kangra district).

Job Cards

Another aspect of the neglect of transparency safeguards in Himachal is the poor design and maintenance of job cards. The back page, where labourers' entitlements are supposed to be spelt out in simple language, is badly written and there is a pressing need for a clearer statement of the basic provisions of the Act (particularly those relating to work applications). An even more serious design flaw is the lack of a column to record wage payments. This defeats one of the main purposes of a job card, which is to enable labourers to verify their wage payment details and keep a written record of this information.

Turning to the maintenance aspect, in more than half of the sample gram panchayats, job cards were not with the labourers themselves. Some labourers even said that they had never seen their job cards, in spite of the fact that their job card numbers were recorded on the muster rolls. Even where labourers were in possession of their job cards, they were inadequately maintained in most cases, with only patchy entries.

SIRMAUR AND KANGRA: A BRIEF CONTRAST

The two survey districts (Kangra and Sirmaur) present a number of contrasts that help to understand the influence of local factors (cultural and administrative, among others) on the operation of

NREGA. As mentioned earlier, Sirmaur belonged to the first phase of implementation of the NREGA (which began on 2 February 2006), while the Act came into force in Kangra only in April 2007. Nevertheless, it is significant that on a number of criteria the programme is operating much better in Kangra than in Sirmaur.

For instance, while labourers' statements in Sirmaur corroborated only 47 per cent of the wage payments shown in the muster rolls, the corresponding figure in Kangra was 87 per cent. This percentage was even higher (98 per cent) in Kangra block, where the 'match' between muster rolls and labourers' statements was almost perfect. Similarly, the participation of women in NREGA was very low in Sirmaur, apparently due to rigid social norms in this regard. In Kangra, on the other hand, women are actively participating in NREGA, and this new employment opportunity appears to make a genuine contribution to their economic independence. Transparency measures were also better observed in Kangra district (there were even two cases where muster rolls were available at the worksite, an unusual achievement).

Within Kangra district, Kangra block was doing particularly well in these respects, and also in other ways, such as the prompt disbursal of wages. This was partly due to the efforts of a dynamic Block Development Officer (BDO), who took active interest in the programme, personally monitored the selection of works, and introduced a schedule of regular surprise inspections of NREGA works. At the time of the survey, payment of wages through bank accounts was being introduced, reinforcing other initiatives to prevent corruption.

In Rajgarh block of Sirmaur district, on the other hand, there were many reasons for concern about the functioning of NREGA, despite some success in initiating a large number of works (as many as 23 in one gram panchayat). In particular, as mentioned earlier, there were major discrepancies between labourers' testimonies and the payment details recorded in the muster rolls. These discrepancies were not necessarily associated with any embezzlement of NREGA funds. In some cases at least, 'adjustments' had been made in the muster rolls for other purposes. At one worksite, for instance, labourers confirmed being paid Rs 100 per day, even though Rs 75 had been entered in the muster rolls. The number of days of work had been correspondingly 'inflated'. This was a case where adjustments had been made to enable the implementing agency to pay more than the minimum wage, as labourers were not willing to work for less than Rs 100 a day. Officials suggested that such 'improvization' is not uncommon in Sirmaur. While these adjustments are perhaps not as serious as the straight embezzlement of NREGA funds (fairly common in other states), they do constitute serious irregularities.

Discussions with PRI representatives suggest that NREGA in Sirmaur has become an opportunity for gram panchayats to execute pending development works, independently of any influence they might have with local MLAs or MPs (political influence has become a prerequisite for getting any work sanctioned under other schemes). This helps to explain the relatively strong performance in terms of asset creation. However, another outcome of this enthusiasm about asset creation has been to relegate questions of employment generation to the background. At Thod-Niwar, a group of residents agreed to sign on the muster rolls without doing any work or taking any wages, so that machines could be hired to speed up the construction of a link road under NREGA. There was little demand for wage labour in this village, and the NREGA was viewed more as a source of funds for village development than as an employment opportunity. There was, thus, little opposition to this double violation of the Act, involving not only fake entries in the muster rolls but also the use of labour-displacing machines.

The contrast between Kangra and Sirmaur suggests that the success of the programme is not just a matter of time. A blind hope that problems are likely to dissolve over time would be misplaced. Fundamental problems such as the neglect of transparency measures require active intervention in the light of local conditions.

POSSIBLE ACTION POINTS

The survey findings suggest that there are, in many ways, outstanding opportunities in Himachal for effective implementation of the Act. They also show, however, that there is a long way to go in making adequate use of these opportunities. This section discusses a few possible steps in this direction.

Awareness Measures

Fresh awareness drives need to be launched in Himachal. Job cards can serve as an excellent means of communication for this purpose. A well-designed entitlements page would be particularly helpful, since literacy rates are relatively higher among NREGA workers in Himachal. Also useful would be a weekly '*rozgar divas*' (employment day) at the gram panchayat level, where discussions are held about NREGA in all its aspects, as recommended in the Operational Guidelines. This can be used as an occasion to demonstrate and practise the various procedures involved—work applications, complaint redressal, disbursement of wages, and so on. Worksites also present excellent opportunities for awareness generation activities. For instance, worksite supervisors (mates) could be trained to convey information about the Act to NREGA labourers or conduct regular group discussions.

More efforts also need to be put into the traditional means of awareness generation, such as wall writing, distribution of NREGA literature, radio or TV features, and so on. 'NREGA camps' could also be held for intensive awareness generation along with other activities such as collecting work applications and redressal of complaints.

Design and Maintenance of Job Cards

The last page of the job card in Himachal needs to be redesigned in lucid language, to explain the basic entitlements and procedures (possibly with pictorial aids). The last page should also contain phone numbers of concerned officials and helpline numbers. The employment record page of the job card should have a column to record the wages paid. All this should be done, at the very least, for the new job cards to be distributed in 'Phase-III' districts, but preferably also elsewhere, by replacing the old job cards with new job cards. While this operation may seem tedious and expensive, it is a small step that could go a long way, and could also be used to conduct a fresh round of much-needed awareness generation activities.

It is also important to fix responsibility for the maintenance of job cards, possibly on the *Gram Rozgar Sevak* (this could also be the joint responsibility of the Gram Rozgar Sevak and Panchayat Secretary). A clear message needs to reach all NREGA functionaries, to the effect that job cards are to be well maintained and should remain with labourers at all times.

Staffing

Under-staffing is one the most crippling problems affecting NREGA in Himachal. It is also widely cited as an excuse for non-compliance with the Act and the Operational Guidelines. General shortfalls of gram panchayat staff also need to be addressed. For instance, it is imperative for every gram panchayat to have its own Secretary, instead of giving charge of several gram panchayats to the same Secretary, as often happens in the present scheme of things. In addition, every gram panchayat should have a *Sahayak Sachiv* (Assistant Secretary) to assist the Secretary, and a Gram Rozgar Sevak dedicated to NREGA-related work.

There are also severe shortages of NREGA-related staff at the block level. In Himachal as in many other states, the role of the 'Programme Officer' has been added to other duties of the BDOs, instead of creating a separate full-time post as required under the Operational Guidelines. Aside from a dedicated, full-time Programme Officer (with rank similar to the BDO), each block should be adequately staffed with computer operators, accountants, and clerks. Other essential staff includes Junior Engineers and/or technical assistants—at least one for every cluster of five gram panchayats.

Piece-rate Work

As mentioned earlier, NREGA works in Himachal are currently based on the daily-wage system. The Act, on the other hand, allows for both daily-wage and piece-rate work. Ideally, there should be some flexibility to choose between the two, depending on the type of work and other local circumstances. This would involve putting in place the nuts and bolts of effective piece-rate work, including fair, accurate, regular, and transparent measurement.

Allowing and facilitating piece-rate work would lead to better work incentives and help to address the problem of low labour productivity in NREGA works, discussed earlier. While piece-rate work is often more demanding for labourers than daily-wage work *per unit of time*, it allows (or at least, should allow) them to go home as soon as they have completed the prescribed task. To put it another way, the piece rate system allows them to earn more per hour, if not per day. In this respect, NREGA workers have something to gain from the piece-rate system.

Bank Payments

Wherever banking services are available within a reasonable radius (say, 5 km from the centre of a gram panchayat), the possibility of paying NREGA wages through banks (or, possibly, post offices) should be explored. Indeed, if implemented with due caution, this innovation can be quite effective as a protection against the embezzlement of wage funds (the beginning of a transition to bank payments has already been made in Kangra block). However, it should not be seen as a magic cure against corruption. As recent field reports from Mayurbhanj (a pioneer of bank payments in Orissa) and other places suggest, the banking system is not beyond manipulation from contractors and other vested interests.[2] Thus, the use of bank payments does not obviate the need for strict enforcement of other transparency safeguards, such proactive disclosure of muster rolls, regular maintenance of job cards, and social audits. Attention also needs to be paid to various issues associated with bank payments, such as the user-friendliness of the system, the possible exclusion of women, and the danger of delays in bank transfers. Bank payments also require intensive awareness drives to familiarize recipients with the practices involved in regular visits to the bank. This should certainly be easier in Himachal than in, say, Orissa (where literacy rates are much lower). However, as the state of awareness about the NREGA itself demonstrates, there is no ground for complacency in this regard.

Equally important, there has to be a streamlining of processes and procedures on the part of the administration. For instance, decisions need to be taken about whether payments are to be dispensed through bearer cheques, account payee cheques, or letters of credit. Without careful preparation, both in terms of procedures and awareness, a sweeping switch from cash payments to bank payments could easily create more problems than it resolves.

Social Audits and Grievance Redressal

In Sirmaur, NREGA was in its second year at the time of the survey and there was no sign of the biannual social audits that are mandatory under the Act. This inertia derives in part from the absence of explicit orders in this regard. The Government of Himachal Pradesh should formulate social audit rules and promote the conduct of social audits according to the Rules.

[2] For further discussion, see Vanaik and Siddhartha (2008); also Drèze and Khera (2008b).

CONCLUSION

The story of NREGA in Himachal is, to a large extent, one of missed opportunities. In many ways, the state enjoys a favourable social environment as far as the implementation of NREGA is concerned: the workforce is highly literate, the institutions of local democracy are relatively active, there is a culture of careful record-keeping, and the administration has a demonstrated ability to implement complex programmes. Yet, there has been limited success so far in terms of translating these favourable conditions into real achievements. For instance, in spite of high literacy rates, awareness levels among NREGA workers remain very low. Similarly, in spite of high potential standards of record-keeping, the transparency safeguards (for example, maintenance of job cards) have been neglected.

This is not to say that NREGA in Himachal is a failure—far from it. In many respects, the standards of implementation of the programme are already higher in Himachal (especially in Kangra district) than in many other states. And where work is provided, it makes a big difference to the lives of the rural poor. But the scale of the programme, the quality of the works, and the procedural standards could be much higher.

These limited achievements seem to reflect the low political visibility of NREGA in Himachal. We noticed, for instance, that the Act was not much of an issue in the Assembly elections (these were held a few days after the completion of the survey). One reason for this may be that, as things stand, NREGA reaches a relatively small proportion of the population, in just a few districts. This situation is likely to change as awareness levels rise, the demand for work increases, and the Act is extended to the whole state. It is not too late to make good use of the vast opportunities associated with NREGA in Himachal.

APPENDIX 11.1 SUMMARY OF KEY FINDINGS

Positive Achievements

1. The state administration and local institutions have a demonstrated ability to implement complex programmes such as NREGA.
2. Block officials and gram panchayats readily disclose information, including the muster rolls, and are developing a culture of transparency.
3. Gram panchayats have been activated around the implementation of NREGA works and are showing keen interest in the programme.
4. PRIs are actively involved in the planning process. For instance, NREGA is being discussed in the gram sabhas and gram panchayats have useful shelves of projects.
5. The programme is highly appreciated by NREGA workers.
6. NREGA makes an important contribution to women's economic independence and empowerment, in areas where they are participating in significant numbers.
7. Minimum wages are paid, and there are no major delays in wage payments.
8. In the sample gram panchayats, contractors have been kept out, with some exceptions (mainly in road works).
9. In Kangra district, there was no discrepancy between the muster rolls and workers' statements, except in Minta gram panchayat. (In Sirmaur, however, there were irregularities in muster roll maintenance.)
10. Pioneer blocks such as Kangra, and pioneer gram panchayats such as Bagli, show that major achievements are possible when the concerned authorities take active interest in NREGA.

Areas of Concern

1. People's awareness of NREGA, and of their entitlements under the Act, is still very low.
2. The scale of employment generation was quite limited in the sample gram panchayats.
3. Job cards are poorly designed (for example, no column for wage payments, no helpline numbers, and the 'entitlements' page is poorly written) and the distribution of job cards is incomplete.

4. The work application process is not in place.
5. There is inadequate technical support for planning and measurement of NREGA works.
6. There are no trained mates and worksite management is quite poor.
7. Labour productivity on NREGA works is quite low.
8. Essential worksite facilities such as first-aid kits are lacking in most cases.
9. Many transparency safeguards are not implemented. For instance, job cards are not being maintained, worksite boards are often missing, and 'dual records' are being kept at many worksites.
10. The scale and quality of NREGA is being held up by shortages of essential staff, including Panchayat Secretaries, Gram Rozgar Sevaks, Junior Engineers, technical staff, and trained mates.

Appendix 11.2 Evidence from the Field Survey

	Himachal (%)	Orissa (%)	Assessment (with reference to Himachal Pradesh)
Proportion of sample worksites where 'few' or 'none' of the labourers were aware of:			
NREGA being in force	0	31	
Right to apply for work	100	100	Awareness levels are low.
Right to unemployment allowance	92	90	
Right to minimum wage	17	55	
Mandatory worksite facilities	100	93	
Did most labourers at this worksite get employed in response to an application for work?			
Yes	44	7	The application process is not in place.
No	56	93	
Proportion of sample worksites where wages had been paid within 15 days	82	41	Wages are paid on time, in most cases.
Proportion of worksites where:			
'All' or 'most' labourers earned the minimum wage	82	48	Minimum wages are paid, in most cases.
'Very few' or 'none' of the labourers earned the minimum wage	18	41	
Proportion of worksites that had:			
Drinking water	42	39	
First-aid kit	0	7	Mandatory worksite facilities are absent.
Child care facility	0	3	

Proportion of sample worksites:			
With an information board	16	59	Transparency safeguards have been neglected.
Where muster rolls were available on site	18	n.a.	
With a vigilance committee	33	56	
Proportion of worksites where evidence of contractor involvement was found	10	56	Contractors have gone.
Economic usefulness of the work, in the assessment of survey team:			
'Very useful' or 'quite useful'	91	59	Most NREGA works are useful.
'Not particularly useful'	0	37	
'Useless'	9	4	
Proportion of sample gram panchayats that had a shelf of projects	100	46	There is a good potential for participatory planning.
Proportion of sample worksites that were selected from a shelf of projects	91	30	

Note: The Himachal survey was conducted in 12 worksites of Kangra and Sirmaur districts. The small size of the sample should be borne in mind while reading the table. To put these figures in perspective, the table also presents the findings of a similar survey conducted in three districts of Orissa (Bolangir, Boudh, and Kalahandi) in October 2007; for further details, see Chapter 10.

12

Dantewada

Guarantee Withdrawn*

Jean Drèze

INTRODUCTION

Studying the National Rural Employment Guarantee Act (NREGA) in conflict areas like Dantewada in south Chhattisgarh may seem like a pointless exercise. Much of this area is a virtual war zone, with little scope—it might seem—for any kind of constructive development work. It is hard to imagine the government organizing relief works in between burning people's villages, hunting Maoist sympathizers, harassing Adivasi women, and other depredations that have become a routine feature of its 'counter-insurgency operations' in Dantewada.[1]

However, it is just possible that NREGA could help to alter the situation, or to repair the damage if and when the hostilities subside. For instance, when displaced people come back to their villages and attempt to rebuild their lives, NREGA could be an initial source of

* This chapter is based on a report prepared for the Central Employment Guarantee Council in September 2008. Thanks are due to Himanshu and Vanvasi Chetna Ashram for facilitating this investigation.

[1] For enlightening first-hand accounts of the situation, Bhatia (2008), Balagopal (2006), and Independent Citizens' Initiative (2006); on the general issue of 'development challenges in extremist affected areas', see the recent report prepared for the Planning Commission by an independent expert group (Planning Commission 2008).

sustenance as well as a means of reviving the local economy. On a more idealistic note perhaps, NREGA could also—in principle—help to build a new rapport between the state and the people in this area, based on constructive work. Considering the repressive character of the state in Dantewada, or for that matter in Chhattisgarh, there are no grounds for optimism in this regard. But the situation seemed exploring at least.

I visited Dantewada district as an individual member of the Central Employment Guarantee Council (CEGC) during 18–20 September 2008.[2] Since time was short, I focused mainly on one block: Bheramgarh, the largest block of the district, with 53 gram panchayats (out of a total of 408 gram panchayats in 'undivided' Dantewada).[3]

Bheramgarh block is effectively divided into two zones, one on each side of the Indravati river which flows through it. One side, where the small town of Bheramgarh is situated, has a functioning administration. But the other side, across the Indravati river, is under Maoist control and most government officials do not go there. Development programmes, public services, and welfare schemes in that area are non-functional, including NREGA. Gram panchayats are also likely to be non-functional in that area, as most of the *Sarpanch*s and *Sachiv*s have deserted it (they are not very popular with the Maoists, who tend to regard them as exploiters).

I conducted this investigation in collaboration with Bela Bhatia, who has done extensive fieldwork in this area and is familiar with local issues. In the short time available (three days), we visited various

[2] In this note, 'Dantewada' refers to the undivided district of Dantewada, including Bijapur, which was recently carved out of it to form a separate district. Even though Bijapur is now a separate district, there is a single zila panchayat for undivided Dantewada, as panchayat elections are yet to be held in Bijapur. Bheramgarh block, the main focus of this chapter, is situated in Bijapur district but is still within the jurisdiction of Dantewada zila panchayat.

[3] This individual visit was a substitute for a team visit of CEGC members, which had been planned for the same dates. Unfortunately, the state government of Chhattisgarh objected to that team visit, apparently on the grounds that elections were due relatively soon—a rather unconvincing excuse.

parts of Bheramgarh block, without any official escort, accompanied by two local volunteers from Vanvasi Chetna Ashram. Among the gram panchayats we visited were Bade Tungali, Bheramgarh, Gadamli, Nelasnar, and Patarpara. All these are situated outside the Maoist-controlled areas—these were out of reach in the absence of adequate preparation. We also spent half a day at the Salwa Judum 'relief camp' (*rahat shivir*) in Nelasnar gram panchayat, and held meetings with various government officials including the Chief Executive Officer (CEO) Bheramgarh, the Programme Officer Bheramgarh, the District Collector Bijapur, the CEO Dantewada, the Assistant Programme Coordinator Dantewada, the District Forest Officer Dantewada, and the Sachiv Gadamli gram panchayat.

This chapter discusses selected aspects of NREGA in Dantewada, as they emerged from this short visit. Unless stated otherwise, the observations below relate to Bheramgarh block. Needless to say, they should not be taken as representative of the general situation in Chhattisgarh. In fact, separate investigations in Surguja (north Chhattisgarh) revealed a more positive picture, with, for instance, a considerable amount of NREGA work being available in every gram panchayat.

ASPECTS OF NREGA IN DANTEWADA

Employment Guarantee in a 'Conflict Zone'

The people of Dantewada, including Bheramgarh block, are bearing the brunt of years of violent conflict. The main protagonists in the conflict are the Communist Party of India (Maoist), the Salwa Judum, and the security forces (including 'Special Police Officers' recruited among the local youth). The area is heavily militarized and there is a general atmosphere of insecurity and fear.

In this atmosphere, it is very difficult for development programmes and public services to thrive. To illustrate, the schooling system is in shambles. Occupation of school buildings by security forces is common—we noticed several cases within a few kilometres of the block headquarters in Bheramgarh. In response to this, many schools have been blown up by Maoist cadre, to pre-empt their occupation. In Gadamli gram panchayat, barely 3 km from the main road that links Bheramgarh with Bijapur, we saw the ruins of a school building and *anganwadi* that had been blown to shreds just a few months earlier—it was a heart-rending sight. According to the CEO Dantewada, more than 100 schools have been blown up in the district (however, this is an unconfirmed figure based on 'informal reports').

As one might expect, the implementation of NREGA in Dantewada has been severely affected by this conflict situation. In areas under Maoist control, the programme is non-functional. Even in other areas, there are widespread violations of workers' entitlements under the Act. As discussed later, however, the main issue is not that the conflict situation has made it impossible to enforce the provisions of the Act. More importantly, it seems to provide a convenient opportunity for the state to abdicate its responsibilities, and undermines people's ability to claim their rights.

Suspension of NREGA Works in the Rainy Season

NREGA works were at a standstill during our visit. According to the CEO Bheramgarh, not a single person was employed under NREGA at that time. In fact, a peculiar and unique feature of Chhattisgarh's Employment Guarantee Scheme (Clause 2.8.8) is that it explicitly 'suspends' the work guarantee during the rainy season—from 15 June to 15 October. This is a violation of the law: under NREGA, people have a legal entitlement to being employed within 15 days of applying, *throughout the year*. If it is not possible to provide work in some areas at that time, the unemployment allowance should be paid to those who apply for work. As far as Dantewada is concerned, rainy weather does not preclude certain types of work, such as plantation. On both counts, therefore, this restriction is unacceptable.

Abysmal Levels of Awareness

People's awareness of their rights under NREGA is often quite low, especially in remote areas with low literacy levels. For instance, in the survey discussed in Chapter 3 (conducted in 10 districts of north India in May–June 2008), barely half of the sample workers knew that they were entitled to 100 days of employment over the year. In Dantewada, however, awareness levels seemed to be even lower—in fact much lower. Most of the people we met *had never heard of NREGA*, and knew *nothing* about their entitlements under the Act. This is shocking, considering that the Act had been in force in this area for almost three years at the time of our visit. Awareness levels in Dantewada were so low that it is hard not to attribute them to an *intentional* attempt to 'keep people in the dark', so that they do not make inconvenient demands on the local administration or question the possible embezzlement of NREGA funds in the area.

There was little evidence of any serious awareness drives having been conducted. For instance, we did not find any trace of 'wall writing' anywhere, in contrast with other districts of Chhattisgarh such as Surguja, where wall-writing is visible in many gram panchayats. In Bheramgarh, we noticed a fair amount of wall-writing related to schooling and education, indicating that it is not impossible to conduct awareness campaigns of this kind.

Hoarding of Job Cards

Chhattisgarh has a relatively well-designed, state-wide job card, with a detailed 'entitlements page' on the back cover. Adequate distribution and regular maintenance of job cards would have been of great help in spreading awareness of NREGA as well as in checking corruption. However, this has been defeated by the large-scale 'hoarding' of job cards by Sachivs and others.

In fact, during these three days, we did not meet a *single person* who was in possession of his or her job card (except in the Nelasnar relief camp). It appeared that the hoarding of job cards on the part of Sachivs and others had become a systematic practice. This is a very serious irregularity, which greatly facilitates embezzlement of NREGA funds.

We also noticed that the distribution of job cards was incomplete. In Matla, a village of 42 households in Bade Tungali gram panchayat, *nobody* had a job card. Everywhere we went, we found evidence that many people had been deprived of a job card. It seemed that the cards had been distributed in a haphazard manner, with some getting a job card and others not, depending, for instance, on whether they happened to be around when the Sachiv turned up to initiate the distribution process. There were also signs of favouritism and arbitrariness in the distribution of the cards (for example, exclusion of hamlets that are seen to be sympathetic to the Maoists).

In short, the situation we observed with respect to job cards was as follows: (i) some people had never seen or heard of a job card; (ii) some people were aware that job cards had been distributed, but did not have one; (iii) some people had a job card, but had surrendered it to the Sachiv or others; (iv) no one (except in Nelasnar relief camp) was in possession of his or her job card. All this put people in a position of extreme helplessness and dependence on the good will of the state for securing their entitlements—the exact opposite of the spirit of NREGA.

Staff Shortages

Shortage of NREGA-related staff is a major issue in Dantewada. To some extent, this is a manifestation of the general problem of NREGA staff shortages across the country, including Chhattisgarh. However, this problem seems particularly acute in Dantewada, due to it being a conflict zone where government officials are reluctant to be posted. According to the District Collector Bijapur, half of the posts of Junior Engineer in Bijapur are vacant (those who get posted there promptly try to 'organize' their transfer to other places).

According to the CEO Dantewada, the zila panchayat has only 11 technical staff appointed, out of 46 posts sanctioned at the sub-engineer level. Similarly, only 83 *Gram Rozgar Sevaks* are in place, against a requirement of at least 408 (one per gram panchayat). There are also shortages of other staff such as accountants and even Programme Officers—three Blocks of Dantewada had no Programme Officer at that time.

Bank Payments: Need for Caution

In mid-2008, the Central Government issued sweeping orders for an immediate 'switch' to bank (or post office) payments of NREGA wages throughout the country, including Dantewada. This was done against the advice of several members of the Central Employment Guarantee Council, who had argued that the transition to bank/post office payments, while commendable in principle, should be undertaken with great caution and adequate safeguards. For one thing, this is not a 'magic bullet' against embezzlement. It is very important to ensure that other transparency safeguards are also enforced, including some (such as wage payments in public and regular maintenance of job cards) that become harder to implement when wages are paid through banks or post offices. For another, attention needs to be paid to the convenience of the public and the reach of the banking system.[4] For instance, a rush to bank payments may not be advisable when people live far away from the nearest bank.

These qualifications are highly relevant in Dantewada. Indeed, the reach of the banking system in this area is quite limited (even outside the areas under Maoist control). According to the CEO Dantewada, there are no banking services beyond the block headquarters. Further, many villages are more than 40 km away from the block headquarters, and some are even 70 km away (this was corroborated by the records). The post office, for its part, refused to get involved in

[4] For further discussion of these issues, see Vanaik and Siddhartha (2008); also Chapter 6 in this volume.

the distribution of NREGA wages in this area, citing security reasons. Needless to say, people's familiarity with the banking system, and their ability to deal with it, are also likely to be very low in Dantewada. In this situation, enforcing an abrupt transition to bank payments could do more harm than good. At the very least, more time should be given in cases where the gram panchayat is beyond a given radius of the block headquarters, and special arrangements (such as mobile 'extension services') for these areas should be explored.

Neglect of Transparency Safeguards

While the Dantewada administration was bending over backwards to implement the mandatory bank payments, other transparency safeguards were sorely neglected. For instance, the systematic hoarding of job cards had defeated their role as a transparency safeguard (purposely so, in all likelihood). Worksite 'boards' were missing at some of the worksites we inspected. And when we asked people who had worked on NREGA whether they had signed a muster roll after being paid, most of them were unsure or confused, and some categorically said that they had not done it.

It was not possible, during this brief visit, to verify muster rolls or conduct other 'audit' activities. Quite likely, social audits would lead to interesting discoveries, including major irregularities in the use of NREGA funds in Dantewada.

Underpayment of Wages

Over three days, we met about a dozen persons who had actually been employed on NREGA works during the preceding 12 months. Most of them mentioned that they had been paid about Rs 60 per *godi* (the prescribed daily task). This is less than the statutory minimum wage of Rs 73 per day, of which none of them were aware. It looked like underpayment of wages had become a standard practice in the area.

There are also other, worse cases of failure to pay minimum wages within 15 days as prescribed under the Act. For instance, in Patarpara gram panchayat (under the work *Nistari Talab Nirman, Shivir Sthal Patarpara*), Kaushila said that about half of her wages were still due, months after the work was completed. Similarly, Channu Ursa of village Ponduru in the same gram panchayat, employed on the same work, stated that he had been promised Rs 60 per godi but paid only Rs 50 per godi. He also mentioned that he had worked without a job card and that he never signed a muster roll.

Quality of Works

In Nelasnar gram panchayat, we inspected four NREGA works, selected at random from the list of completed works. There were three approach roads on the list, and one *talab* (pond).

Work had been done in each case, suggesting that there were at least no 'ghost works' in the list. However, quality standards left much to be desired. Two of the three 'approach roads' were covered with bushes, to the extent that they had become almost indistinguishable from the surrounding jungle. Their location appeared to be faulty, and in the absence of regular traffic, they had reverted to the status of footpaths.

The third approach road in Nelasnar gram panchayat (from Nelasnar to Bangapal) had much potential value, and seemed to be in high demand from the local residents. Unfortunately, the construction of this road (more precisely, the laying of *morrum* or gravel) had been interrupted mid-way, apparently because a culvert was needed there, and no provision existed for it. According to the CEO Dantewada, this is a common problem: approach roads require culverts, and building of culverts under NREGA is hard to do within the mandatory 60:40 labour–material ratio. Dovetailing of NREGA with the Backward Regions Grant Fund (BRGF) has begun, but this may not go far enough. This is an important issue, as there is much scope for improved rural connectivity in Dantewada, and much potential for employment generation under this category of permissible NREGA works.

The fourth work inspected in Nelasnar was a pond (*Nistari Talab Nirman, Chhote Surokhi*). This pond seemed to be of good quality. It had been built on private land, probably under close supervision from the landowner (a local Adivasi). It was well located, with good potential as a source of irrigation, and 3 kg of fish seeds had already been released in the pond. This was a heartening sight, and a useful illustration of the possibility of doing good work under NREGA even in this troubled area.

Official Apathy

On 19 September, I met the District Collector Bijapur, L.S. Ken, and apprised him of some of the irregularities I had observed, such as the systematic hoarding of job cards and the neglect of transparency safeguards. He was extraordinarily cool about it. He openly admitted that this was the situation, and that implementing agencies were fudging the records. He seemed to accept this as the normal state of affairs, and was not planning to take any specific action to enforce the transparency safeguards.

Political Uses of NREGA

Though time was too short to probe this matter, we heard allegations of NREGA being used for political purposes in the area, and some of these allegations had a ring of truth. For instance, it was clear that NREGA had been used in 2006–7 to build facilities in and around the 'relief camps', while villages under Maoist influence were being sidelined. There were also allegations that NREGA funds had been siphoned off to support the illegal activities of the Salwa Judum. We were unable to probe these rumours, but they were certainly consistent with our limited observations, and quite plausible in the light of other investigations of the Salwa Judum's activities (often sponsored by the state).

NREGA in 'Maoist Areas'

According to NREGA data from the block office in Bheramgarh, NREGA works have been implemented in about 30 of the 53 gram panchayats located in this block. The remaining gram panchayats are situated in areas under Maoist control, mainly across the Indravati river. As mentioned earlier, government officials have stopped going to these areas, as have most Sarpanchs and Sachivs, bringing NREGA to a standstill. According to the District Collector Bijapur, implementing the Act in those areas would require 'permission' [sic] from the Maoist high command. Even with permission, it would be difficult to activate NREGA there, given the reluctance of government officials to move in those areas. The CEO Dantewada expressed his unwillingness to sanction NREGA works in areas where government officials (himself included) are not able to go and monitor the works. This includes not only areas under Maoist control but also some other areas, where gram panchayat functionaries (for example, Sarpanch and Sachiv) are willing to work but not other government officials.

In Maoist-controlled areas as elsewhere, people have a legal entitlement to work under NREGA. It is not clear how this entitlement can be protected in the present situation. Since the legal entitlement is to work within the block (and not necessarily within 5 km of residence, though that is the recommended pattern), one option would be to open relatively large works outside those areas, within the block. However, this may not be adequate, as many of those living in areas under Maoist control reside quite far from these potential sites, and may also be reluctant to go there at all, as from their point of view, it is the government-controlled area that is 'unsafe' (for example, they may be targeted as alleged Maoist sympathizers) and not the Maoist-controlled area. The only obvious alternative would be some sort of negotiated implementation of NREGA in Maoist-controlled areas, possibly, through the Forest Department, which continues to have a presence in some of these areas.

Potential Role of Forest Department

According to the District Forest Officer (DFO) Dantewada, the Forest Department is the only department that has an active presence in the Maoist-controlled areas. In those areas, there appears to be some 'accommodation' between the Forest Department and the Maoists. They never deal with each other directly, but the Forest Department 'negotiates' with the villagers, who are presumed to be in touch with the Maoist leadership. For instance, the Forest Department occasionally asks for 'permission' to initiate some works or activities, and local residents answer their requests after a few days (based, presumably, on consultations with the Maoist cadre). The Forest Department is never allowed to construct roads in those areas, or to initiate activities that might attract outsiders. But some activities are permitted, for example, purchase of minor forest produce (such as *imli* or *mahua*), plantation, and construction of ponds. The DFO stressed that the department had no 'enmity' with the people in those areas and tried to 'avoid conflict' (giving up, if necessary, any activities that might antagonize people). He also said that the Forest Department personnel were safe in those areas, though they had to 'move cautiously', always respecting the 'instructions' they get from local residents. This account suggests that the Forest Department has some sort of rapport with the residents of Maoist-controlled areas, and perhaps even—implicitly—with the Maoist leadership.

Since the Forest Department is already conducting some activities in those areas, and is one of the permissible 'implementing agencies' under the Act, it may be possible to implement NREGA in Maoist-controlled areas through the Forest Department. The DFO himself felt that this was feasible, and indeed, the Forest Department had already implemented some NREGA works in those areas, on a small scale (with the required 'permission'). There is a case for exploring this possible approach to the activation of NREGA in areas under Maoist control.[5]

[5] It should be mentioned, however, that in many of the other investigations of NREGA reported in this book, the Forest Department emerged as a particularly corrupt implementing agency.

CONCLUDING REMARKS

This brief investigation suggests that the implementation of NREGA has barely begun in Dantewada, three years after the Act came into force in the area. Large sums have been spent, but the Act is being implemented in much the same fashion as earlier 'schemes' such as the Sampoorna Grameen Rozgar Yojana (SGRY) and the National Food for Work Programme. People have no awareness of their entitlements, no idea as to how to enforce them, and no recourse in the event where these entitlements are violated. The basic administrative and technical structures required to make NREGA work are also missing.

Perhaps it is not surprising to find that NREGA is at a standstill in this conflict zone. What is less obvious is that the reason for this does not lie in any impossibility of implementing the Act in Dantewada. Quite likely, the programme could do wonders here as elsewhere, if it were a political priority. What is striking is that no attempt has even been made to activate NREGA. This is evident, for instance, in the absence of awareness drives, the incomplete distribution of job cards, and, last but not least, the fact that job cards have been hoarded.

Hoarding of job cards is typically associated with forging of muster rolls and embezzlement of NREGA funds. The Act is particularly vulnerable to fraud in Dantewada, where transparency safeguards are systematically ignored and public vigilance is stifled by fear and repression. It is reasonably safe to assume that large amounts of NREGA money have been diverted, and possibly used to fund the Salwa Judum's activities. Hopefully, time will tell.

13

Tamil Nadu

Slow and Steady…*

Reetika Khera and Karuna Muthiah

The National Rural Employment Guarantee Act (NREGA), enacted in 2005, has had a varied record so far. In many states, implementation has been lame (for example, Bihar and Gujarat) or marred by corruption (for example, Jharkhand and Uttar Pradesh), but some states, notably, Andhra Pradesh and Rajasthan, have raced ahead and are widely regarded as NREGA 'success stories'. Less well-known are Tamil Nadu's achievements in this regard. This essay, based on field visits to Viluppuram (in 2007 and 2008), Cuddalore (in 2008), and Dindigul (in March 2010), seeks to convey some of these achievements.

The scale of NREGA employment (average person-days per rural household) in Tamil Nadu has increased steadily between 2006–7 and 2009–10: from 9 to 42 days in the 'Phase-I' districts. In the initial years of implementation, the focus of the state government seems to have been on putting systems and staff in place. At the outset, it took innovative steps to prevent corruption. For instance, recognizing that the procurement of materials requires contractors, and that contractors are a major source of corruption, the state issued orders to implement only *kachha* works, that is, works with no material component. Similarly, while the Act allows line departments (such as the Forest Department) to implement NREGA works, in Tamil Nadu all NREGA funds are spent through gram panchayats.

* Originally published as 'Slow but Steady Success', *The Hindu Magazine*, 25 April 2010.

As gram panchayats are relatively accessible to NREGA workers, they tend to be more accountable than line departments. Further, the state has built a strict monitoring system for NREGA—one of the best in the country. This is combined with firm and swift action against those who are found guilty of fraud. Though this does not happen in each case, the demonstration effects of selective action are significant.

Two other achievements in Tamil Nadu deserve mention. First, women's participation in NREGA. The share of women in the NREGA workforce in Tamil Nadu has remained high (around 80 per cent) from the beginning and is the highest in the country. Women are also employed in sizeable numbers as NREGA staff at the gram panchayat and block level as worksite supervisors (*Makkal Nala Panniyalars*, or MNPs), data entry operators, and so on. Second, the involvement of gram panchayats in the implementation of NREGA is also noteworthy. The gram panchayat plays an active role in selecting NREGA works, monitoring implementation, and so on. Gram panchayats are well-equipped (with proper buildings, furniture, computers, stationery, and staff), which enables them to perform these roles. Regular and well-attended gram panchayat meetings indicate that gram panchayats are functional and lively. Here too, high participation of women is noticeable.

TIMELY AND CORRUPTION-FREE WAGE PAYMENTS

In Dindigul, our main focus was on whether wage payments were being made in a timely manner and whether there was any evidence of corruption. According to the Management Information System (MIS), Tamil Nadu is one of two states (along with Andhra Pradesh) where there are no significant delays in wage payments. This was indeed true, we found. None of the workers we spoke to had any complaints of delayed payment. Tamil Nadu has a weekly schedule to process wage payments. The work week ends with the submission of muster rolls on Thursday, and the engineer measures output on

Friday. Cheques are issued and encashed on Monday, and wages are paid on Tuesday. Payments are made in a public place and job cards are updated at this time. The weekly schedule is strictly adhered to. This is a significant achievement given that delays in wage payments have caused great hardship to NREGA workers in many other parts of the country.

In 2008, the Central Government ordered all wage payments to be made directly to workers' bank and post office accounts, as an anti-corruption measure. Payment of wages through banks and post offices ensures separation of the implementing agency from the payment agency, making corruption more difficult. Tamil Nadu is the only state that continues to make wage payments in cash, on the ground that it helps to avoid delays. To see if corruption was an issue, we verified entries in a sample of electronic job cards (downloaded from the NREGA website, www.nrega.nic.in). All muster rolls are entered on the MIS, and from there, each person's workdays and wages are automatically transferred to the 'electronic' job cards. It is, therefore, possible to use the electronic job card to verify whether any wage money has been embezzled. We verified 23 job cards (from three gram panchayats spread over two blocks) with the concerned workers. According to the official records, the labourers on these job cards had earned Rs 92,050 as wages. Of this, Rs 1,395 was not corroborated by the labourers, suggesting that only 1.5 per cent had been siphoned off.

This is consistent with other reports on Tamil Nadu's success in controlling corruption in NREGA works. The main reason why Tamil Nadu is able to check corruption, in spite of cash payments, is its effective monitoring system. Unlike in most other states, muster rolls are maintained at the worksites. Labourers sign the muster roll every day. This simple measure is important as it gives labourers a chance to verify the names on the muster roll on a daily basis. (In Dindigul, a District Collector who felt that thumbprints were being forged issued instructions for all those labourers to be taught how to sign in evening classes.) There are strict instructions on maintenance of muster rolls—the total number of male and female workers is entered below the name of the last labourer, so that no more can names be added, absent labourers have to be marked on the muster roll with a red-ink rubber stamp by 10 AM, and so on. By 10 AM, all MNPs report that day's attendance to the block, for immediate uploading on an internal government website. Once this is done, officials send out squads to carry out random checks to verify reported attendance. Many MNPs have been visited by such squads and are, therefore, careful about muster roll maintenance. Tamil Nadu's system of random checks presents an interesting alternative to Andhra Pradesh's system of institutionalized social audits, as it is less expensive.

This is not to say that there is no corruption: for instance, during a study in 10 gram panchayats of Cuddalore, one of us found massive corruption in one gram panchayat. Petty corruption also continues (for example, as mentioned earlier in the case of workers who use thumbprints). An easy way to reduce corruption further would be to make daily attendance public (through the website) so that everyone can monitor these worksites.

ALL IS NOT WELL

There were two main complaints in Dindigul: lack of work and the non-payment of minimum wages. Though the average person-days per year for the job cards we verified was 57 days, most labourers wanted more. Further, the daily wage earned ranged from Rs 70 to Rs 85 (the minimum wage in Tamil Nadu is Rs 100/day).

Speaking to one Panchayat *Thalaivar* (President), we learnt that there is no dearth of funds. Though the gram panchayat has money, it had only one MNP. Running more than one worksite simultaneously (or managing too many workers at one worksite) with only one MNP worried him, because it would mean poor supervision. If labour productivity fell to unacceptably low levels, he would get into trouble. One MNP, he said, can handle only up to 100 workers effectively. To deal with this constraint, the Thalaivars rotate work from one habitation to another. This allows them to give work for each habitation and keep the numbers under control. However, rotation of work across habitations creates a potential for caste-based discrimination in the allocation of work. This is because hamlets within a gram panchayat tend to be along caste lines. If there were more MNPs, the Thalaivar could provide more work, avoid rotation (which can be discriminatory), and also improve labour productivity.

There are at least two possible solutions. One is to link the appointment of MNPs to the size of the gram panchayat (population or number of habitations) in a realistic manner. Another possibility is to train 'mates' (worksite supervisors) to perform some functions of the MNP. For example, mates can be given the responsibility of maintaining muster rolls, marking out the task for each week, and reporting daily attendance to the MNP/block. The time of the MNPs thus freed up could be utilized to monitor mates, and one MNP could handle more than one worksite.

During our worksite visits, we felt that apart from increasing supervision, labour productivity could be improved by selecting works that labourers themselves perceive as being useful. When we raised the question of labour productivity at a check-dam where its usefulness seemed questionable, a female worker's prompt replied, 'You should see how nicely we made the pond before this one. It is full of water. Now it's hot, that's why we are working like this.' Perhaps the list of permissible works for gram panchayats to choose from could be expanded. For instance, land improvement (land levelling, farm ponds) on the lands of Dalit farmers could be added to the list. When NREGA works are undertaken on the private lands of farmers, landowners have a self interest in improving labour productivity.

Tamil Nadu's emergence as NREGA success story fits into a more general pattern of a relatively well-governed state with a strong commitment to social welfare. Most social welfare schemes (Integrated Child Development Services [ICDS], mid-day meals, public health, and so on) perform better there than in other parts of the country. For a researcher working mainly in the northern states (as one of us is), Tamil Nadu is heartening. The attention to detail (even, say, column widths in the design of muster rolls) is quite remarkable. The openness with which officials admit to faults in the system, crucial if one wants to make improvements, is refreshing. The sense of commitment and duty among government employees is palpable. Perhaps, this has been fostered by accountability mechanisms in the system as well as a more demanding public (for example, road-blocks to protest payment of very low wages, 'petition' writing, and the use of helplines are quite common). Either way, one thing is certain: there is a lot to learn from Tamil Nadu.

PART IV

TROUBLE SPOTS

14

Breaking the Nexus of Corruption*

Jean Drèze

Once upon a time, public employment programmes in rural India were safely in the hands of private contractors and their political masters, with a little help from corrupt bureaucrats. The game was roughly as follows. Private contractors were the direct recipients of 'work orders', and of the corresponding funds. They made money by submitting fudged muster rolls, with inflated employment and wage figures. A substantial part of the loot was recycled through the so-called 'PC' (percentage) system, whereby various functionaries received fixed percentages of the amounts released. The contractors also had to pay tribute to their political bosses, for whom these funds came handy during election campaigns. In return for this, the political masters helped them to get contracts and escape scrutiny. This is the sort of situation that led writer P. Sainath to say that 'everybody loves a good drought'—the peak season for rural employment programmes. Labourers, for their part, worked hard and earned a pittance.

RESTORING TRANSPARENCY

The National Rural Employment Guarantee Act (NREGA) was supposed to bring about a radical change in this state of affairs. Under NREGA, rural labourers have a legal entitlement not only to work

* This chapter is an updated version of two earlier articles: 'NREGA: Dismantling the Contractor Raj' (*The Hindu*, 20 November 2007) and 'Corruption in NREGA: Myths and Reality' (*The Hindu*, 22 January 2008), co-authored with Reetika Khera and Siddhartha.

on demand but also to minimum wages. To prevent corruption, a wide range of transparency safeguards have been built into the Act. For instance, muster rolls are supposed to be kept at the worksite, displayed at the Panchayat Bhawan, and read out in public at the time of wage payments (today, they are also posted on the internet). Employment and wage details also have to be entered on the labourers' 'job cards', to enable them to verify the records for themselves. Social audits are to be conducted regularly by the gram sabha.[1] Contractors are banned.

The effectiveness of these transparency safeguards is a matter of empirical investigation. On the one hand, there is considerable evidence that *if* the safeguards are implemented, they can go a long way in preventing the embezzlement of NREGA funds (at least in the wage component of the programme). On the other hand, the transparency safeguards are often neglected or even deliberately sabotaged. This is not surprising, since they are supposed to be enforced (or, at least, monitored) by the same corrupt machinery that benefits from leakages in the first place. As discussed in Chapter 18, transparency safeguards are incomplete without an independent system of grievance redressal, which is sorely lacking in NREGA as things stand.

In the early days of NREGA, claims were often made that the bulk of the funds failed to reach the poor. For instance, in January 2008, this impression was sought to be created by a section of the media, based on misleading accounts of a draft report of the Comptroller and Auditor General (CAG) on NREGA.[2] 'It's official: In poorest states, job funds don't reach the poor' is how *Indian Express* summarized the report in a front-page headline, in spite of the fact that the CAG report contained very little evidence on the extent of corruption in NREGA.

It is partly to arrive at a more objective assessment of the situation that a series of 'muster roll verification' exercises were conducted in

[1] Mandatory payment of NREGA wages through banks and post offices was introduced later on (in mid-2008) as a further safeguard; see Chapter 6.

[2] See Chapter 5.

2007–8 in different parts of the country by a group of researchers based at Allahabad University. The survey teams consisted of carefully-trained students from University of Delhi and elsewhere, working with local volunteers. The muster rolls were selected through random sampling and obtained just before the survey, leaving little scope for window-dressing. The investigators interviewed the labourers listed in a particular muster roll and asked them to confirm the details of days worked and wages earned.[3]

MUSTER ROLLS UNDER THE SCANNER

This series of verification exercises began during May–June 2007, in Chhattisgarh and Jharkhand, in areas where we had found large-scale corruption just two years earlier, under the National Food for Work Programme (NFFWP). For instance, in Surguja district of Chhattisgarh, there was virtually no check on the embezzlement of NFFWP funds at that time. The situation was so bad that we were constrained to describe NFFWP as a 'Loot for Work Programme' (*Times of India*, 2 July 2005).

Two years later, in the same district, we heard from a wide range of sources that the enactment of NREGA had led to a steep decline in the incidence of corruption. This was borne out by the muster roll verification exercises: in a random sample of nine works implemented by gram panchayats, we found that 95 per cent of the wages that had been paid according to the muster rolls had actually reached the labourers concerned. A similar exercise conducted in Koriya, the neighbouring district, led to similar estimates of 'leakages' in the labour component of NREGA—only 5 per cent or so.

In Jharkhand, detailed muster roll verification in five randomly-selected gram panchayats of Ranchi district suggested leakages

[3] The methodology of muster roll verification was developed in Rajasthan in the context of the right to information movement. Many of the transparency safeguards that were later incorporated in NREGA (or in the Operational Guidelines) emerged from this learning process.

of around 33 per cent. Clearly, this is totally unacceptable, but by Jharkhand's dismal standards, even this high figure suggested some improvement compared with earlier years, when it was not uncommon to find that entire muster rolls had been manufactured from top to bottom. There were also other signs of a gradual retreat of corruption in NREGA works, at least in Ranchi district.[4]

Next we went to Tamil Nadu to participate in a social audit of NREGA in Viluppuram district, conducted in July–August 2007. There we found much evidence of serious efforts to prevent corruption. For instance, the government of Tamil Nadu had initiated an imaginative system of muster roll maintenance, whereby each labourer has to enter her signature or thumbprint in the muster roll every day by way of marking attendance. This ensures not only that the muster roll is available for public scrutiny at the worksite, as required by the NREGA Guidelines, but also that large numbers of people actually see it every day. An impressive system of regular worksite inspections had also been put in place. In these and other ways, much progress had evidently been made towards eliminating corruption in NREGA. Unfortunately, it was not possible to quantify the leakages, as the Viluppuram social audit did not include systematic muster roll verification exercises.[5]

A brief follow-up visit to Andhra Pradesh, also in 2007, enabled us to observe further initiatives to prevent corruption in NREGA. For instance, the government of Andhra Pradesh had already taken

[4] It should be mentioned, however, that Ranchi district is not typical of Jharkhand in this respect. Follow-up investigations in other districts (including Deoghar, Giridih, Khunti, Latehar, and Palamau) unearthed a whole series of scams. It is only after the introduction of bank payments of NREGA wages that substantial progress began to show in Jharkhand. Even bank payments were initially subverted by corrupt middlemen in many areas, for example, by operating bank accounts on behalf of NREGA workers (Drèze and Khera 2008b) or simply by continuing with cash payments, against the law (Drèze and Herenj 2010).

[5] For further discussion of Tamil Nadu's experience, see Chapter 13. For a detailed report on the Villupuram social audit, see NREGA Watch Tamil Nadu (2007).

the bold step of paying all NREGA wages through post offices. This is an example of the 'separation of payment agencies from implementing agencies', which virtually removes any incentive the latter may have to fudge muster rolls, since the payments are beyond their reach.[6] In addition, Andhra Pradesh had put in place a system of institutionalized social audits, involving routine verification of NREGA records through participatory processes. Judging from our brief visit, and from the social audit reports, these safeguards are quite effective. While various forms of petty corruption (such as bribes being taken by postmasters) have emerged from the social audits, there is no evidence of the sort of large-scale fraud that plagued public works schemes in Andhra Pradesh just a few years ago.[7]

After these relatively upbeat discoveries, we had a rude shock in Orissa, where muster roll verification exercises were conducted in October 2007 for 30 randomly-selected worksites spread over three districts (Bolangir, Boudh, and Kalahandi). The findings pointed to a quiet sabotage of the transparency safeguards, aimed at perpetuating the traditional system of extortion in rural employment programmes (see Chapter 10). The extent of the loot was hard to estimate, given thc near unverifiability of the muster rolls, but the infamous PC system (alive and well in Bolangir and Kalahandi) provided some useful clues. According to fairly reliable sources, including several contractors, the PC system absorbed about 20–25 per cent of NREGA funds in the sample blocks. The 'profit' of the contractors, for its part, appeared to be of the order of 10–15 per cent. This suggests that 30–40 per cent of NREGA funds were siphoned off in this area. The silver lining is that even in this corruption-ridden region, there were indications of positive change (especially in Boudh district). As checks and

[6] See Chapter 6.

[7] Andhra Pradesh was notorious for large-scale fraud under the National Food for Work Programme (see, for example, Deshingkar et al. 2005). On the social audit process in Andhra Pradesh, see Aiyar and Samji (2009), Gopal (2009), Singh and Vukuturu (2008), and Aakella and Kidambi (2007a, 2007b).

balances were put in place, the system was becoming harder for vested interests to manipulate.

After this, it was refreshing (literally) to head for the hills of Himachal Pradesh in December 2007. A sharp contrast emerged there between the two survey districts—Kangra and Sirmaur. In Kangra, we found a remarkable culture of transparency in public records, including NREGA. The muster rolls and other NREGA records were usually available for public scrutiny at the gram panchayat office, often in computerized form. Further, with one major exception (Minta gram panchayat), there was an almost perfect match between the muster rolls and workers' testimonies. In Sirmaur, however, there was evidence of significant irregularities in the muster rolls. In some cases, 'adjustments' had been made (illegally) to augment the material component of the scheme, without any embezzlement of funds, but there were also cases where embezzlement was involved.

Finally, we returned to Rajasthan—the cradle of India's right to information movement—in February 2008, for a brief reconnaissance of Jhalawar district. Ten randomly-selected gram panchayats were surveyed in a single block—Manohar Thana. The findings consolidated earlier evidence of Rajasthan's pioneering achievements as far as imparting transparency in NREGA is concerned. Job cards were well maintained, and, what is more, workers understood the job card entries and monitored them. Muster rolls were generally available at the worksite, and again, elicited much public scrutiny. Verification of the 'last paid muster roll' at 10 randomly-selected worksites in the 10 sample gram panchayats suggested that leakages in the labour component of NREGA were relatively small: less than 5 per cent for these worksites. However, these achievements were threatened by growing official hostility to social audits initiated by citizens' organizations (and even to their involvement in the mandatory social audits conducted by the gram sabhas). This has been a contested terrain ever since.[8]

[8] See, for example, Roy and Dey (2010), Sivakumar (2010), and Subrahmaniam (2009a, 2009b).

RECENT DEVELOPMENTS

More extensive investigations are obviously required to consolidate these findings, but even small-scale surveys of this kind yield rich insights. Behind the diversity of these findings is one overarching lesson. Corruption can be eradicated from NREGA, and the way to do it is to enforce the transparency safeguards that are built into the Act and the Guidelines. Along with this, swift action needs to be taken whenever corruption is exposed.

In the debate that led to the enactment of NREGA, one of the main arguments against the Act was that it would just be money down the drain. Rajiv Gandhi's reported statement that only about 15 paise of every rupee spent on rural development programmes reach the poor was routinely cited in this context, or rather out of context.[9] While corruption has been a major hurdle for NREGA from the beginning, the evidence does not justify these fatalistic pronouncements.

Himanshu's (2010) recent analysis of National Sample Survey (NSS) data for 2007–8 sheds further light on the extent of corruption in NREGA. The author 'matches' NSS survey data on NREGA employment with official employment generation figures from the Ministry of Rural Development, and finds that about 70 per cent of the total person-days (and 74 per cent of the wage payments) officially generated by NREGA are reflected in the household survey. If anything, this is likely to be an underestimate, since NSS surveys are not particularly well designed to capture NREGA employment. As the author observes, 'even a 25% leakage in MGNREGA is cause for concern', yet the findings hardly vindicate 'the usual claim that only 15% of government money reaches the people'. These findings

[9] This figure is often presented as a semi-official 'estimate' of the extent of leakages in rural development programmes, but it was just a rhetorical statement. Further, this statement did not refer primarily to corruption; it was actually a comment on bureaucratic inefficiency and administrative costs. In that respect, NREGA is doing quite well—the administrative costs are below 6 per cent of the total expenditure.

should also be read in the light that the NSS survey *preceded* the transition to bank (or post office) payments of NREGA wages. [10]

There have been further developments in the last two years, both positive and negative. As far as transparency safeguards are concerned, a major development (in mid-2008) was the mandatory payment of NREGA wages through banks and post offices. The findings presented in Chapter 6 suggest that this is, in principle, a fairly effective safeguard, and that NREGA workers themselves often welcome payment through bank or post office accounts (except when they live far away from the nearest bank, which is of course a common situation).[11] Even in Jharkhand, a hotbed of crime and corruption, this approach has shown substantial results. On the other hand, the transition to bank payments has been associated with a growing problem of delays in wage payments, which is threatening to undermine the entire programme (see Chapter 6). Urgent action is required to address this problem and streamline the system of bank payments.

There are also new vulnerabilities. The ill-conceived drive to construct 'Rajiv Gandhi Bharat Nirman Seva Kendras' under NREGA threatens to become a backdoor entry for corrupt contractors (see Chapter 16). Transparency safeguards for material expenditure (as opposed to wage payments) are still at an early stage of development, and need much greater attention as corrupt elements increasingly target this component of NREGA. In Rajasthan, the trail-blazer in this field, there have been disquieting accounts of a revival of corruption in the run-up to the Assembly elections in 2008, and to

[10] However, a more recent analysis of NSS data by Clément Imbert and John Papp suggests somewhat higher NREGA leakages in 2007–8 (around 50 per cent)—see Chapter 19. Interestingly, the authors found an almost perfect match between official employment figures and NSS survey data in Andhra Pradesh, Himachal Pradesh, and Tamil Nadu, confirming the positive findings reported here for these states.

[11] Another important study, involving interviews with more than 1,500 NREGA workers across the entire state of Chhattisgarh, points in the same direction. The sample workers reported getting 41 days of NREGA work on average in the preceding 12 months, compared with 44 days according to the official records (Chaupal Sansthan 2010).

the gram panchayat elections in 2010, when NREGA funds became a tempting resource for election campaigns. Along with this, as mentioned earlier, there has been a backlash against social audits, led by corrupt *Sarpanch*s and other vested interests.

In short, the last few years have seen major gains in the battle against corruption in public works programme. There are significant prospects of extending these gains in other domains, such as the proposed National Food Security Act, or for that matter the entire field of rural governance. However, the battle is far from over, and even setbacks cannot be ruled out.

15

Wage Payments

Live without Pay?*

Reetika Khera

When the National Rural Employment Guarantee Act (NREGA) was enacted in 2005, it was celebrated as a 'people's Act. It was an Act that focused on labourers rights—to employment, minimum wages, and timely payments. Besides, the involvement of people's groups in its drafting, the transparency provisions therein, and so on, earned the NREGA this tag.

For over a year now, serious delays in the payment of NREGA wages have been recorded across the country. Apart from violating the law (the Act stipulates that wages be paid within 15 days of work being done), delays cause great hardship to NREGA labourers. When wages are delayed, they are forced to resort to lower-paid or exploitative employment, and even distress migration. The delays have diminished the interest of labourers in the Act, so much so that this people's Act faces the danger of those very people turning against the NREGA.

For instance, in May 2009, labourers in Khunti (Jharkhand), who had not been paid for up to six months, insisted on earlier dues being cleared before taking on more NREGA work. More recently, in February 2010, in Banswara (south Rajasthan), I noticed that the highway to Gujarat was dotted with migrant labourers. One of them

* Originally published as 'Wages of Delay', *Frontline*, 27 (10), 8–21 May 2010.

was Amro Jitra Garasiya (Satra Khuta panchayat), who had not been paid for afforestation work done exactly 12 months ago! Now, he said, he was not sure if he would be paid at all. He did not want to 'risk' NREGA work any more.

Such complaints—lack of work, delays in payments, and labourers turning against NREGA—have been pouring in from several states, including Chhattisgarh, Gujarat, Jharkhand, Madhya Pradesh, Rajasthan, Uttar Pradesh, and West Bengal. This essay is based on field visits to these states.

FALLOUT OF PAYMENTS THROUGH BANKS AND POST OFFICES?

What has caused these delays? In 2008, the Centre had directed that all NREGA wages be paid through banks and post offices. This move was motivated by the need to separate the implementing agency from the payment agency. This separation, it was hoped, would end the embezzlement of NREGA wages. The administration is quick to blame banks and post offices for the delays. Government officials often claim that they do their work in a timely manner, but that banks and post offices are unable to cope with the volume of payments.

It is true that the transition from cash to payments through accounts created a 'jam', as banks and post offices were overburdened with the opening of thousands of accounts in each branch. In the case of banks, that initial hurdle seems to have been largely overcome, though the opening of accounts remains incomplete. Where the account opening process is complete and banks are computerized, they are able to cope with NREGA payments reasonably efficiently. Generally, banks do not take more than 2–3 days to credit wages into the accounts of labourers after they receive the cheque from the administration.

The case of post offices is different. Take, for instance, Surguja district (Chhattisgarh) where they rely on post offices because there are hardly any rural banks. In one block, the post office had only one employee who was responsible for opening and operating thousands of NREGA accounts. All the work is done manually, as there are no computers. In addition, the post master complained that account opening formalities remained incomplete because he did not have enough passbooks (its supply had been delayed by the district for months)! Similar problems have been reported wherever post offices are being used for NREGA payments, including Rajasthan and Jharkhand.

SOURCES OF DELAYS

There are, however, several steps in the wage payment process. Once work is complete, muster rolls have to be submitted to the implementing agency. The next step is the measurement of work, since most states pay wages on the basis of work done, not on attendance alone ('daily wage'). After this, payment orders, listing the labourers and the wages due to them, are prepared. These payments have to be sanctioned by concerned officials (for example, Block Development Officer, Sarpanch, Junior Engineer). Then, the cheques and payment orders are sent to the bank or post office so that wages can be credited into the accounts of individual labourers. Delays are creeping in at some, or all, of those steps.

On tracking the payment process, one finds that there are several other sources of delays. Often the delay occurs *before* the cheques reach the bank/post office. After the payment orders have been generated, the signatures of the sanctioning authority take time. An important reason behind this foot-dragging is that the separation of the payment and implementing agency has made embezzling NREGA wages very difficult. Even if the implementing agency inflates measurements and attendance on muster rolls, they can no longer embezzle that money as it goes directly into the accounts of the labourers. In order to cheat, they would either have to collude with labourers, or illegally operate the labourers' bank accounts, or forcibly extract wages from labourers after they withdraw the money. This 'loss' seems to have affected the motivation of concerned officials. This is the *indirect* way in which payments through accounts has led to delays.

In the present system, where payments are made on the basis of measurements rather than attendance alone, the Junior Engineer exercises a lot of power. Attendance has to be reconciled with measurement before payments are processed. Though the law requires it, in many states, muster rolls are not maintained at the worksite. Notable exceptions are Andhra Pradesh, Rajasthan, and Tamil Nadu. In other states, the practice that has evolved is to maintain *kachha* attendance and measurement records, which are faired out later on official muster rolls, after the Junior Engineer approves informal measurements maintained by the worksite supervisors.

However, delays have also emerged in Rajasthan where strict enforcement of transparency measures had had a noticeable impact on reducing corruption, at least in the labour expenditure. If the loss of opportunities for embezzling wages were the only cause of delays, then bank payments would not have affected Rajasthan. Here, it seems that apart from post offices causing delays, another issue is the scale of employment. During the peak season, up to 2,000 workers are known to report for work. When all workers show up for payments at the bank or post office, even computerized banks find it hard to cope with the crowds.

'Flow of funds' is another important source of delays. This is especially true in states like Bihar, Jharkhand, and Karnataka. It is not clear whether this is due to poor planning by the district administration (for example, delaying demand for funds, low standards of record-keeping) and/or due to Centre–State politics, whereby funds are withheld or delayed by the Centre (for instance, incomplete reports being submitted by the state, frequent changes in the norms for release of funds). Recently in Bihar, I was told that funds are being transferred just before the close of the financial year. This shows up as a large opening balance and becomes an excuse for holding up further release.

Record-keeping requirements of the NREGA also put a strain on the system. After the muster rolls, the payment orders have to be generated. Many states do not use a printed format for the payment orders. NREGA staff, often already overstretched and untrained, prepare these formats manually (including, wasting their time drawing rows and columns) each week, slowing things down and also leading to errors. Ideally, this process should be computerized. At the very least printed formats should be provided.

Finally, it is worth mentioning that distance, though an *inconvenience*, has rarely been mentioned as the source of delay. Therefore, the ministry's technological solution of a 'business correspondent model' (whereby an intermediary will withdraw wages from the bank or post office and deliver wages at the doorsteps of the labourers) cannot go very far in dealing with delays. The use of the biometrics machine (used in Andhra Pradesh post offices) can help in cases where the volume is very high. However, wherever this model is introduced, adequate safeguards must be put in place to ensure that business correspondents do not demand an 'informal fee' from labourers in exchange for the service they provide.

WHAT CAN BE DONE ABOUT THESE DELAYS?

No significant delays have been reported in Andhra Pradesh and Tamil Nadu though the scale of NREGA employment is substantial. In Andhra Pradesh, computerization of the payment process has helped to ensure timely payments. One reason for timely payments in Tamil Nadu is that it continues to pay wages in cash in spite of the Central Government's order on payment through accounts. The state has done this as it was felt that the transition to payments through accounts would cause labourers a lot of inconvenience. What other lessons can we learn from these states?

Both states have streamlined the process of wage payments, by putting in place a weekly schedule. There is a deadline for each step in the payment process (submission of muster rolls, measurement, sanctioning of payments, disbursal of wages). This weekly schedule is accompanied with intensive monitoring, for example, MIS tracking of which step in the process has been delayed and setting up alerts to deal with them. Apart from this, both states have appointed additional staff, especially technical staff, to ensure timely measurement of NREGA works. Each person involved in the payment process seems to be aware of the schedule and faces pressure to meet deadlines. For instance, in Dindigul district (Tamil Nadu), the data entry operator in Shanarpatti block told me that if the NREGA website (www.nrega.nic.in) reports any delays in wage payments for Tamil Nadu, it had to be on account of a data entry error. 'In all of Tamil Nadu, wages are paid on Tuesdays,' he confidently declared. This suggests the need for a transparent system to track the payment process and to fix responsibility for delays at each step.

Going beyond Andhra Pradesh and Tamil Nadu, it is essential to go back to the basics, including the maintenance of muster rolls at the worksite and regular updating of job cards, so that labourers have official evidence of the dates on which work was done. The present 'dual record-keeping' system (whereby kachha records are faired out only after measurements are passed by the Junior Engineer), makes it vulnerable to delays and corruption.

Strict measures must be taken to ensure greater accountability of the implementing bodies towards labourers. There are provisions in the NREGA that can be activated. For instance, the penalty clause (NREGA Section 25) which allows for a fine of up to Rs 1,000 when any officer fails to do his/her duty should apply automatically in cases of delays that exceed 15 days. This measure would go a long way in ensuring the accountability of officials. In places where payments are being held up due to delays in measurement by the Junior Engineer, states could consider paying labourers on a daily wage basis (at least as a short-term measure until adequate staff is appointed).

Further, Schedule II of the NREGA mandates that labourers be compensated for delays in accordance with the provisions of the Payment of Wages Act, 1936. As far as we are aware, this has been used only once when 265 workers were paid Rs 2,000 as compensation in Khunti district, Jharkhand in May 2009. (There is some evidence that there has been some improvement in Khunti where wages are now paid within one month.)

Other longer-term measures would include upgrading post offices, increasing staff in rural post offices, providing stationery, and computerized facilities so that they are better equipped to deal with the workload.

For a government that believes that NREGA played an important role in its re-election in 2009, such delays cannot be ignored. Indeed, when Prime Minister Manmohan Singh and UPA Chairperson Sonia Gandhi spoke at this year's NREGA *sammelan* on 2 February, they noted that delays in payments presented one of the most serious challenges in the implementation of the Act. The Ministry of Rural Development should focus on the electoral promises made in the Congress manifesto where it 'pledges at least 100 days of work at a real wage of Rs 100 a day for everyone as an entitlement under the NREGA'. These two promises assume greater importance for labourers in a year of drought and spiralling food inflation. To the extent that the Congress is interested in cashing in on votes through the NREGA, this is where its efforts should be directed. The Ministry, however, seems to believe that measures such as prefixing 'Mahatma Gandhi' to the name of the Act and constructing '*Bharat Nirman Rajiv Gandhi Sewa Kendras*' under the NREGA, would consolidate its vote-catching potential. The disconnect between the Ministry's understanding regarding the priorities under NREGA and that of the labourers is likely to boomerang.

16

The Perils of Gandhigiri

Jean Drèze

The National Rural Employment Guarantee Act (NREGA) has been widely credited for the electoral victory of the Congress Party in the latest Lok Sabha elections. Much as I would like to believe this story, I am a little sceptical—not because I doubt the popularity of NREGA, but because I suspect that the Act is not particularly associated with the Congress Party (or the UPA government) in the minds of rural voters. A limited confirmation of this emerged from a recent mini-survey of 44 NREGA workers in Khunti district, Jharkhand. When they were asked which political party or coalition was responsible for the enactment of NREGA, a vast majority (77 per cent) were unable to answer. When they were asked which political leader, in their view, deserved most credit for the enactment of NREGA, and presented with a list of options including Sonia Gandhi and Manmohan Singh, again, most of the respondents (84 per cent) were unable to answer. A similar, larger poll conducted in rural areas of Gujarat, Madhya Pradesh, and Rajasthan by John Papp, a research scholar from Princeton University, led to similar results.

Perhaps it is to correct this incorrigible failure of the masses to give the Congress its due that the Ministry of Rural Development is doing its best to put the 'Gandhi' stamp on NREGA. About a year ago, the Act was renamed, with 'Mahatma Gandhi' as a prefix. It is possible, of course, that this was a genuine tribute to the Mahatma, rather than a surreptitious attempt to reclaim NREGA for the Congress Party. Be that as it may, the change of name led to a fair amount of confusion and chaos. Just when 'narega' (as it is known in the Hindi belt) had become a household name, helping the Act to become a matter of wide interest in rural areas, the government spoilt this achievement and forced the people to learn a new and incomprehensible acronym—'MGNREGA'. Sweeping orders were issued, making it mandatory to pepper all relevant terms and documents with the 'Mahatma Gandhi' prefix, and also to use the new NREGA logo inclusive of the Mahatma's photograph. Incidentally, the mandatory use of this logo on the job cards is a violation of the Central Government's earlier order (dated 12 February 2008), whereby 'no photograph, name or details of any person other than that of the registered adult members of the household to whom that Job Card belongs will be affixed or recorded in the Job Card'. It is no secret that the purpose of this earlier order was to prevent enterprising Chief Ministers and other political leaders from putting their own photograph on the job card and 'hijacking' NREGA. The Central Government is now doing exactly what it has been trying to prevent others from doing, in violation of its own order!

All this is perhaps of little consequence. But another, far more insidious development is taking place today—this time in the name of Rajiv Gandhi. For reasons best known to itself, the Ministry of Rural Development insists on top priority being given to the construction of *Bharat Nirman Rajiv Gandhi Seva Kendra*s (BNRGSKs) in the selection of NREGA works. The Kendras are supposed to be first-class premises for gram panchayat offices and NREGA functionaries, complete with IT facilities, toilets, and an amphitheatre for public meetings—a noble idea, no doubt, but potentially very disruptive for NREGA.

No efforts were spared, and all norms were violated, to thrust this new priority on the state governments. First, a dubious 'consultation process' was engineered (in July–August 2009), to claim that this idea had wide support, notably, from the Central Employment Council. Second, the Act was amended by stealth, on 11 November 2009, to add the construction of BNRGSKs to the list of permissible works. Third, the Central Government overstepped its mandate by insisting on priority being given to this particular item in the list of permissible works. Even states like Tamil Nadu, that already have well-built Panchayat Bhawans in most gram panchayats, are being asked to get on with the BNRGSK programme. Fourth, the Central Government suddenly declared that the ceiling of 40 per cent on the material component of NREGA expenditure would apply at the district level, rather than at the gram panchayat or block level. This would 'make room' for material-intensive construction activities, but only by depriving other works of material expenditure. Fifth, in another creative move, progress with the construction of BNRGSKs became a new 'conditionality' for the timely release of NREGA funds. Indeed, in a circular dated 31 May 2010, the Ministry linked the release of the second tranche of NREGA funds to provisions being made for BNRGSKs. In a follow-up letter dated 12 July 2010, the Ministry requested all the Principal Secretaries to furnish district-wise information on the progress of construction of BNRGSKs in their respective states within two days. This is an unprecedented interference with the prerogatives of the state governments and the Panchayati Raj Institutions under the Act.

Last but not least, the Central Government obviously decided to turn a blind eye to the re-entry of private contractors in NREGA. The involvement of private contractors is banned under the Act, and for good reasons—private contractors have an appalling record of corruption and exploitation in rural public works programmes. The gradual replacement of private contractors with Panchayati Raj Institutions as the main implementing agencies in NREGA was one of the major achievements of the last few years. This achievement is now being reversed: buildings like BNRGSKs (costing around Rs 10 lakh each) cannot be constructed without private contractors. And if private contractors are allowed in one component of the programme, how will they be kept out of other NREGA works?

The worst part of the BNRGSK programme, however, is that it reopens the door to unbridled corruption, just when a battery of transparency measures (including the mandatory payment of wages through bank accounts) had substantially reduced the levels of embezzlement. Preventing corruption in the material component of

NREGA is notoriously difficult, and the BNRGSK programme is likely to become a smooth conduit for siphoning off material expenditure on a large scale.

This is not to deny that better infrastructure, including well-designed Panchayat Bhawans, is needed in many gram panchayats. But NREGA is not an appropriate umbrella for this infrastructure programme. Other centrally sponsored schemes, such as the Backward Regions Grant Fund (BRGF) and Bharat Nirman, would be more appropriate. In fact, one way of containing the damage done so far would be to restrict the BNRGSK construction programme to BRGF districts, and to insist that the material component of this construction programme should be charged to BRGF.

The BNRGSK programme falls in a larger, disturbing pattern whereby the UPA-II government seems to be doing its best to ruin NREGA. Other examples include the non-payment of minimum wages, a resilient failure to speed up wage payments, the backlash against social audits, and the impending invasion of NREGA by inappropriate UID technology. As Aruna Roy and Nikhil Dey observe in the next chapter, NREGA is a remarkable example of 'the capacity of India's policymakers to turn a progressive piece of legislation upside down'.

I would like to think that, in the next Lok Sabha elections, rural workers will give due credit to whoever defends their rights under NREGA—whether it is the Congress Party, or other parties. Cosmetic attempts to claim credit where none is due are, at any rate, unlikely to work.

17

The Wages of Discontent*

Aruna Roy and Nikhil Dey

If anyone wants to study the capacity of India's policymakers to turn a progressive piece of legislation upside down, the wage policy under the Mahatma Gandhi National Rural Employment Guarantee Act (MGNREGA) is a good place to start. It has been used to blatantly violate and undermine the Minimum Wages Act, 1948—one of the few means of protection for India's vast and exploited unorganized sector. The right to minimum wages has been recognized as a fundamental right by the Supreme Court of India, which has held non-payment of minimum wages to be a violation of Article 23 and, therefore, declared it to be 'forced labour'.

In January 2009, the Ministry of Rural Development (MoRD) of the Government of India delinked MGNREGA wages from 'minimum wages' through a notification, under Section 6(1) of the MGNREGA. This fundamentally undermined the sanctity of the Minimum Wages Act for all workers in India. Questions of (un)constitutionality have been considered and ignored, responsibilities passed from one government to the other, and fiscal concerns invoked to override fundamental, human rights and issues of morality and ethics.

Perhaps, even the limited success of the MGNREGA was too unpalatable for the few people who have steadily cornered most of the resources for themselves since Independence. Entrenched vested interests are adept at using their power and skill to entangle any potential or real benefits to the poor in a web of bureaucratic subterfuge.

* Originally published as 'The Wages of Discontent', *The Hindu*, 22 October 2010.

The MGNREGA had proved its critics wrong in important ways. It had raised the earning capacity of the rural workforce. This happened without a budgetary emergency or fiscal collapse, as many economists had wildly predicted. In fact, the Act was seen as being responsible for shielding large parts of rural India from the ill-effects of the economic downturn. Even in places where the Act was not implemented very well, it had facilitated the capacity of workers to demand minimum wages from all employers, including feudal landlords and contractors. People asserted their right to work on an MGNREGA work site, rather than accept a lower wage. In fact, it is now clear that even more than the bogey of budgetary collapse, it is the impact on the availability of cheap labour that is the concern of the powers that influence policy.

An MoRD notification of 1 January 2009 capped MGNREGA wages at Rs 100, and froze minimum wages in states where it was higher than Rs 100 a day. The Government of India thus made it clear that it disregarded any responsibility to pay minimum wages. There had been disputes on the issue of minimum wages from the time of the drafting of the Act. Neo-liberal economists said there was a need for 'a minimum below the minimum'. One of the 'safety measures' that had been inserted by policymakers was the 'non-obstante' clause that asserted: 'Notwithstanding anything contained in the Minimum Wages Act 1948, the Central Government may, by notification, specify the wage rate for the purposes of this Act.' Officials in the MoRD took the view that this allowed them to fix any wage rate, and the state governments could pay what they could 'afford'.

In Rajasthan, the minimum actually functioned as a maximum, and now, even the maximum is below the 'minimum wage'. Supposedly, the humpty dumpty (non-obstante) clause would continue to protect the Minimum Wages Act. If all this sounds like complicated double-speak, it is. For instance, it allows the government to 'legally' justify the payment of Re 1 a day to 99 workers in Tonk district. In this world of deliberate make-believe, technical is above legal, and legal above constitutional.

The Supreme Court held in 1983 that:

> where a person provides labour or service to another for remuneration which is less than the minimum wage, the labour or service provided by him clearly falls within the meaning of the words 'forced labour' and attracts the condemnation of Article 23... if anything less than the minimum wage is paid to him, he can complain of violation of his fundamental right under Article 23 and ask the Court to direct payment of the minimum wage to him so that the breach of Article 23 may be abated.

The 1 January 2009 notification was discussed in the MoRD on 10 July 2009, and the Labour Department recorded its view thus: 'Minimum Wages Act, 1948 guarantees minimum wages to workers and there cannot be a wage rate less than the minimum wage rate in any circumstances.' This was simply ignored, with the financial adviser in the MoRD asserting that 'the wage rate notified under section 6(1) is independent of Minimum Wages Act 1948'.

Labour groups took the non-payment of minimum wages to the Andhra Pradesh High Court, which suspended the 1 January 2009 notification of the MoRD. The Andhra Pradesh government was ordered to pay the notified minimum wage of the state. The Central Government reviewed the matter in a meeting and decided to pass the burden on to the states. The Financial Adviser and the Additional Secretary stated: 'Our stand with the Andhra Pradesh Government should be that while the State Government is obliged to pay the minimum wages as notified by it, the GoI shall reimburse the amount to the extent permissible under Section 6(1) of MGNREGA.'

The states say that they do not have the money to pay, and believe they should be provided 100 per cent of the wage component by the Central government, as Section 22 (1) of the MGNREGA says, 'the Central government shall meet the cost of... (a) the amount required for payment of wages for unskilled manual work under the scheme...'. Since the Central Government refuses to pay beyond its notified wage rate, the states have passed the burden on to the workers. In Andhra Pradesh, as in Kerala, Bihar, Himachal Pradesh, Karnataka, Jharkhand, Chhattisgarh, and now Rajasthan, MGNREGA workers are being paid less than the minimum wage by the respective governments. The Andhra Pradesh government wrote to the MoRD on 12 August 2009, pointing out that the state and Central Governments 'face the risk of contempt of court', but this fell on deaf ears.

Additional Solicitor General Indira Jaising was unequivocal in providing her legal opinion to a wage committee set up by the Central Employment Guarantee Council on Section 6(1),: 'The non-obstante clause in sub section (1) of Section 6 by itself will not enable the Central Government to fix a wage rate at a rate lower than what is provided under the Minimum Wages Act. The payment of wage below minimum wage would amount to forced labour.' Based on this, the committee made an emergency recommendation that under no circumstances should the provisions of the Minimum Wages Act be overridden and that the notification under Section 6(1) of the Act should be withdrawn. The Ministry responded thus: 'This is not feasible. The wage rates fixed under Section 6 (1) of the Act are distinct from the minimum wages. The provisions of the Act have to be respected.' The MoRD, obviously, does not see the need to pay the same level of respect to the Minimum Wages Act, the High Courts, the Supreme Court, and the Constitution of India.

The irony is that the Minimum Wages Act is being snuffed out by a showpiece legislation that is purportedly designed to liberate people from poverty and exploitation. The wage policy of the MoRD is, consequently, crippling the twin objectives of the MGNREGA—to provide 100 days of work a year with non-exploitative wages.

To keep a drowning population's nose just above the water might be the government's concept of economic growth with a human(e) face. While the poor have to be subsumed by the financial crunch, the ineffective 'steel frame' continues to get its dearness allowance of 10 per cent for six months, without batting an eyelid.

This hypocrisy must end. The country has to make up its mind whether the gloss will justify injustice and inequality. The writing on the wall is clear—insensitivity and continual erosion of basic rights will lead to conflict and violence. Both MGNREGA and the Minimum Wages Act are 'minimum measures', where one needs to be used to strengthen the other.

At a time when claims are being made to the status of an economic superpower, the government has no moral or logical grounds to deny the obligation to the payment of minimum wages to the most deprived.

18

The Accountability Gap*

Jean Drèze

In a recent Budget Speech, the Finance Minister described the National Rural Employment Guarantee Act (NREGA) as a 'magnificent success'. There is a sense in which he is right. The fact that the Act is in place, and provides dignified employment at minimum wages to millions of rural workers every year, is a success of sorts. However, as a statement about the status of implementation of NREGA, the Hon'ble Minister's statement is bound to sound a trifle heroic to anyone who is familiar with the situation on the ground.

In a series of field surveys spread over a dozen states during the last three years, we have observed routine violations of the entitlements of NREGA workers, whether it is their entitlement to work on demand, or to minimum wages, or to payment within 15 days, or to basic worksite facilities. This state of affairs reflects the absence of any grievance redressal system worth the name. This defeats the very purpose of the Act, which is to give people enforceable entitlements.

The Employment Guarantee Act includes many provisions for grievance redressal. However, these provisions have been quietly ignored or sidelined. A few illustrations may help.

One of the key accountability mechanisms in the Act is the unemployment allowance: if someone is not employed within 15 days of applying, he or she is entitled to an unemployment allowance. However, with a few exceptions, the state governments have resist-

* Originally published as 'Act Fair, Give Rural Workers their Due', *The Times of India*, 12 July 2009.

ed this tooth and nail. A common stalling tactic is to reject work applications, or refuse to issue a receipt when someone applies. Without a receipt showing that they have demanded work, they cannot even apply for the unemployment allowance.

Another accountability provision is Section 25 of NREGA, whereby anyone who fails to perform his or her duty under the Act is liable to a fine of up to Rs 1,000. Recent experience shows that even relatively small fines can be of great help in keeping government officials on their toes. When a fine of Rs 1,000 was slapped on the Block Development Officer (BDO) of Karon block in Jharkhand two years ago, he spared no effort to find an escape route. So did the BDO of Manika block (also in Jharkhand), a year later. Thus, wider use of Section 25 could make a big difference—unfortunately, no state government, other than that of Jharkhand, has used it so far.

There is also a provision, under Schedule II Section 30 of NREGA, for compensating workers for delays in wage payments. If wages are not paid within the stipulated limit of 15 days, workers are entitled to compensation under the Payment of Wages Act. But this, again, has never happened, except in one isolated instance (in Khunti district, Jharkhand). Meanwhile, delays in wage payments appear to be getting worse, causing immense hardship to NREGA workers. What greater injustice can there be than to extract hard labour from undernourished women and men and then fail to pay them for months on end?

State governments bear the primary responsibility for putting in place grievance redressal systems. Under Section 19 of NREGA, they are bound to formulate Grievance Redressal Rules for 'dealing with any complaint by any person'. To my knowledge, no state government has done that so far. Interesting ideas have been floated, such as the appointment of Ombudsmen at the district level, but they are yet to see the light of day.

At the national level, the Central Employment Guarantee Council was supposed to be an active, independent watchdog for NREGA. It has a broad mandate and wide powers under the Act. Unfortunately, the Council is not doing its job, nor has it been enabled to do it.

Further, the government seems to consider the Council as a purely advisory body, and to treat it like most advisory bodies—taking on board whatever advice turns out to be convenient and ignoring the rest. A telling example of disregard for the Council's advice was the 'freezing' of NREGA wages in January 2009, against the unanimous advice of Council members. As it happens, this notification has recently been suspended by the High Court of Andhra Pradesh.

These are just some examples of the 'dormant' provisions and institutions that could be activated to restore accountability in NREGA. The real question is—will the Central and state governments have the courage to make themselves accountable to the people?

19

Estimating Leakages in India's Employment Guarantee

Clément Imbert and John Papp[#]

INTRODUCTION

We compare the administrative data on the implementation of the National Rural Employment Guarantee Act (NREGA) with estimates of public works employment from India's National Sample Survey (NSS). A widely held concern is that the administrative employment records are inflated by corrupt officials and, therefore, do not reflect the true employment provided. By comparing the administrative data with independent household survey data, we provide an estimate of the fraction of officially reported days that are actually worked.

The employment estimates from the survey data are between 42 per cent and 56 per cent of the employment reported in the administrative data. These numbers are similar in magnitude though generally lower than existing estimates. In particular, using a similar approach, Himanshu (2010) estimates that 70 per cent of the reported days are independently confirmed by the NSS data. Bhalla (2010) estimates the number to be 50 per cent for an earlier time period.

[#] We are grateful to Amita Sharma (Joint Secretary, Ministry of Rural Development) and to Ashutosh Gupta and Ritesh Saxena (Ministry of Rural Development) for sharing the Monthly Progress Report data.

We describe later how estimates based on similar data lead to different results and emphasize the tentative nature of estimates based on the NSS data. In particular, our estimates are based on 2007–8 since that is the reference period for the most recent available NSS data set. Much has changed since then, and the figures reported are likely only a rough approximation of the current extent of over-reporting. For example, as explained in Chapter 6, the introduction of wage payments through banks around mid-2008 is likely to have reduced it.

DATA

Our data come from two sources. The administrative data are taken from the Monthly Progress Reports (MPRs) available for each district on the NREGA website.[1] These figures reflect the person-days that are reported by each state to the Central Government for disbursement of funds, including any inflation of person-days due to corruption. Our analysis uses the MPR data from July 2007 to June 2008.

We compare the administrative data to household survey data from the NSS—an all-India employment survey which collects detailed information about activities performed by all persons in each sample household during the last seven days. In particular, the NSS records how many days each person worked in public works. Most of the analysis will use the 64th Round of the employment survey, which was conducted from July 2007 through June 2008. We will also use the 61st Round, which was conducted from July 2004 to June 2005 for one of our estimates.

The NSS survey methodology minimizes the risk of recall bias, since respondents are asked about their activities in the last seven days. Systematic under-reporting is also unlikely, because for each day at least one activity must be recorded, and respondents are allowed to report up to two activities on a given day.

[1] The official NREGA website address is http://nrega.nic.in.

A full discussion of the NSS survey methodology is provided in the survey reports.[2] The NSS surveys a random sample of households stratified at the district, sector, sub-round level, where sector is either rural or urban and sub-round is a period of three months. Using the survey weights described in National Sample Survey Office (2010), we are able to construct estimates of the number of person-days worked in public works in rural areas.

We restrict the state-level analysis to the 20 largest states by population. Together, these states account for 98.5 per cent of India's rural population. The total sample size for the 64th Round is 262,396 adults aged 14 years or older from 79,045 households. Although this is a relatively large sample by survey standards, it is still small enough that sampling error is a concern especially for the state-level results presented later.

METHODOLOGY

Our analysis covers the period July 2007 to June 2008, since it is the only year for which we have both NSS and MPR data. We use the NSS data to construct estimates of person-days worked in public works:

$$NSS = n_p^m \hat{X}_m + n_p^f \hat{X}_f$$

where n_p^m and n_p^f are the number of rural males and females, respectively, based on census projections, and $\hat{X}_m$ and $\hat{X}_f$ are the per capita estimates of public works using the NSS survey data for males and females surveyed in rural India.

We present two primary estimates using the NSS data which differ only in how we estimate the per capita days worked in public works $\hat{X}_m$ and $\hat{X}_f$.[3] Our first estimate is based on whether the per-

[2] See, for example, NSSO (2010).

[3] All per capita estimates are constructed using survey sampling weights as described in NSSO (2010).

son reports working in any type of public works. This estimate is a natural upper bound for total NREGA employment as it includes non-NREGA public works. Our second estimate is obtained by computing the increase in public works from 2004–5 (just before the introduction of NREGA) to 2007–8. This estimate assumes that non-NREGA public works did not change between 2004–5 and 2007–8. We take this estimate as a lower bound for total NREGA employment since the NREGA most likely crowds out existing public works.

The 2007–8 NSS employment survey introduces a specific category of public works labeled NREGA public works. We also present estimates based only on persons who report work in NREGA public works. This estimate will be biased downwards if some people who were provided work under the NREGA mis-report their activity as generic non-NREGA public works. Such mis-reporting is a serious concern as, at that time, the NREGA had been active for less than a year in most districts of India and awareness levels were likely to have been low. Confirming these concerns, the estimates based on NREGA public works are significantly lower than the estimates computed using the change in public works from 2004–5 to 2007–8.

We compare the estimates based on the NSS survey data with the person-days reported in the MPRs. In comparing the results, we compute both the ratio of the NSS to MPR estimates as well as the MPR estimates less the NSS estimates. The ratio provides an estimate of the fraction of official days of work that are independently reported as being worked by survey respondents. This number gauges the proportional leakage for each state. However, we are also interested in the absolute amount of over-reporting. For example, we may be more concerned about a state that reports 100,000 person-days but only provides 50,000 compared with a state that reports 2,000 person-days but only provides 1,000. For this reason, we also present the simple difference between the MPR and NSS estimates.

RESULTS

The last row of Table 19.1 shows the two estimates of person-days generated from the NSS data as well as the MPR data at the national level. From July 2007 to June 2008, the government disbursed funds for 1.84 billion person-days.[4] Based on the estimates from the NSS survey, respondents reported working 1.02 billion person-days (56 per cent of the official figure) in public works (NREGA and non-NREGA). If we compare the 2007–8 to the 2004–5 survey, the increase in person-days spent in public works is 777 million (42 per cent of the official figure).

We further disaggregate our results by state, as shown in Table 19.1. There is significant variation across states in terms of person-days generated by the NREGA. The state-level variation corresponds well with the on-the-ground evidence presented in earlier chapters of this book. Some states have performed exceptionally well: in Andhra Pradesh, Himachal Pradesh, and Tamil Nadu, the MPR and NSS match each other almost exactly. In Rajasthan, 76 per cent of the MPR figures are reflected in NSS data according to the higher bound estimate. For this state, the lower bound estimate is artificially driven down by the discontinuation of non-NREGA relief works between 2004–5 and 2007–8.

Together with Andhra Pradesh and Rajasthan, the states of Madhya Pradesh and Chhattisgarh lead in terms of employment generated both using MPR and NSS figures. According to our estimates, in Madhya Pradesh, between 58 per cent and 64 per cent of the officially reported work show up in the NSS survey data, which is higher than the national average. For Chhattisgarh, proportional leakages are close to the average, with 38–55 per cent of administrative records matched by survey data. Still, in both states the absolute amount of over-reporting is substantial: 117 to 137 million person-days were over-reported in Madhya Pradesh and 68 to 92 million in Chhattisgarh.

[4] Our estimates are not directly comparable to the figures reported in Chapter 2 since we use the period from July 2007 through June 2008 rather than April 2007 through March 2008 and since we also include 'phase three' districts where the NREGA was started in April 2008.

Table 19.1 Matching NREGA Employment Estimates: NSS vs MPR (July 2007 to June 2008)

State	NSS-1	NSS-2	MPR	MPR − NSS-1	MPR − NSS-2	NSS-1/MPR	NSS-2/MPR
Andhra Pradesh	290,464,268	284,131,135	291,935,000	1,470,732	7,803,865	0.99	0.97
Assam	8,121,708	7,904,764	57,192,000	49,070,292	49,287,236	0.14	0.14
Bihar	35,940,273	29,918,327	116,419,000	80,478,728	86,500,673	0.31	0.26
Chhattisgarh	81,070,298	56,966,488	148,591,001	67,520,703	91,624,513	0.55	0.38
Gujarat	0	−4,346,844	8,584,000	8,584,000	12,930,844	–	–
Haryana	6,397,936	6,397,936	4,273,000	−2,124,936	−2,124,936	1.50	1.50
Himachal Pradesh	12,159,935	7,520,130	11,798,000	−361,935	4,277,870	1.03	0.64
Jammu & Kashmir	1,563,504	−16,559,034	3,590,500	2,026,996	20,149,534	0.44	–
Jharkhand	12,693,080	10,101,779	87,074,000	74,380,920	76,972,221	0.15	0.12
Karnataka	39,437	−1,099,974	22,554,000	22,514,563	23,653,974	0.00	–
Kerala	4,622,487	3,780,207	6,699,000	2,076,513	2,918,793	0.69	0.56
Madhya Pradesh	209,425,542	188,962,467	326,343,999	116,918,457	137,381,532	0.64	0.58
Maharashtra	4,614,372	−14,176,488	27,254,000	22,639,628	41,430,488	0.17	–
Orissa	24,427,873	13,476,005	44,080,000	19,652,127	30,603,995	0.55	0.31
Punjab	2,145,844	2,145,844	2,144,000	−1,844	−1,844	1.00	1.00
Rajasthan	136,562,872	28,971,840	180,468,000	43,905,128	151,496,160	0.76	0.16

State	NSS-1	NSS-2	MPR	MPR − NSS-1	MPR − NSS-2	NSS-1/MPR	NSS-2/MPR
Tamil Nadu	64,255,929	64,255,929	63,061,000	−1,194,929	−1,194,929	1.02	1.02
Uttar Pradesh	63,246,208	56,384,342	136,967,000	73,720,792	80,582,658	0.46	0.41
Uttarakhand	10,698,427	9,544,703	41,155,000	30,456,573	31,610,297	0.26	0.23
West Bengal	37,701,374	29,761,131	102,207,999	64,506,625	72,446,868	0.37	0.29
All-India	**1,023,032,696**	**776,892,063**	**1,840,875,000**	**817,842,304**	**1,063,982,937**	**0.56**	**0.42**

Notes:

1. Estimates are from 64th and 61st Rounds of the NSS Employment and Unemployment Survey. All estimates are adjusted using survey sampling weights.
2. The All-India estimates are greater than the sum of the state estimates since they include all states in India while state-level estimates are computed only for the largest 20.
3. NSS-1 is an estimate of the total number of person-days worked in any type of public works based on NSS surveys.
4. NSS-2 is an estimate of the change in the total number of person-days worked in any type of public works between 2004–5 and 2007–8.
5. MPR is the total number of person-days worked according to the NREGA administrative data (see the text for more details).

On the other hand, some states exhibit large numbers in the official data with very little employment reported in the NSS data. Jharkhand and, to a lesser extent, Bihar have substantial employment based on the MPR data but relatively little employment reported in the survey data. Our results reveal below average performance in Orissa, Uttarakhand, and Uttar Pradesh as well. Finally, some states have seen a fall in public works employment between 2004–5 and 2007–8, yielding a negative estimate for NSS-2. The fall is sharpest in Maharashtra, which had its own employment guarantee programme prior to 2004–5 and took little interest in NREGA in the initial years (see Chapter 2).

In closing, we emphasize that the employment numbers constructed using NSS survey responses are only estimates of the true person-days worked. The true employment generated will be different due not only to possible mis-reporting but also due to sampling error. This is especially relevant for the state-level estimates. For example, the estimate of zero days for Gujarat does not imply that no public works were provided.

ALTERNATIVE ESTIMATES

We are not the first to provide estimates of the degree of employment inflation in the NREGA administrative data. Table 19.2 presents some of the previous estimates using the NSS and MPR data alongside the results presented here. We will briefly discuss these studies.

One could compare the NSS data from July 2007 to June 2008 with the administrative data for the NREGA fiscal year from April 2007 to March 2008. This method is followed by Himanshu (2010). The drawback of this approach is that the NSS and administrative years do not correspond to the same time period. Since employment provided by the NREGA has increased each year, employment from the MPR is higher for the NSS survey year than the NREGA fiscal year. As a result, this approach will tend to overestimate the fraction of days confirmed by the NSS survey data.

Table 19.2 Ratio of NSS Employment Estimates to MPR Employment

Article	Administrative source	Survey source	Survey question	Estimate (%)
Himanshu 2010	MPR, financial year 2007–8	NSS survey 64th Round (July 2007 to June 2008)	Person-days in public works in the last 7 days	70
Bhalla 2010	MPR, financial year 2006–7	NSS survey 63rd Round (July 2006 to June 2007)	Person-days in public works in the last 12 months	51
Present paper: upper bound	MPR, July 2007 to June 2008	NSS survey 64th Round (July 2007 to June 2008)	Person-days in public works in the last 7 days	56
Present paper: lower bound		NSS survey 64th (2007–8) and 61st (2004–5) Rounds		42
Present paper: alternative estimate		NSS survey 64th Round (July 2007 to June 2008)		34

Bhalla (2010) compares the July 2006 to June 2007 NSS survey data with the April 2006 to March 2007 administrative data and finds that the survey estimates are 51 per cent of the administrative numbers. The key difference between this estimate and the others is that the 2006–7 NSS survey asked about work performed in the past 365 days rather than the past 7 days. If respondents are unable to recall all person-days worked in the past year, this estimate is likely to be biased downwards. However, for the same reasons outlined earlier, the estimate may be biased upwards.

Finally, the last row of Table 19.2 presents estimates using public works explicitly categorized as NREGA by respondents. The estimate of 34 per cent is substantially below even the lower bound estimate based on the change in public works.[5]

FINAL REMARKS

Our estimates suggest that roughly half of the person-days reported by the government are independently confirmed by household survey responses. While the leakages in 2007–8 are high, the aggregate estimates mask considerable heterogeneity across states. The results confirm the state patterns presented in this volume that corruption is much less of a concern in the four high-performing states of Andhra Pradesh, Himachal Pradesh, Tamil Nadu, and Rajasthan. For the first three of these four states, MPR and NSS data match each other almost exactly, suggesting negligible leakages—a significant achievement. As discussed earlier, these estimates likely provide only a rough guide to the current extent of over-reporting. The upcoming release of the 2009–10 NSS data, as well as the possibility of a nationally representative survey focused solely on the NREGA are both reasons to be hopeful that we will soon have more reliable estimates of employment generated by the NREGA.

[5] Inflation of NREGA wages may also be a concern, but cannot be easily assessed using NSS data, because at the time of the survey, it is likely that workers have not yet received payment for work performed during the past seven days.

Bibliography

Aakella, K.V. and S. Kidambi (2007a) 'Social Audits in Andhra Pradesh: A Process in Evolution', *Economic and Political Weekly*, 24 November, 42 (47): 18–19.

——— (2007b) 'Challenging Corruption with Social Audits', *Economic and Political Weekly*, 3 February, 42 (5): 345–7.

Abhay (2006) 'Status of National Rural Employment Guarantee Scheme in Raichur, Karnataka. Satyagraha on 14–15 August 2007 at Raichur, Karnataka for NREGS'.

Acharya, Shankar (2004a) 'Bad Ideas Are Winning', *Business Standard*, 28 December.

——— 'Guaranteeing Jobs or a Fiscal Crisis?', *Business Standard*, 30 November.

——— (2005) 'Populism Rides Again', *Business Standard*, 27 December.

Aiyar, Swaminathan S. Anklesaria (2004) 'Poverty Reduction by Helicopter', *Times of India*, 19 December.

Aiyar, Y. and S. Samji (2006) 'Improving the Effectiveness of National Rural Employment Guarantee Act', *Economic and Political Weekly*, 28 January, 41 (4): 320–6.

——— (2009) 'Transparency and Accountability in NREGA: A Case Study of Andhra Pradesh', Working Paper, Accountability Initiative, Centre for Policy Research, New Delhi.

Ambasta, P., P.S. Vijay Shankar, and M. Shah (2008) 'Two Years of NREGA: The Road Ahead', *Economic and Political Weekly*, 23 February, 43 (8): 41–50.

Asha Parivar (2006) 'Findings of Social Audit of NREGS in Bharawan and Sandila Blocks of Hardoi District in U.P. during 25th November–2nd December'.

——— (2007) 'Findings of Social Audit of NREGA in Behendar Block of Hardoi District'.

Bagchee, Aruna (2005) 'Political and Administrative Realities of the EGS', *Economic and Political Weekly*, 15 October, 40 (43): 4531–7.

Balagopal, K. (2006) 'Chhattisgarh: Physiognomy of Violence', *Economic and Political Weekly*, 3 June, 41 (22): 2183–6.

Banerjee, A. and P. Bardhan (2004) 'Food for Thought', *Hindustan Times*, 15 December.

Banerjee, K. and P. Saha (2010) 'The NREGA, the Maoists and the Development Woes of Indian State', *Economic and Political Weekly*, 10 July, 45 (28): 42–8.

Barret, B.C., S. Holden, and D.C. Clay (2002) 'Can Food-for-Work Programme Reduce Vulnerability?', Discussion Paper 2002/24, World Institute for Development Economics Research, Helsinki.

Benbabbaali, Dalel (2009) 'Implementation of the National Rural Employment Guarantee Act in a Tribal State: Meghalaya', mimeo.

Besley, T. and S. Coate (1992) 'Workfare vs Welfare: Incentive Arguments for Work Requirements in Poverty Alleviation Programmes', *American Economic Review*, 82 (1): 249–61.

Bhaduri, Amit (2005) *Development with Dignity: A Case for Full Employment*. New Delhi: National Book Trust.

Bhalla, Sheila (2005) 'India's Rural Economy: Issues and Evidence', Institute of Human Development, New Delhi.

Bhalla, Surjit S. (2004a) 'Corruption with a Human Face', *Business Standard*, 11 December.

——— (2004b) 'Ten Lies and an Act: I', *Business Standard*, 25 December.

——— (2005) 'Ten Lies and an Act: III', *Business Standard*, 8 January.

——— (2011) 'Does NREGA Really Work?', *Business Standard*, 27 March.

Bhargava, Rajeev (2006) 'Indian Democracy and Well-Being: Employment as a Right', *Public Culture*, 18 (3): 445–51.

Bhatia, Bela (2008) 'Salwa Judum: Internal War as Counter-Insurgency', mimeo, National Institute of Rural Development; also partly reprinted in Bhatia, B. (2008) *Aspects of the Naxalite Movement in India*, report to the Indian Council of Social Science Research.

Bhatia, Bela and Jean Drèze (2006) 'Employment Guarantee in Jharkhand: Ground Realities', *Economic and Political Weekly*, 22 July, 49 (23): 3198–202.

Bhatia, Kartika (2009) 'NREGA: A Guarantee against Migration?', mimeo, G.B. Pant Social Science Institute, Allahabad.

Bhatty, Kiran (2006a) 'Employment Guarantee and Child Rights', *Economic and Political Weekly*, 20 May, 41 (20): 1965–7.

——— (2006b) 'Social Equality and Development: Himachal Pradesh and Its Wider Significance', PhD thesis submitted to the London School of Economics.

——— (2008) 'Falling Through the Cracks', *The Hindu, Sunday Magazine*, 16 March.

Bisht, Arvind Singh (2006) 'Rural Employment: No Guarantee Yet', *Times of India,* 19 February.

Breman, Jan (1996) *Footloose Labour: Working in India's Informal Economy*, Contemporary South Asia Series. Cambridge: Cambridge University Press.

——— (2003) *The Labouring Poor in India: Patterns of Exploitation, Subordination and Exclusion.* New Delhi: Oxford University Press.

Burra, Neera (2006) 'NREGA—A Stock Taking', New Delhi.

Centre for Budget and Governance Accountability (2006) 'Draft Report on Implementation of NREGA in Andhra Pradesh, Chhattisgarh, Jharkhand and Madhya Pradesh', Report. New Delhi: Centre for Budget and Governance Accountability.

Centre for Planning, Monitoring and Evaluation (2008) 'Evaluation of Implementation of NREGS in Orissa', Social Audit Report. Hyderabad: National Institute for Rural Development.

Centre for Science and Environment (CSE) (2008a) *NREGA: Opportunities and Challenges*. New Delhi: CSE.

——— (2008b) *An Ecological Act: A Backgrounder to the National Employment Guarantee Scheme.* New Delhi: CSE. Available at http://www.world-governance.org/IMG/pdf_572_-_NREGA_Briefing_CSE.pdf, accessed on 1 February 2011.

Chakraborty, Pinaki (2007) 'Implementation of the National Rural Employment Guarantee Act in India: Spatial Dimensions and Fiscal Implementation', Working Paper No. 55, NIPFPF and The Levy Economics Institute, July 2007.

Chakraborty, P., C.B. Rao, D.K. Srivastava, and S.K. Sanyal (2007) 'Rural Poverty in Madhya Pradesh: Looking Beyond Conventional Measures', *Economic and Political Weekly*, 3 February, 42 (5): 381–8.

Chari, Anurekha (2006) 'Guaranteed Employment and Gender Construction: Women's Mobilisation in Maharashtra', *Economic and Political Weekly*, 16 December, 41 (50): 5141–8.

Chary, Venkat R. (2005) 'REGS: Grossly Miscalculated?', *Hindu Business Line*, 9 September.

Chathukulam, J. and K. Gireesan (2007) 'Impact Assessment of NREGS in Kerala: Evaluation of Systems and Processes', mimeo, Centre for Rural Management, Kerala.

Chaupal Sansthan (2010) 'Study of Implementation of MGNREGA in Chhattisgarh', mimeo, Chaupal Gramin Vikas Prashikshan Evam Shodh Sansthan, Ambikapur.

Chen, Martha (1989) 'Women's Work in Indian Agriculture by Agro-ecologic Zones: Meeting Needs of Landless and Land-Poor Women', *Economic and Political Weekly*, 28 October, 24 (43): WS79–89.

Cherian, Thomas (2005) 'Adding Jobs but at What Cost?', *International Herald Tribune*, 14 September.

Chikermane, Gautam (2008) 'It is not Worth CAG's while to Look at Rs 100 Telephone Bills or Rs 200 Staff Car Bills', *Indian Express*, 13 February.

Chopra, Deepta (2010) 'National Rural Employment Guarantee Act, India: Towards an Understanding of Policy Spaces', PhD thesis, University of Cambridge.

Citizen's Initiative for the Rights of Children under Six (2006) *Focus on Children under Six*. New Delhi: Secretariat of the Right to Food Campaign. Available at www.righttofoodindia.org, accessed on 1 February 2011.

Comptroller and Auditor General (2007) 'Performance Audit of Implementation of National Rural Employment Guarantee Act, 2005 (NREGA)', draft report, New Delhi.

——— (2008) *Performance Audit of Implementation of National Rural Employment Guarantee Act (NREGA)*. Available at http://www.cag.gov.in/html/reports/civil/2008_PA11_nregacivil/contents.htm, accessed on 1 February 2011.

——— (n.d.) *Performance Auditing Guidelines—SAI India*. Available at http://cag.nic.in/html/peraudguid-regbod.htm, accessed on 1 February 2011.

Dandekar, Kumudini (1983) *Employment Guarantee Scheme—An Employment Opportunity for Women*. Pune: Gokhale Institute of Politics and Economics.

Das, Upasak (2009a) 'NREGA: Can It be Sustained in India?', mimeo, Indira Gandhi Institute for Development Research, Mumbai.

——— 'Three and a Half Years of NREGA: A Journey through Some Parts of Jalpaiguri District', mimeo, Indira Gandhi Institute for Development Research, Mumbai.

Das, Vidhya and Pramod Pradhan (2007) 'Illusions of Change', *Economic and Political Weekly*, 11 August, 42 (32): 3283–7.

Dasgupta, Swapan (2005) 'Rename REGA as Corruption Guarantee Scheme', *Pioneer*, 14 August.

——— (2008) 'Flawed Job Scheme', *Times of India*, 10 February.

Datar, Chhaya (2007) 'Failure of National Rural Employmnet Guarantee Scheme in Maharashtra', *Economic and Political Weekly*, 25 August, 42 (34): 3454–7.

Debroy, Bibek (2004a) 'The Rs. 208,000 Crore Puzzle', *Indian Express*, 23 October.

——— (2004b) 'Jobs, Not the Government's Job', *Indian Express*, 13 October.

Deshingkar, P., C. Johnson, and J. Farrington (2005) 'State Transfers to the Poor and Back: The Case of the Food for Work Program in India', *World Development*, 33 (4): 575–91.

Dey, N., J. Drèze, and R. Khera (2006) *Employment Guarantee Act: A Primer*. New Delhi: National Book Trust.

Dey, N., J. Drèze, and A. Roy (2008) 'Finish the Job', *Hindustan Times*, 31 January.

Dey, N. and A. Roy (2009) 'Dalits, Poor and the NREGA', *The Hindu*, 27 August.

Dey, S. and A.S. Bedi (2010) 'The National Rural Employment Guarantee Scheme in Birbhum', *Economic and Political Weekly*, 9 October, 45 (41): 19–25.

Dhuru, Arundhati (2007) 'National Rural Employment Guarantee Act and Mid Day Meal Scheme Review of Uttar Pradesh', unpublished report, Movement for Right to Food and Employment, Uttar Pradesh.

Dhuru, A. and S. Pandey (2009) 'The Wages of Protest', *The Hindu*, 5 April.

Dogra, Bharat (2005) 'Rural Employment Guarantee Scheme: Rhetoric and Reality', *Economic and Political Weekly*, 30 April, 40 (18): 1809–10.

Drèze, Jean (2004a) 'Employment as Social Responsibility', *The Hindu*, 21 November.

——— (2004b) 'Unemployment Guarantee Bill', *The Hindu*, 31 December.

——— (2005a) 'Employment Guarantee and Its Discontents', *Times of India*, 12 August.

——— (2005b) 'Promise and Demise', *Yojana*, April.

——— (2006) 'India's National Employment Guarantee Inaction', *The Hindu*, 12 September.

——— (2007a) 'Dismantling the Contractor Raj', *The Hindu*, 20 November.

——— (2007b) 'India's Employment Guarantee Act: Reclaiming Policy Space', in A. Deshpande (ed.), *Globalization and Development*. New Delhi: Oxford University Press.

——— (2008a) 'Employment Guarantee: Beyond Propaganda', *The Hindu*, 11 January.

——— (2008b) 'NREGA: Ship without Rudder?', *The Hindu*, 19 July.

——— (2008c) 'NREGA in Dantewada', Report to the Central Employment Guarantee Council, September.

——— (2009a) 'Act Fair, Give Rural Workers Their Due', *Times of India*, 12 July.

——— (2009b) 'Employment Guarantee or Slave Labour?', *The Hindu*, 19 September.

——— (2010) 'Democracy and the Right to Work: India's Employment Guarantee Act', in N. Jayal and P.B. Mehta (eds), *Oxford Companion to Politics in India New Delhi*. New Delhi: Oxford University Press.

Drèze, Jean, with Kartika Bhatia and Reetika Khera (2009) 'Making NREGA Work', Report for the National Commission for Enterprises in the Unorganized Sector (NCEUS), New Delhi, April.

Drèze, J. and J. Herenj (2010) 'State of NREGA in Manika Block (Latehar): Summary Report', mimeo, Department of Economics, Allahabad University.

Drèze, J. and R. Khera (2008a) 'Uttar Pradesh: On the Move', *Hindustan*, March.

——— (2008b) 'From Accounts to Accountability', *The Hindu*, 6 December.

——— (2009) 'Lok Adalat or Joke Adalat?', *The Hindu*, 22 February.

Drèze, Jean, R. Khera, and Siddhartha (2008) 'Corruption in NREGA: Myths and Realities', *The Hindu*, 22 January.

Drèze, J. and S. Kidambi (2007) 'Long Road to Employment Guarantee', *The Hindu*, 2 August.

Drèze, J. and S. Lal (2007) 'Employment Guarantee: Unfinished Agenda', *The Hindu*, 13 July.

Drèze, J. and C. Oldiges (2007) 'Commendable Act', *Frontline*, 27 July.

——— (2009) 'Work in Progress', *Frontline*, 14 February.

Drèze, J. and N. Sharma (1988) 'Palanpur: Population, Society and Economy', in Peter Lanjouw and Nicholas Stern (eds), *Economic Development in Palanpur over Five Decades*. Oxford: Clarendon Press.

Gaiha, R., V.S. Kulkarni, M. Pandey, and K. Imai (2009) 'National Rural Employment Guarantee Poverty and Prices in India', ASARC Working Paper, March.

Ganapathy, Nirmala (2005) 'Rural Employment Bill: World is Watching India', *Indian Express*, 1 September.

Ganesh-Kumar, A., Srijit Mishra, and Manoj Panda (2004) 'Employment Guarantee for Rural India', *Economic and Political Weekly*, 18 December, 39 (51): 5359–61.

Ghose, Sagarika (2008) 'The Idiocy of Urban Thinking', *Hindustan Times*, 14 February.

Ghosh, Jayati (2008) 'Far from Failure', *Frontline*, 2–15 February.

——— (2009) 'Equity and Inclusion through Public Expenditure: The Potential of the NREGS', paper presented at an international conference on NREGA convened by the Ministry of Rural Development, New Delhi. Available at http://www.macroscan.org/pol/jan09/pol290109NREGS.htm, accessed on 1 February 2011.

Gopal, K.S. (2005) 'Is the Euphoria Justified?', *Economic and Political Weekly*, 15 October, 40 (42): 4523–4.

——— (2009) 'NREGA Social Audits: Myths and Reality', *Economic and Political Weekly*, 17 January, 44 (3): 70–1.

Government of India (1992) *Towards Employment Guarantee*, Final Report of Department of Rural Development. New Delhi: Ministry of Agriculture.

——— (2006) *NREGA: Operational Guidelines 2006*. New Delhi: Ministry of Rural Development.

——— (2008) *NREGA Operational Guidelines*, third edition. New Delhi: Ministry of Rural Development. Also available at www.nrega.nic.in, accessed on 1 February 2011.

Gupta, Santanu (2006) 'Were District Choice for NFFWP Approriate', *Journal of Indian School of Political Economy*, Oct–Dec, pp. 641–8.

Harriss-White, Barbara (2003) 'India Working: Essays on Society and Economy', *Contemporary South Asia*. Cambridge: Cambridge University Press.

Herman, Edward S. and Noam Chomsky (1988) *Manufacturing Consent: The Political Economy of the Mass Media*. New York: Pantheon Books.

Herring, Ronald and Rex Edwards (1983) 'Guaranteeing Employment to the Rural Poor: Social Functions and Class Interests in the Employment Guarantee Scheme in Western India', *World Development*, 11 (7): 575–92.

Himanshu (2010) 'Five Heady Years of MGNREGA', *Livemint*, 31 August.

Hirway, Indira (2004a) 'Providing Employment Guarantee in India: Some Critical Issues', *Economic and Political Weekly*, 27 November, 39 (48): 5117–25.

——— (2004b) 'Employment Programmes for Protecting the Vulnerable Poor, Lessons from the Past Experiences in India', paper presented at a National Workshop on Protecting the Vulnerable Poor in India: The Role of Safety Nets, by World Food Programme at Delhi, 6–8 October.

——— (2006) 'Enhancing Livelihood Security through National Employment Guarantee Act: Towards Effective Operationalisation of the Act', Centre for Development Alternatives and Levy Economics Institute, Economics Working Paper No. 437.

——— (2008) 'Plan for Long Term', *The Indian Express*, 2 February.

Hirway, Indira and Piet Terhal (1994) *Towards Employment Guarantee in India: Indian and International Experiences in Rural Public Works Programme*. New Delhi: Sage Publications.

Imai, Katsushi (2003) 'The Employment Guarantee Scheme as a Social Safety Net—Poverty Dynamics and Poverty Alleviation', Economic Series Working Paper No. 149, Department of Economics, University of Oxford.

Independent Citizens' Initiative (ICI) (2006) *War in the Heart of India: An Enquiry into the Ground Situation in Dantewada District, Chhattisgarh*. New Delhi: ICI.

Institute of Applied Manpower Research (2009) *All India Report on Evaluation of NREGA: A Survey of Twenty Districts*. Delhi: Institute of Applied Manpower Resources.

Institute of Social Studies Trust (2006) *Women and the NREGA*. New Delhi: Institute of Social Studies Trust and International Labour Organization.

Iyer, Yamini (2007) 'A Happy Tale from Two States', *Indian Express*, 27 December.

Jacob, Arun and Varghese Richard (2006) 'Reasonable Beginning in Palakkad, Kerala', *Economic and Political Weekly*, 2 December, 41 (48): 4943–5.

Jadhav, Vishal (2006) 'Elite Politics and Maharashtra's Employment Guarantee Scheme', *Economic and Political Weekly*, 16 December, 41 (50): 5157–61.

Jain, Devaki (2005) 'Guaranteeing Employment: Immeasurable Benefits for Women', mimeo, Institute of Social Studies Trust, Bangalore.

Jain, Sonu (2005) 'Rich, Poor, All States are in Job Guarantee Net', *Indian Express*, 8 December.

Jain, Sunil (2005) 'Problems in Panchayati Paradise', *Business Standard*, 28 November.

——— (2007) 'Wages of Meddling?', *Business Standard*, 12 March.

Jandu, Navjyoti (2008) 'Employment Guarantee and Women's Empowerment in Rural India', mimeo, National Federation of Indian Women, New Delhi.

Jaswal, Anshuman and Paulomee Mistry (2007) 'Diwas Uge Ne Dadi Male, Work Guarantee Must be as Certain as the Rising of the Sun, Will NREGA Ensure Security Against Hunger? A Study–Summary Report, by Disha', Ahmedabad. Available at http://www.disha-india.org/Diwas%20Uge%20Ne%20Dadi%20Male.pdf, accessed on 1 February 2011.

Jha, Raghbendra, Raghav Gaiha, and Shylashri Shankar (2008) 'Reviewing the National Rural Employment Guarantee Programme', *Economic and Political Weekly*, 15 March, 43 (11): 44–8.

Johnson, Doug (2009a) 'Does NREGA Help the Rural Poor to Cope with Bad Weather?', Working Paper No. 32, Institute of Financial Management and Research, Centre for Microfinance, Chennai.

——— (2009b) 'How Do Caste, Gender and Party Affiliation of Locally Elected Leaders Affect Implementation of NREGA?', Working Paper No. 33, Institute of Financial Management and Research, Centre for Microfinance, Chennai.

Joseph, Shaji (2006) 'Power of the People: Political Mobilisation and Guaranteed Employment', *Economic and Political Weekly*, 16 December, 41 (50): 5146–9.

Kaboub, Fadhel (2007) 'Employment Guarantee Programs: A Survey of Theory and Policy Experiences', Working Paper No. 498, The Levy institute of Brad College.

Kannan, K.P. (2005) 'Linking Guarantee to Human Development', *Economic and Political Weekly*, 15 October, 40 (42): 4518–22.

Kar, Anirban (2009) 'Don't Bank on Them', *Business Standard*, 1 February.

Karat, Brinda (2005) 'Towards Implementing the Rural Employment Guarantee Act', *People's Democracy*, 16 October.

Kareemulla, K., K. Srinivas Reddy, C.A. Rama Rao, Shalander Kumar, and B. Venkateswarlu (2009) 'Soil and Water Conservation Works through National Rural Employment Gurantee Scheme (NREGS) in Andhra Pradesh—An Analysis of Livelihood Impact', *Agricultural Economics Research Review*, Vol. 22 (Conference No.), pp. 443–50.

Khera, Reetika (2005a) 'Maharashtra's Experience with the Employment Guarantee Scheme', mimeo, Centre for Development Economics, Delhi School of Economics, University of Delhi.

——— (2005b) 'Employment Guarantee in Maharashtra and India', UNDP report, Delhi.

——— (2006) 'Employment Guarantee and Migration', *The Hindu*, 17 June.

——— (2008) 'The Black Hole of NREGA Records in Orissa', *Yojana*, August.

——— (2011) 'The UID Project and Welfare Economics', *Economic and Political Weekly*, 26 February, 46 (9): 38–44.

Krishnaraj, M., D. Pandey, and K. Aruna (2004a) 'Does EGS Require Restructuring for Poverty Alleviation and Gender Equality?', *Economic and Political Weekly*, 17 April, 39 (16): 1597–604.

Krishnaraj, M., D. Pandey, and A. Kanchi (2004b) 'Does EGS Require Restructuring for Poverty Alleviation and Gender Equality?', *Economic and Political Weekly*, 24 April, 39 (17): 1741–7.

Krishnamurty, J. (2005) 'Employment Guarantee and Crisis Response', *Economic and Political Weekly*, 4 March, 41 (9): 789–90.

Kumar, Himanshu (2009) 'Who is the Problem, the CPI (Maoist) or the Indian State', *Economic and Political Weekly*, 21 November, 44 (7): 8–12.

Kumar, Rohit (2007) 'Seeds of Revolution @ 73', NREGANET, Knowledge Network for NREGA, Series 1, Ministry of Rural Development, Department of Rural Development, Government of India.

Kundu, Amitabh and Niranjan Sarangi (2005) 'Issue of Urban Exclusion', *Economic and Political Weekly*, 13 August, 43 (33): 3642–6.

Lakin, J. and N. Ravishankar (2006) 'Working for Votes: The Politics of Employment Guarantee in India', paper presented at the annual meeting of the American Political Science Association, Marriott, Loews Philadelphia, and the Pennsylvania Convention Center, Philadelphia, PA, 31 August.

Lakshman, Narayan (2009) 'NREGS a Boon for Agriculture in Delta Area', *The Hindu,* 31 August.

Lakshman, Nirmala (2006) 'Employment Guarantee—Signs of Transformation', *The Hindu*, 11 May.

Long, S. (2004) 'Guaranteed to Disappoint', *The Economist*, 29 December.

Louis, Prakash (2006) 'Birth Pangs in Bihar', *Economic and Political Weekly*, 2 December, 41 (48): 4946–7.

M S Swaminathan Research Foundation (2005) 'Recommendations for the Amendment of the Employment Guarantee Act', workshop on 'Gender Sensitivity of the Employment Guarantee Act', 28 January, M S Swaminathan Research Foundation, Chennai.

MacAuslan, I. (Forthcoming) 'How and Why are Anti-poverty Laws Made? The Passage of India's National Rural Employment Guarantee Act', IDS Working Paper, Institute of Development Studies, Brighton.

Mahapatra, R. (2011) 'Channels of Change', *Down to Earth*, 15 March Available at http://downtoearth.org.in/content/channels-change, accessed on 30 March 2011.

Mahapatra, R., N. Sakhuja, S. Das, and S. Singh (2008) 'The National Rural Employment Guarantee Act (NREGA): Opportunities and Challenges', CSE Policy Paper. Available at http://old.cseindia.org/programme/nrml/pdf/NREGA_Policy_Paper_2008.pdf, accessed on 1 February 2011.

Mahendra Dev, S. (1995) 'Alleviating Poverty and Maharashtra Employment Guarantee Scheme', *Economic and Political Weekly*, 14 October, 30 (41–2): 2663–76.

Mahendra Dev, S. (1996a) 'Experience of India's (Maharashtra) Employment Guarantee Scheme: Lessons for Development Policy', *Development Policy Review*, 14 (3): 227–54.

——— (1996b) 'Food Security: PDS vs EGS—A Tale of Two States', *Economic and Political Weekly*, 6 July, 31 (27): 1752–64.

——— (2000) 'Economic Liberalisation and Employment in South Asia', *Economic and Political Weekly*, 14 January, 35 (3): 135–46.

——— (2002) 'Bold Initiatives Needed on Agriculture and Rural Employment', *Economic and Political Weekly*, 23 March, 37 (12): 1088–91.

Mahendra Dev, S. and A. Ranade (2001) 'Employment Guarantee Scheme and Employment Security', in S. Mahendra Dev, Piyush Anthony, V. Gayathri, and R.P. Mamgain (eds), *Social and Economic Security in India*. New Delhi: Institute of Human Development.

Mathur, Lalit (2007) 'Employment Guarantee: Progress So Far', *Economic and Political Weekly*, 29 December, 42 (52): 17–20.

——— (2008) 'Transforming Rural India', *The Hindu*, 4 May.

——— (2009) 'Silent but Successful Initiative', *The Hindu*, 1 March.

Mazdoor Kisan Samiti (2007) 'Fact Finding Report on the Status of Implementation of Scheme under NREGA in Bengabad Block of Giridih District Jharkhand'.

Mehrotra, Santosh (2004) 'Job Laws Can Sharply Cut Poverty This Decade', *Economic and Politcal Weekly*, 18 December, 39 (51): 5657–8.

——— (2008) 'NREGA Two Years On: Where Do We Go From Here?', *Economic and Political Weekly*, 31 October, 43 (31): 27–35.

Mehta, A.K., S. Ghosh, and S. Gupta (2000) 'Monitoring of NREGA in Rajasthan: Analysis Based on Reports of Field Visits to Villages in Two Districts by National Level Monitors', Draft Report, MoRD.

Moore, M. and V. Jadhav (2004a) 'The Employment Guarantee Scheme in Comparative and Historical Perspective', mimeo, IDS, Brighton.

——— (2004b) 'The Politics and Bureaucratics of Rural Public Works: Maharashtra's Employment Guarantee Scheme', *Journal of Development Studies*, November, 42 (8): 1271–300.

Mosse, D., S. Gupta, and V. Shah (2007) 'On the Margins in the City: Adivasi Seasonal Labour Migration in Western India', *Economic and Political Weekly*, 9 July, 40 (28): 3025–38.

Mulji, Sudhir (2005) 'Employment Guarantee Scheme', *Business Standard*, 20 January.

Murgai, R. and M. Ravallion (2005a) 'Employment Guarantee in Rural India: What Would It Cost and How Much Would It Reduce Poverty?', *Economic and Political Weekly*, 30 July, 40 (31): 3450–5.

——— (2005b) 'Is a Guaranteed Living Wage a Good Anti-Poverty Policy?', World Bank Policy Research Working Paper 3640, June.

Nanavaty, Reema and Divya Pandya (2005) 'National Rural Employment Guarantee Programme: SEWA's Perception and Implications', mimeo, SEWA, Ahmedabad.

National Advisory Council (2004) 'Financial Implications of an Employment Guarantee Act'. Available at www.nac.nic.in

National Council of Applied Economic Research and Public Interest Foundation (NCAER) (2009) *NCAER–PIF Study on Evaluating Performance of National Rural Employment Guarantee Act*. New Delhi: NCAER.

National Commission for Enterprises in the Unorganized Sector (NCEUS) (2007) *Report on Conditions of Work and Promotion of*

Livelihoods in the Unorganised Sector. Available at http://nceus.gov.in/Condition_of_workers_sep_2007.pdf, accessed on 1 February 2011.

National Federation of Indian Women (2008) 'Socio-economic Empowerment of Women under NREGA', report prepared for the Ministry of Rural Development.

National Sample Survey Office (2010) Employment and Unemployment Situation in India 2007–8, NSS 64th Round, July 2007 to June 2008, Appendix B.

Nayak, Nandini (2008) 'Songs of Hope', *The Hindu*, 14 September.

NREGA Consortium (2009) 'NREGA Reforms, Building Rural India', First Annual Report of the National Consortium of Civil Society Organizations on NREGA 2008–09.

NREGA Watch Tamil Nadu (2007) 'A Report for Action Based on the First Mass Social Audit of National Rural Employment Guarantee Act in Viluppuram District, Tamil Nadu'. Available at www.righttofoodindia.org, accessed on 1 February 2011.

Olson, Maxine (2005) 'Work for Pro-poor Growth', *Economic Times*, 20 October.

Olsen, W. and S. Mehta (2006) 'Female Labour Participation in Rural and Urban India: Does Housewives' Work Count?', *Radical Statistics*, Vol. 93, 2006. Available http://www.radstats.org.uk/no093/OlsenMehta93.pdf, accessed on 5 January 2009.

Pankaj, Ashok (2008) 'The National Employment Guarantee Act: Guaranteeing the Right to Livelihood', *India Social Development Report 2008*. New Delhi: Oxford University Press.

Pankaj, A. and A. Sharma (2006) 'Evaluation and Impact Assessment of NREGS in Bihar', Report by Institute for Human Development.

Pankaj, A. and R. Tankha (2010) 'Empowerment Effects of the NREGS on Women Workers—A Study in Four States', *Economic and Political Weekly*, 24 July, 45 (30): 45–55.

Papola, T.S. (2005) 'A Universal Programme is Feasible', *Economic and Political Weekly*, 12 February, 40 (7): 594–9.

Participatory Research in Asia (2006) 'Role of Panchayat Raj Institutions in Implementation of NREGA', Report by PRIA, New Delhi.

Patnaik, Ila (2005) 'Will It Reduce Poverty or Fill Corrupt Pockets? A 7-item Reality Check', *Financial Express*, 19 August.

Patnaik, Prabhat (2005) 'On the Need for Providing Employment Guarantee', *Economic and Political Weekly*, 15 January, 40 (3): 203–7.

Planning Commission (2008) *Development Challenges in Extremist Affected Areas*, Report of an Expert Group. New Delhi: Planning Commission.

Radhakrishna, R. (2002) 'Agricultural Growth, Employment and Poverty: A Policy Perspective', *Economic and Political Weekly*, 19 January, 37 (3): 243–9.

Radhakrishnan, R.K. (2007) 'Stalin Welcomes Core Findings of Social Audit', *The Hindu*, 4 August.

Ramanathan, Ramesh (2004) 'Time to Reflect on the Rural Jobs Bill?', *Financial Express*, 17 December.

Ranade, Ajit (1998) 'Maharashtra's Employment Guarantee Scheme: Regional Patterns, Scope for Reforms and Replication', *Indian Journal of Labour Economics*, 41 (2): 249.

Rao, V.M. (2007) 'Making Safety Nets Effective For Poor', *Economic and Political Weekly*, 18 August, 42 (33): 3397–403.

Ravallion, Martin and Rinku Murgai (2005) 'Employment Guarantee in Rural India: What Would It Cost and How Much Would It Reduce Poverty?', *Economic and Political Weekly*, 30 July, 40 (31): 3450–5.

Ravi, S. and M. Engler (2009) 'Workfare in Low Income Countries: An Effective Way to Fight Poverty? The Case of the NREGS in India', draft manuscript.

Ridge, Mian (2008) 'India's Job Plan Goes Nationwide', *Christian Science Monitor*, 8 April. Available online at http://www.csmonitor.com/2008/0408/p06s02-wosc.html, accessed on 1 February 2011.

Roy, A. and N. Dey (2008) 'Act on the Apathy', *The Indian Express*, 2 February.

——— (2009) 'NREGA: Breaking the New Ground', *The Hindu*, 21 June.

——— (2010) 'Auditing Employment Guarantee', *Indian Express*, 26 August.

Sainath, P. (2007) 'NREGP: No Place for Single Women', *The Hindu*, 22 May.

Saith, Ashwani (2005) 'Poverty Lines versus the Poor, Method versus Meaning', *Economic and Political Weekly*, 22 October, 40 (43): 4601–10.

Sankaran, Kamala (2004) 'Decent Work, Women and Family: The Dilemma Facing the Employment Guarantee Law', paper presented at NIRD Foundation Day Seminar on 'Guaranteed Employment for the Rural Poor', 4–5 November 2004, Hyderabad.

Sathe, Madhusudhan D. (1991) *Rural Employment and Employment Guarantee Scheme in Maharashtra: A Summary*. Pune: Development Group.

Savale, Sanjay (2006) 'Is Local Really Better? Comparing EGS and Locally Managed Rural Works Programme in Nasik District', *Economic and Political Weekly*, 16 December, 41 (50): 5133–9.

Shah, Mihir (2004) 'National Rural Employment Gurantee Act: A Historic Opportunity', *Economic and Political Weekly*, 11 December, 39 (50): 5287–91.

——— (2005) 'Saving the Employment Guarantee Act', *Economic and Political Weekly*, 12 February, 40 (7): 599–602.

——— (2006) 'Delivering on the Employment Guarantee', *The Hindu*, 4 May.

——— (2007) 'Employment Guarantee, Civil Society and Indian Democracy', *Economic and Political Weekly*, 17 November, 42 (45–6): 43–51.

——— (2009a) 'Governance Reform Key to NREGA Success', *The Hindu*, 14 March.

——— (2009b) 'Multiplier Accelerator Synergy in NREGA', *The Hindu*, 4 April.

——— (2009c) 'UPA's Challenge—Rural Governance Reform', *The Hindu*, 28 May.

——— (2009d) 'Taking Goals of NREGA-1 Forward', *The Hindu*, 14 August.

Shah, M. and P. Ambasta (2008) 'NREGA: Andhra Pradesh Shows the Way', *The Hindu*, 8 September.

Shankar, Shylashri (2010) 'Can Social Audits Count?', ASARC Working Paper 2010/09.

Sharma, Alakh N. (2005) 'Agrarian Relations and Socio-Economic Change in Bihar', *Economic and Political Weekly*, 5 March, 40 (10): 960–72.

Singh, R. and V. Vukuturu (2008) 'Enhancing Accountability in Delivery of Public Services through Social Audits: A Case Study of

Andhra Pradesh, India', Working Paper, Accountability Initiative, Centre for Policy Research, New Delhi.

Singh, Tavleen (2005) 'Why We are a Poor Rich Country', *Indian Express*, 7 February.

Sivakumar, Sowmya Kerbart (2006) 'Walking with a Purpose', *Frontline*, 6 May.

——— (2010) 'No Guarantees Anymore', *The Hindu*, 2 October.

Sridhar, V. (2005) 'Bias in the Criticism', *Frontline*, 23 September.

Srinivasa-Raghavan, T.C.A. (2004) 'Can the State Really Help the Poor?', *Business Standard*, 18 December.

Srinivasan, T.N. (2005) 'Guaranteeing Employment: A Palliative?', *The Hindu*, 3 January.

Srivastava, Pradeep (2004) 'Poverty Targeting in Asia: Country Experience of India', Discussion Paper No. 5, ADB Institute.

Subrahmaniam, Vidya (2009a) 'The System Strikes Back', *The Hindu*, 17 December.

——— (2009b) "Violence and Threats Bring a Government to its Knees', *The Hindu*, 16 December.

——— (2009c) 'Social Political Dividends from NREGA', *The Hindu*, 18 October.

Swaminathan, M. (1991) 'Childcare Services in Tamil Nadu', *Economic and Political Weekly*, 28 December, 26 (52): 2988–92 .

Tambe, Sandeep (2010) 'MGNREGS—Performance Evaluation in 2009–10 and Planning for 2010–11 in Sikkim', mimeo, Rural Management and Development Department, Government of Sikkim.

Tiwari, R. and G. Pandey (2008a) 'UPA Guaranteed 100 Days of Work to Poor, over 96% Didn't Get It, Says First Audit', *The Indian Express*, 7 January.

——— (2008b) 'It's Official: In Poorest States, Job Funds Don't Reach the Poor', *The Indian Express*, January 8.

——— (2008c) 'Cong ka Haath Kiske Saath?', *The Indian Express*, 9 January.

——— (2008d) 'In Opposition Camp Too, Delays, Mismanagement', *The Indian Express*, 10 January.

Tiwari, Rakesh, H.I. Somashekhar, V.R. Ramakrishna Parama, Indu K. Murthy, M.S. Mohan Kumar, B.K. Mohan Kumar, Harshad

Parate, Murari Varma, Sumedha Malaviya, Ananya S. Rao, Asmita Sengupta, Ruth Kattumuri, and N.H. Ravindranath (2011) 'MGNREGA for Environmental Service Enhancement and Vulnerability Reduction', *Economic and Political Weekly*, 14 May, 46 (20): 39–47.

Unni, Jeemol (1998) 'Non-agricultural Employment and Poverty in Rural India: A Review of Evidence', *Economic and Political Weekly*, 28 March, 33 (13): A36–A44.

Uppal, Vinayak (2009) 'Is NREGS a Safety Net for Children?', *Young Lives Student Paper*, Young Lives, Department of International Development, University of Oxford.

Vaidyanathan, A. (2005a) 'Panchayats and Employment Guarantee', *The Hindu*, 15 February.

——— (2005b) 'Employment Guarantee and Decentralisation', *Economic and Political Weekly*, 16 April, 40 (16): 1582–7.

Vanaik, Anish (2008a) 'NREGA and the Death of Tapas Soren', *Economic and Political Weekly*, 26 July, 43 (30): 8–10.

——— (2008b) 'Tale of Two Cites', *Yojana*, August.

Vanaik, Anish and Siddhartha (2008) 'Bank Payments: End of Corruption in NREGA?', *Economic and Political Weekly*, 2 May, 43 (17): 33–9.

Vijayanand, S.M. (2008) 'NREGA and Panchayati Raj Institutions: Learnings from Kerala', Government of Kerala, mimeo.

Vijayshanker, P.S., Rangu Rao, Nivedita Banerji, and Mihir Shah (2006) 'Government's "Schedule of Rates"', *Economic and Political Weekly*, 29 April, 41 (17): 1616–19.

Contributors

Anindita Adhikari Independent Researcher, Bihar

Anish Vanaik PhD student, History, University of Oxford

Aruna Roy Activist, Mazdoor Kisan Shakti Sangathan

Christian Oldiges PhD student, Economics, University of Heidelberg

Clément Imbert PhD student, Economics, Paris School of Economics

Jean Drèze Visiting Professor, Department of Economics, University of Allahabad

John Papp PhD student, Economics, Princeton University

Kartika Bhatia PhD student, Economics, Toulouse School of Economics

Karuna Muthiah Independent Researcher, Tamil Nadu

Nandini Nayak PhD student, School of Oriental and African Studies, University of London

Nikhil Dey Activist, Mazdoor Kisan Shakti Sangathan

Reetika Khera Assistant Professor, Indian Institute of Technology Delhi

Siddhartha Research Fellow, National Judicial Academy, Bhopal

Sudha Narayanan PhD, Economics, Cornell University

Name Index

Subject Index